Civil Justice in China

Representation and Practice in the Qing

Law, Society, and Culture in China

Philip C. C. Huang and Kathryn Bernhardt, Editors

THE OPENING OF archives on legal case records and judicial administration in China has made possible a new examination of past assumptions about the Chinese justice system. Scholars can now ask where actual legal practice deviated from official and popular conceptualizations and depictions. In the process, they can arrive at a new understanding not only of the legal system, but of state-society relations and the nature of the Chinese social-political system as a whole.

Studies of Chinese justice also permit the joining together of social and cultural history. Historians of society and economy, on the one hand, and of mentalities and culture, on the other, have long tended to go their separate ways. Law, however, is a sphere of life in which the two are inseparable. Legal case records contain evidence for both practice and representation. A study of law can tell us about the interconnections between actions and attitudes in ways that segmented studies of each cannot.

This series will comprise, after an initial conference volume (*Civil Law in Qing and Republican China*), major new studies by the editors themselves, as well as other contributions from a new generation of scholarship, grounded both in the archives and in new theoretical approaches.

Civil Justice in China

Representation and Practice in the Qing

Philip C. C. Huang

STANFORD UNIVERSITY PRESS, STANFORD, CALIFORNIA 1996

Stanford University Press
Stanford, California
© 1996 by the Board of Trustees of the
Leland Stanford Junior University
Printed in the United States of America

CIP data are at the end of the book

Stanford University Press publications are distributed
exclusively by Stanford University Press within the United
States, Canada, Mexico, and Central America; they are
distributed exclusively by Cambridge University Press
throughout the rest of the world

Preface

THIS BOOK IS A departure for me, taking up as it does the subject of law after 15 years and two books on China's rural society and economy. Even more than the subject itself, the departure has been in the nature of the source materials, which differ greatly from the kinds of historical materials I had been used to. Legal materials, unlike, say, cropping records, involve of necessity both representation and practice. The plaints and counterplaints of case files contain both the litigants' representations of the facts and evidence of their actions; the court judgments both the magistrates' proffered rationales and their actual rulings; and the Qing code and magistrate handbooks both ideological statements and practical instructions. For me, what became most striking in the end were the disjunctions between representation and practice in the legal system. Those remind us of the relative autonomy of the two dimensions and the need to consider both in our efforts to comprehend historical reality. They form the central focus of this book.

One thing that has not changed is my general approach. As with my 1985 and 1990 books, I began this one by searching out a large body of little-explored materials (in this case, court records) and immersing myself in them. As before, I eventually learned that the materials contradict a number of the conventional assumptions of our field. My task was then to develop concepts to take account of the empirical findings. For that, I once again drew liberally from the theoretical literature, while taking care to avoid common traps like applying a given model mechanically or arguing that China is not, as some theorists hold, a different (and by implication inferior) "other," but the same as (and by implication equal to) the West. I have looked to theory simply for useful ideas that might shed light on the evidence or help to forge connections, and have not hesitated to modify or develop theoretical notions as needed. Though I owe a good deal to numerous theorists, my arguments in the end again bear only a limited resemblance to their original ideas.

This book also builds on my earlier work in one important respect. As it happens, the ethnographic materials produced by Japanese researchers of the South Manchurian Railway Company (Mantetsu), on which I relied so heavily, contain the best information available on intravillage disputes. My acquaintance with those materials has helped me to put the legal case records into their larger societal context. This book deals with both the official legal system of the state and the informal justice of the village community.

I have had the good fortune of sharing my journey into this subject with a number of outstanding scholars. Kathryn Bernhardt, my colleague and wife, began her project on women and the law from the Song through the Republic at the same time as I began mine. I have benefited immensely from working with her on related though separate topics. Learning and discovery become that much more fun when shared. We were fortunate also to work with four exceptional graduate students who elected to study related topics—Yasuhiko Karasawa, Bradly Reed, Matthew Sommer, and Zhou Guangyuan. I have probably learned as much from them as they from me. Their dissertations, referred to in the text, should not be far from publication as books.

In the past seven years, I have benefited from discussions with Chang Wejen, Jing Junjian, Zheng Qin, Zhang Jinfan, and Fuma Susumu during their successive stints as visiting professors at UCLA. The numerous workshops and conferences Kathryn Bernhardt and I organized at UCLA under our Luce Foundation grant provided the opportunity to learn from senior legal scholars like David Buxbaum, Jerome Cohen, Randle Edwards, and Stanley Lubman, even as I disagreed with some of them, as well as from younger historians like Mark Allee and Melissa Macauley. My debt to the foundational works of other scholars, especially those of Derk Bodde and Clarence Morris, Tai Yen-hui (Dai Yanhui), Shiga Shūzō, and Huang Tsing-chia, will be obvious to all my readers. William Alford, Lucien Bianco, William Rowe, and Hugh Scogin gave me helpful comments at different stages of the manuscript, and Kathryn Bernhardt, especially, read and commented on several different drafts. For the final version of the book, I had the privilege of working once more with Barbara Mnookin, who amazed me again with all the ways she found to improve even a relatively finished manuscript.

My final debt is to the Chinese archivists, as well as once again to the Mantetsu researchers. Without their work, I could not have seen the legal system in practice or placed it into the context of informal justice. Grants from the Committee on Scholarly Communication with China (CSCC) and from the Luce Foundation made possible trips to the archives in 1988 and 1990 and the reproduction of the case records.

Readers of the book should be forewarned that records of lawsuits, unlike many other historical documents, always contain a story within a story. Each case file provides documentation for various subjects of interest, say, legal procedure and magisterial adjudication, or land transactions and inheritance practices, but each also records a tale of human drama. The choice of what to include and what to leave out of those tales has been a special problem; I hope I have included enough to breathe life into the story without obscuring its main themes.

Pacific Palisades   P.H.
February 1996

Contents

Tables

Text

Civil Justice in China

Representation and Practice in the Qing

CHAPTER ONE

Introduction

THIS BOOK TAKES AS its starting point this question: to what extent, if at all, do newly available case records bear out the Qing state's own representations of its legal system? Is it true, for example, that Qing courts rarely handled civil lawsuits? Is it true that decent people did not resort to the courts, and that lawsuits increased only when immoral people and corrupt yamen clerks/runners instigated them for gain? And is it true that magistrates generally relied more on moral predilections than codified law and acted more like mediators than judges in dealing with the cases that did reach them?

Those Qing representations have greatly shaped our conventional assumptions about the Qing legal system. Past scholarship—Western and Japanese as well as Chinese—have to varying degrees accepted at least parts of them. In the absence of alternative documentation, we were largely at the mercy of official representations. This book reexamines these representations in the light of actual practices. My aim is to define the nature of the Qing legal system as it actually was.

The empirical focus is on those parts of the legal system that dealt with the four most common kinds of popular disputes and lawsuits, namely, those related to land, debt, marriage, and inheritance. By Qing representations, such cases—if they were acknowledged at all— were insignificant "minor" or "trivial matters" (xishi), at some remove from the "weighty matters" (zhongqing), or "weighty cases" (zhong'an) that were of serious concern to the state. Republican (1912–49) and contemporary Chinese law, by contrast, came to acknowledge the widespread existence of such lawsuits and carefully distinguished these "people's matters" or "civil matters" (*minshi*) from "punishable matters" or "criminal matters" (*xingshi*). As discussed later in this chapter, I use the term "civil" in the same meaning as Republican and contemporary Chinese law.

My choice of civil matters over criminal matters for study is related to the questions posed above. It was in the civil realm that the greatest disjunctions between official representation and actual practice emerged. And it was in this realm where we can talk about what kind of people chose to go to court for what reasons. This area, in other words, makes a good testing ground for two of our past assumptions.

In addition, since the Qing code paid much less attention to civil matters than to criminal and administrative ones, if it is true that magistrates acted not by codified law but by extralegal and mediatory predilections, then that must have been doubly true of the civil part of the system. In the terms of Chinese political discourse, Qing civil law must have been based even more than criminal law on the moral "rule of men" (*renzhi*) rather than on the harsh "rule of law" (*fazhi*). And in the terms of Western theoretical discourse, à la Max Weber, Qing civil law must have been even more like the arbitrary "*kadi* justice" based on magisterial whims than "rational" modern law (Weber 1968, 976–78; 2: 812–14, 844–48; see also 2: 644–46).* On the other hand, if our prevailing notions turn out to be incorrect for civil cases, they must be incorrect also for criminal cases.

The civil realm of the legal system, moreover, constituted arguably *the* major area of contact between the state apparatus and the populace. Outside of tax payments, most people dealt directly with state authority only when they needed official intercession in disputes over everyday matters like land transactions and inheritance. The way in which the magistrates dealt with these matters, therefore, tells us fundamental things about the relations between state and society: how the state represented itself to society, how state officials actually exercised authority, how the common people looked upon the state, and how they actually behaved toward official authority. If we were to revise our common images of the civil legal system, we would also have to revise our picture of the nature of the Qing state and how it and society related to each other.

Furthermore, law differs from other aspects of the state and of

---

*The term *kadi*, referring to Moslem magistrates, is rendered inconsistently by the translators; it occurs also as *Kadi* and *khadi*.

state-society relations in the sense that it involved most explicitly both representation and practice. Legal administration came with elaborate ideological justifications; a study of the legal system is of necessity also a study of the ideology of the state. At the same time, legal records document not only the rationalizations given by the state and its officials for their actions, but also the actions themselves. Legal sources thus differ fundamentally both from the ideological pronouncements of the state and the annals of imperial actions. Case records allow us to look at the entire process stretching from representation to action, and to ask about the congruences and disjunctions between them. Instead of assuming congruence between words and deeds, we need to ask about the possibility of the state saying one thing and doing another.

Yet it will not do to dismiss what the state said as mere words, and argue that the true nature of the system is told only by what was actually done. This book will make clear that the Qing legal system, like the Qing state itself, can be understood only in terms of a systemic coupling of moralistic representations with practical actions. It was the disjunctions between representation and practice that truly defined the nature of that system.

Magistrate and litigant mentalities and actions need to be understood accordingly. The moralizing words and practical actions of magistrates seem contradictory on the surface, just as the timid demeanor and brazen maneuverings of many litigants seem difficult to reconcile. My argument in this book is that those seemingly contradictory aspects of Qing legal culture become readily understandable only in the light of a system that encompassed paradoxical representation and practice.

The Sources

This study is based in large part on the records of 628 civil cases from three counties: Baxian in the southwestern province of Sichuan from the 1760's to the 1850's, Baodi near Beijing (and in the capital Shuntian prefecture) from the 1810's to the 1900's, and Danshui subprefecture and Xinzhu county in the frontier province of Taiwan from the 1830's to the 1890's.* Though the Danshui-Xinzhu materi-

---

* Though Danshui subprefecture (Danshui *ting*) was divided in 1875 into Danshui and Xinzhu counties, the Danshui subprefect continued to handle cases until a Xinzhu county magistrate was appointed (late 1878). I will refer to the entire set of cases simply as the Dan-Xin archives, or as records of the Danshui-Xinzhu court.

als have been available for some time, the Baxian and Baodi materials
were not open to researchers until the 1980s.*

On average, the file of a relatively simple but complete court case
contains about seven sheets and typically includes the initial plaint,
on which the magistrate usually wrote his reactions and instructions; the counterplaint if any, again with the magistrate's comments; the original depositions of the plaintiff and defendant if those
were taken; the report of the runners if any; the court summons if
one was issued; the testimony of the litigants taken at the court session; the magistrate's brief written judgment; and the pledge by the
litigants to accept that judgment. Where multiple plaints and counterplaints were submitted with documentary evidence or supporting petitions from members of the community, the records can be
substantially longer. When multiple court sessions were involved,
the record can become quite bulky and run to hundreds of sheets.

For purposes of comparison, I have also used Republican-period
case records. For that period, I have drawn on previously unavailable
records of 128 civil cases from Shunyi county, near Beijing, from the
1910's to the 1930's. Those files typically include the original plaint
and counterplaint of the litigants, any supportive evidence submitted, the court summons if any, and, by the late 1920's, the steno-
graphic recording of the court session and a detailed formal "judgment" (*panjue*) that summarizes the representations made by the
litigants, the judge's view of the facts of the case, and the legal basis
for his decision.

During the Republican period, it will be seen, the legal system
changed more in the cities than the countryside, and more in representation than in practice. Comparing Republican with Qing case records will bring out the essential continuity in the practice of civil
justice at the local level of villages and county towns. Representational change, also an integral part of the Republican story, and extremely important when seen in the light of contemporary Chinese
law, will be considered more fully in my sequel volumes on civil justice in the Republican and contemporary periods.

Finally, for a picture of the societal context that gave rise to these
lawsuits, I have drawn on ethnographic information about disputes

---

*The Danshui-Xinzhu materials were used by David Buxbaum (1971) and Mark
Allee (1987, 1994). For an early report on the Baxian materials, see P. Huang 1982.
Madeleine Zelin (1986) subsequently used those materials to analyze landlord-tenant
relations. My North China book (P. Huang 1985) used the Baodi materials for analyz-
ing the role of the subcounty quasi-official *xiangbao* in the nineteenth century.

on the village level, where the vast majority of the population lived. Since most civil lawsuits in the Qing and Republican periods began as village disputes and went on to the courts only when they could not be resolved by community or kin mediation, we need to look closely at the origins of those suits. Unfortunately, there is to my knowledge virtually no available documentation on village disputes in the Qing period. Accordingly, I have had to rely on Republican-period information to fill the gap. The best such information I have been able to find is in three of the village surveys that the Research Department of the South Manchurian Railway Company (Minami Manshū Tetsudō Kabushiki Kaisha, or "Mantetsu" for short) conducted in North China from 1940 to 1942, those for Shajing in Shunyi county, Sibeichai in Luancheng county, and Houjiaying in Changli county, all in Hebei province.* Those surveys contain detailed material on 41 disputes spanning the 1920's down to 1942, of which 18 went on to become lawsuits.

The ethnographic data make clear that village practices of community and kin mediation changed little in the Republican period. When used in conjunction with information garnered from county court records from both that period and the Qing, they also make clear that the role and content of formal law in village life remained much the same as before. Major changes did not really come until after the Communist Revolution. The village materials, therefore, can be relied on to provide the larger societal context needed for the lawsuits studied.

"Civil Law" and "Civil Justice"

Before I elaborate on the findings of this book, let me explain my usage of the categories "civil law" and "civil justice." I use "civil law" in the same meaning as the modern Chinese term *minfa*, or *minshi falü*. It refers to codified legal stipulations dealing with "people's matters" (*minshi*), distinguished from "punishable matters" or "criminal matters" (*xingshi*).[†] Its scope and content are well

---

* For a detailed discussion of the Mantetsu surveys, see P. Huang 1985: chap. 2. In the Qing, Hebei was part of Zhili, which also included portions of Daming prefecture, now in Henan province. Shunyi county is now a part of Beijing municipality. For the exact location of the villages, see the map in ibid., p. 36.

[†] In the words of one early attempt at systematic formulation, "Criminal litigation seeks to establish whether a crime has been committed," while "civil litigation seeks to determine right and wrong" ("Geji shenpanting shiban zhangcheng," 1907: Art. 1).

indicated by the headings of the four substantive books of the Republican Civil Code of 1929–30: "Obligations," "Rights Over Things,"
"Family," and "Inheritance."*

As it turned out, those headings neatly fit the categories of cases
that my materials revealed to be the most common kinds of civil
disputes and lawsuits in the Qing and the Republic. Land, debt,
marriage, and inheritance are the principal concerns of "Rights Over
Things," "Obligations," "Family," and "Inheritance," respectively.

Those headings are congruent also with what Qing law called
"Minor Matters Relating to Family [Household], Marriage, and Land"
(*hu, hun, tiantu xishi*; Substatute 334–8). In the conception of the
Qing code, such matters were supposed to be dealt with mainly by
society itself; they were "minor" in terms of both the state's concern and the punishments to be imposed. The Qing code dealt with
such matters mostly under the statutes and substatutes in its "book"
on "Household Law" (Hulü), divided into seven chapters, including
"Land and House" (*tianzhai*), "Marriage" (*hunyin*), and "Debt"
(*qianzhai*); Inheritance (*jicheng*) fell under "Household and Tax" (*hu
yi*).† This "book" on "Household Law," "minor" though much of its
content might have been by official representation, accounted for 82
of the Qing code's 436 statutes (from 1740), and 300 of its 1907 substatutes (in Xue Yunsheng's compilation, circa 1900). Those statutes
and substatutes make up the main body of what I refer to as Qing
civil law.

The Republican code's conception of "civil law," it should be
pointed out, approximates that of the continental tradition of modern Western law. The code was in fact modeled closely on the German Civil Code of 1900. It was divided into the same five books; with
a few exceptions, it employed essentially the same language and conceptual approaches; and it took the vast majority of its 1,225 articles
from its German model (*The German Civil Code*, 1907).

My use of "civil law," however, differs from two common Western usages. For the contemporary English reader, in particular, the
word civil in its legal application unavoidably calls to mind much
more than things like property and debt, and family and inheritance;

*Books I ("General Principles"), II, and III were promulgated in 1929, Books IV
and V in 1930.
†The *hu* in Hulü may also be rendered "family" or "revenue." I prefer "household" because it conveys to some degree the twin concerns of these sections of the
Qing code with revenues and with family law. The other chapters of this "book" are
"Markets" (*shichan*), "Granaries and Treasuries" (*cangku*), and "Customs and Duties"
(*kecheng*).

it also embraces the notion of political rights, as for example in the terms civil liberties and civil rights, and by extension, individual human rights. "Civil law" is often used interchangeably with "private law," calling to mind further the "private rights of individuals." Implicit in the notion of "civil," in fact, is the conceptual juxtaposition between society or individuals (private) on the one hand and the state (public) on the other, as in the term "civil society."

The clustering of these associations and usages around the word civil can lead to the expectation that civil law must include human rights, and that, failing this fundamental notion, there can be no civil law. From such a point of view, one would conclude that there was simply no civil law in Qing or post-1949 China before the 1980's reforms, whereas Republican China and reformist China after the 1980's might be seen as evincing tentative steps in the direction of civil law. That kind of perspective, in turn, can provoke counterarguments to assert an equivalence between China and the West.*

I believe we need to set aside such normative arguments by acknowledging at the outset that there was and is little in the way of liberal-democratic civil liberties in China.[†] In fact, I would argue, Chinese political discourse as a whole has difficulty conceptualizing an opposition between state authority and individual rights, or state authority and civil society, the starting point of much of Western liberal-democratic thought (P. Huang 1993a). It tends to insist on a view of the essential harmony between the state and the individual or society, which is surely a product in good measure of the imperial state's long domination of intellectual activity through its civil service examination system. That long tradition has remained in force to a great extent in twentieth-century Chinese law.

But are civil liberties in fact a sine qua non of civil law? Hardly.

---

*William Jones, in his analysis of post-1949 China, has perhaps carried the first tendency to its most extreme. As Jones would have it, there was no civil law at all after 1949, only administration, until the coming of market and capitalistic reforms in the 1980's. Marriage law, the most important of contemporary Chinese statutes dealing with civil matters, Jones dismisses as something that "deal[s] only with fringe activities and in an erratic way" (Jones 1987: 318). The second tendency can be seen in David Buxbaum (1971), who (after a persuasive empirical demonstration on the basis of the Dan-Xin archives that local courts in the Qing dealt extensively with civil matters) attempted to argue that Qing law was as "rational" in Weberian terms as modern Western law.

[†] Roberto Unger's comparative theoretical treatise (1976: especially chap. 2) makes this point forcefully. William Alford (1986), on the other hand, points out how Unger's culture-bound universalizing of Western liberal values led to an oversimplification of the Chinese legal tradition. See also my discussion of the debate in P. Huang 1991a: 322–24.

The German Civil Code of 1900, for example, has nothing to say about political rights. To insist that civil law must be predicated on the entire complex of individual rights in the liberal-democratic tradition can lead to arguments that are really more about what we ourselves think (civil) law should or should not be than about the empirical reality of China. What we need to do instead is to focus on the body of civil law that did exist in Qing China and to attempt to understand its logic and practice.

The other usage of "civil law" that should not be confused with mine is the one that restricts the term to *the* Civil Law, as exemplified by the French Civil Code of 1803 and the German Civil Code of 1900. To accept this usage is to accept that civil law must bring with it the features that we associate with modern Western civil law, including an approach to civil matters in terms of rights, not of prohibitions and punishments as in Qing law, and a view of law as independent of the administrative authority of the ruler, not as emanating from the absolute power of the ruler as in the Qing. Some specialists of comparative law would also distinguish this continental tradition from Anglo-American common law, with its notable lack of national civil codes (e.g., Watson 1981).

My problem with such a view of "civil law" is that it leaves us with no conceptual rubric for thinking about Qing laws that dealt with civil matters. It too can lead us into an unproductive argument about whether or not Chinese law matched up to a preconceived standard. Here again I propose to set aside arguments about what civil law ought or ought not to be by acknowledging at the outset that Qing law did indeed conceive civil stipulations mainly in terms of prohibitions and punishments rather than of positively stated rights, as Bodde and Morris (1967) made crystal clear. That was certainly true on the level of official representations. But as we will see shortly, in practice the Qing legal system almost never applied punishments in civil cases and acted routinely to protect property rights and contracts. There was in fact an essential continuity of practice between the Qing and the Republic, despite radical changes after 1929–30 in the conceptual approach and language of civil law. The issues raised by the disjunctions between representation and practice in both the Qing and the Republic will be addressed more fully later in this Introduction.

The important point here is that my less restrictive usage of the term civil law enables us to examine how Chinese law dealt with civil matters at the level of both representation and practice. It will not do to dismiss Qing law from the subject of civil law simply because of the manner in which it was represented, just as it will not do to equate Republican civil law with modern Western civil law simply because it adopted a civil code based on a German model. Such approaches would reduce our inquiry to representation alone.

My usage is intended also to allow us to deal with the question of the continuities and discontinuities between Qing and Republican civil law. Like its German model, the Republican Chinese civil code built on a long tradition of legal dealings with civil matters, even as it departed importantly from that tradition. We can only understand Republican civil law by comparing it with Qing civil law, and vice versa.

Perhaps the strongest testimony to the relevance of Qing civil law comes from the early Republican lawmakers themselves: instead of adopting the newly drafted civil code (modeled after the German code) of the late Qing, as they did the newly drafted criminal code, they opted to retain in use for nearly two decades the civil portions of the (revised) old Qing code as the operative civil law of the new Republic. They did so because they wished to allow for a period of transition and because they thought the old code closer to Chinese realities than the newly drafted one. The new code was not to be promulgated until after revisions had been made to bring it closer in line with Chinese social practices.* We would be foolish to ignore what the Republican lawmakers did and dismiss the Qing code as just a criminal code.

Finally, let me briefly explain some other important terminological distinctions I make in this book. I reserve "civil law" for the codified law and the official legal system. But in fact most disputes were settled by kin/community mediation without becoming lawsuits. I use "civil justice" as an umbrella term for both this "unofficial" or "informal" justice system and the "official" or "formal" system.† It includes also what I call "third-realm justice," in which lawsuits were resolved by informal mediation before they reached formal

---

* This subject is explored in detail in my sequel volume on civil justice in the Republic.

† I will use in this book the terms "official" and "formal," and "unofficial" and "informal," interchangeably. The terms "formalist" and "substantive" will be used only when I am referring specifically to Max Weber's theories.

court adjudication, usually under the influence of some preliminary indications of the court's opinion.

In my view, formal Chinese law is not comprehensible without being seen in conjunction with the informal justice system. Perhaps the most striking distinction between the imperial Chinese and modern Western justice systems is the great reliance of the former on informal and semiformal justice. Codified civil law remains relatively unspecific in China even today, and most civil disputes continue to be resolved outside the court system at the points of origin in the community. That is why the topic of this book is not limited to the formal legal system.

Some Preliminary Considerations and Findings

Having engaged in some self-conscious reflection about our own culture-bound constructions, one is easily tempted to move next to a position of cultural relativism: to argue that Chinese law should be studied simply in terms of Chinese categories. This book maintains, however, that Qing constructions can be just as misleading as our own. Our critical searchlight must be brought to bear not only on our own categories but also on those of the Qing. We need to differentiate not only between our own constructions and Chinese practice, but also between official Chinese constructions and actual Qing practice.

Official representation and the actual practice of civil law. In the codified construction of Qing law, as noted, "minor matters" were seen as concerns mainly of society itself and not of the state. If civil disputes intruded into the official system, they were to be accepted only on selected days and months and handled at the local magistrate's discretion (*zhouxian zili*), unlike "weighty matters," which had to be taken up immediately and reported upward in detail for review and approval. Civil lawsuits were officially construed and represented as trivial annoyances for a system concerned mainly with administrative and penal matters. Ideally, civil lawsuits were not to exist at all.

Small wonder, then, that an earlier generation of scholarship should have pictured a legal system that was little concerned with civil disputes. Without access to actual case records, we were at the mercy of official representations of the system, as contained in codes and regulations, magistrate handbooks, and collections of model cases. We followed by and large the representations of the state and its bureaucrats in our image of the legal system.*

Archival records of the courts will demonstrate instead that civil or "minor" matters in fact accounted for perhaps one-third of the total caseload of the local courts. Far from not dealing with civil matters, the local courts of the Qing in fact expended much time and effort on them. Far from being insignificant, civil cases constituted in practice a major and integral part of the state's legal system.[†]

Official Qing representations would also have us believe that civil litigation only abounded when the system failed to function as it should and abusive individuals or corrupt clerks and runners instigated lawsuits for immoral gain; decent people stayed away from the courts. This is a picture that has not been challenged in past scholarship because of our lack of access to court records.[‡] This book will show instead that most litigants were common people who turned to the courts to protect their legitimate interests and settle unresolved disputes. Enough simple peasants turned to the courts to make lawsuits part of the collective memory of most villages.

The fact that common folk frequently did turn to the courts raises also the question: what are we to make of the Qing state's picture of yamen clerks and runners as rapacious evildoers? Would not their supposed extortionate practices have kept most people away? My evidence on lawsuits and litigants, in fact, argues for a rethinking of the conventional picture of pervasive abuse by yamen personnel.

Our common image that magistrates behaved more like mediators than judges is an inference that followed directly from the original presumption that there was little civil litigation, and that the official legal system concerned itself little with civil matters. By

---

* See, for example, Bodde and Morris 1967, the best of our earlier generation of scholarship; it includes just 21 civil cases in its selection of 190 cases for translation. The influence of this picture on our field in general is shown in, for example, the summary treatment of imperial Chinese law in John Fairbank's text (1983: 117 ff, especially 122–23). Mainland Chinese scholarship, by contrast, has long maintained that there was civil law in imperial China. (The latest of many textbooks is Zhang Jinfan 1994.)

† Buxbaum's (1971) earlier argument to this effect on the basis of the Dan-Xin archives has not been given as much attention as it deserved, perhaps because of the excessive claims he made for the Qing system, or perhaps because the evidence, coming from the frontier province of Taiwan, was seen as exceptional. There can be no further argument on this point, given the new evidence from other counties. See the fuller discussion in Bernhardt and Huang 1994a: 3–6.

‡ Even Zheng Qin's excellent monograph (1988), which drew on the Baodi archives and paid more attention to actual legal practice than other works emanating from China, left unchallenged these official representations (see especially 234–35, 243–44).

Confucian constructions, state law (*guofa*) was but the selective crystallization of larger moral principles.* Since state law had relatively little to say about civil matters, the unmistakable implication was that such matters would be settled mainly by the moral principles of society and not by law. In civil disputes particularly, magisterial practice would be guided chiefly by what Shiga Shūzō has termed "didactic conciliation."† In that image, magistrates worked more like kindly and peacemaking parents for squabbling children than referees applying positive regulations (Shiga 1981).

The case records we will examine demonstrate that magistrates were in fact guided closely by the code in adjudging civil disputes. To be sure, they preferred to defer to extrajudicial community/kin mediation whenever possible, in accordance with official ideology. But when confronted in a formal court session with suits not resolved by extrajudicial mediation, they almost always adjudicated forthwith by the code. They acted, in other words, as judges and not as mediators. Indeed, the standard magistrate handbooks that have been much used in past research, as we will see, directed magistrates to study the code closely and adjudicate accordingly. Examining actual magisterial judgments in civil cases brings into focus some of the most frequently used substatutes of the code, often buried under misleading statutes.

Community mediation. The disjunction between representation and practice in the official legal system extended also to the informal justice system. By Confucian idealization, informal justice, even more than formal justice, was governed chiefly by human compassion (*renqing*) and "heavenly [moral] principles" (*tianli*), or *qingli* for short. Law (guofa) mattered little.

The actual practice of community justice differed from its official representation in several respects. First, the meaning of *li* in community mediation actually approximates more closely commonsense right and wrong, or *daoli* ("reason"), than the high-flown construction lent it by Confucian idealization. Similarly, *qing* ("feeling") meant the renqing ("human feeling") of human relations, in which

---

* Much as, in Shiga Shūzō's metaphor, icebergs are to the ocean (Shiga 1981, 1984).
† A term Shiga borrows from Dan Fenno Henderson (1965), who uses it in reference to Japanese law. This image of the magistrate acting as mediator/arbitrator rather than judge has influenced most existing writings on civil justice in the Qing. Contemporary Chinese scholarship customarily accepts the representation as fact and glorifies it as the distinguishing characteristic of the Chinese legal system (e.g., Zheng Qin 1988: especially 241–46).

the emphasis was on maintaining decent relationships among those living in close promixity to one another, rather than the moralistic "human compassion" of Confucian constructions, in which it approximated the concept of *ren* or humaneness.* Operationally, qing meant the resolution of disputes through mediated compromise.

Of the triad of principles—law, common-sense right and wrong, and peacemaking compromise—that guided informal justice, compromise was the most important. But that is not to say that state law did not matter. The fact that the imperial state sought in its representations to deny, or at least to trivialize, civil law has encouraged an image of the informal justice system as essentially unaffected by official law. The records show, however, that state law, far from playing no role in community mediation, in fact made up the frame within which compromise took place. Contrary to official representation, the resort to, or threat of, a lawsuit was ever-present in village life. A party to a dispute could almost always opt for official justice over community or kin mediation. All parties knew, moreover, that if and when community mediation failed, resort to the courts of the state might follow. Thus, state law figured as a significant factor in informal mediation. This is as one might expect, given that Qing courts were in fact quite accessible and were regularly turned to for the settlement of civil disputes.

This study highlights also the intermediate realm between the formal and informal parts of the justice system. The majority of the civil cases examined were settled without a formal court session, by a process that combined the workings of informal community mediation and magisterial opinion. Once a case entered the court system with the filing of a plaint, efforts at community mediation would be intensified. At the same time, expressions of magisterial opinion in the form of comments on the plaints and counterplaints, generally available to the litigants, provided a preliminary indication of the likely verdict of a formal court session. Informal mediations were generally worked out under the influence of such magisterial opinion.

* Readers familiar with Shiga's explanation of the meanings of tianli, renqing, and guofa might find a surface resemblance here between my analysis and his. But Shiga uses the terms in connection with the formal legal system, whereas I apply them here to the informal system. What is more, Shiga does not distinguish clearly between official representation and practical meanings (Shiga 1984: 263–304).

Representationism versus objectivism. On the first level of analysis, then, this book takes advantage of the newly available case records, supplemented by ethnographic information, to make some statements about how the Qing justice system actually worked, despite official representations. My choice of civil justice as the focus of this book was guided in part by a concern to correct past misimpressions stemming from those representations, for it was in the civil realm that there was the greatest divergence between official representation and actual practice.

The issues raised by Qing civil justice, however, do not stop there. My intention is not to make the simple "objectivist" argument against a "representationist" one: that the "true" nature of the Qing legal system lay in what it actually did, not what it said it did.* Instead, I have focused on disjunctions between practice and representation to highlight and problematize the complex issue of the relationship between objective actions and subjective constructions. Disjunctions between representation and practice can and should lead us to further questions beyond the simple objectivist argument. To begin with: what light might legal practice throw on representation itself? How, for example, might the text of the code be read differently from the perspective of actual legal practice?

Here the record on civil adjudications brings into focus the multilayered nature of the text of the imperial code. What began as a Legalist-inspired administrative and penal code came to be infused with Confucian notions of social hierarchy and moral relations. Those aspects of the code have been well analyzed and documented by an earlier generation of scholarship (Ch'ü T'ung-tsu 1961; Bodde and Morris 1967). What can still use special emphasis is the practice that evolved in the Ming-Qing period of distinguishing between unchanging statutes (*lü*) embodying moral and administrative-penal principles and changing "substatutes" (*li*) added as the state adapted to new social and political realities.† The case records highlight the most widely employed of the li, often buried under statutes that seemingly addressed very different issues. When one reads the full

---

*I have opted for the word "representationist" over "subjectivist" here because of the multiple connotations that the words "subject" and "subjectivity" have taken on in recent years. Here, of course, I would be using "subjectivist" in its old-fashioned opposition to "objectivist."

†William Jones's recent (1994) translation of the Qing code does not include any of the substatutes. Huang Tsing-chia's 1970 introduction to Xue Yunsheng's 1905 compilation of the Qing code, however, distinguished well the lü from the li.

texts in conjunction with case records, it becomes starkly apparent that the Qing code in fact contained an intentional coupling of moralistic packaging with practical stipulations.

But we must not stop here. We need also to turn a representationist searchlight on objectivist concerns. A purely objectivist perspective overlooks the powerful ways in which representational constructions shaped practice. For one thing, the representation of administrative authority as benevolent but absolute kept the court system from developing in the direction of judicial autonomy or of liberal-democratic civil rights. For another, the conception of civil matters as "minor," subject to the discretion of local officials acting as representatives of the emperor, kept the system from a fuller elaboration and standardization of civil stipulations. Despite the fact that the magistrates generally acted in accordance with the code, therefore, the judicial system remained vulnerable to administrative whims. This is just one important example of the practical consequence of the official representations.

The paradoxical structure of the justice system. This book argues that a view that takes into account both representation and practice and both official and unofficial aspects of the Qing justice system points up the extent to which that system was characterized by built-in paradoxes. To identify the "real" system with the constructions of the state is as much off the mark as to identify it with the actions and consequences of the system. Rather, the system is really only understandable in terms of its paradoxical dimensions.

The law's approach to property rights illustrates the point. The Qing code does not speak in terms of "rights of ownership," merely of punishments for violating others' property or legitimate land transactions. Qing law, then, could be said to be concerned only with social order; it had no conception of property rights in the sense of absolute rights, independent of the administrative and penal concerns of the ruler. Yet the fact is that many litigants successfully turned to the courts to safeguard their property. Regardless of the intentions of the law, we might say, its practical consequence was to protect property rights. Thus, one might conclude, there were real property rights in Qing law, representations to the contrary notwithstanding.

The same was true of the official representation of court adjudication. As Shiga has pointed out, in the idealized vision of the Qing state, magistrates did not decide the truth of a matter; rather, they served to facilitate the revelation of the truth through the voluntary confessions of the accused. Under the precepts of modern Western law, by contrast, the court's judgment is held to be the nearest possible approximation to the actual truth. The Western view derives directly from an emphasis on the standardization of procedures, such that "legal truth" comes to be distinguished from substantive truth; truth is what is established within the boundaries of established procedures, regardless of the "real" substantive truth (Shiga 1974–75, especially 33: 121–23; Weber 1968, 2: 809–15). From the representationist point of view, then, there is really no such thing in Chinese justice as magisterial adjudication.

. Yet the reality was that Qing magistrates routinely made decisions about what they thought to be true. They pressured people into "confessions" that conformed to their own judgments by one means or another, including severe torture in the case of criminal offenses. In their reports to upper levels, it was standard practice for magistrates to narrate the facts of a case in such a way as to support the sentences they recommended (Zhou Guangyuan 1993). Since the ostensibly verbatim confession was a standard part of a report, it was not uncommon for magistrates to put words in the mouths of the accused to achieve the desired effect (Karasawa 1994). Despite the representation that judges merely facilitated the revelation of the truth, therefore, they routinely acted on the basis of their own perceptions and opinions. From an objectivist point of view, in other words, they routinely made adjudicatory judgments.

Here again, a purely objectivist view that ignores representation cannot capture the reality of the Qing legal system because the representation that magistrates did not adjudicate had practical consequences. It led, for example, to the practice in civil cases of requiring litigants to pledge to accept court judgments. That requirement served in practice as something of a check on magisterial authority. By refusing to accept a judgment, a litigant could keep a magistrate from formally disposing of the case and thereby exercise some small measure of recourse against arbitrary adjudication. We need to view the system as one whose very structure comprised mutually informing representation and practice.

Magistrate choices and actions, similarly, become understandable only in the light of paradoxical representation and practice. On the one hand, the magistrate supposedly acted as the personal agent of the emperor and as the "father-mother official" (*fumu guan*) of the local populace, wielding absolute and undivided authority, in the same manner as the emperor.* With civil disputes, moreover, he was ostensibly to act at his own discretion. On the other hand, the magistrate was also someone at the bottom rung of a well-articulated bureaucracy, with established rules of behavior and an elaborate report and review system. In the judicial realm, his actions were further governed by a code that spelled out both general principles and specific practices. There was also always the check of possible appeal and review, even in civil cases. In practice, therefore, the magistrate was a lowly functionary who had to tread carefully within established rules and regulations, lest his career be harmed.

Under those conditions, the majority of magistrates chose to adjudicate according to the code. This should not be surprising really, given the elaborate bureaucratic review system for evaluating magistrates' performance. Yet, at the same time, those magistrates who wrote handbooks and compiled records of their judgments tended to abide by the Confucian representations; most highlighted moralistic rather than code-based rulings and played up their discretionary and moral acumen rather than their close observance of the code in disposing of civil cases. Such apparently contradictory choices and actions become understandable in the light of the paradoxical structure within which they had to operate.

The Qing justice system was paradoxical also in its combination of official and unofficial justice. Shiga Shūzō, as has been seen, tended to conflate the two. That led to a view of magistrates as concerned mainly with mediation rather than adjudication. But the Qing civil justice system was in fact based on a coupling of a formal system guided mainly by adjudication and an informal system guided mainly by compromise. The workings of the system depended on a co-reliance on the two and a negotiatory space between them. The burden placed on official justice would be lightened by the operations of community justice. The proportion of civil disputes becoming lawsuits would be kept low through community mediation.

Almost all litigants, despite their fear of the system, took advantage of their simultaneous access to both the formal and the informal system of justice. Many of them filed suits just to leverage the informal mediation process in progress, without going through to final court adjudication. Many made intricate choices to arrive at a desired

---

*Indeed, one can be easily led to equate this one-sided official representation with reality.

mix of court opinion and community or kin mediation. What is striking and to be kept in mind is that the side-by-side operation of the two systems gave them room to maneuver between the two.

The defining characteristic of the Qing system, indeed of Chinese legal culture as a whole, then, is its simultaneous reliance on the official and unofficial, and the moralistic and the practical. It would be an error to equate the entire system with just one dimension or the other.

Long-term tendencies. It is through the interplay of systemic structure and litigant agency that we can discern the long-term tendencies in the system. To be sure, the paradoxes built into the system were crucial to its flexibility and longevity. Yet they also opened the system to abuse and manipulation by resourceful and sophisticated litigants. The system worked best with lowly naifs who were easily intimidated. It did not work so well with those who had access to the services of knowledgeable advisers and agents.

My county records reveal that the system operated in two distinctively different patterns. One, in nineteenth-century Baodi and in Baxian down to the mid-nineteenth century, was relatively simple and straightforward, with the system working pretty much as it was intended to. Most cases were settled relatively expeditiously and usually by a single court session. The other, in more highly commercialized and differentiated Danshui-Xinzhu, shows rich and powerful litigants who, often with the help of litigation specialists, were able to prevent the court from taking definitive action by entangling it in mazes of complex petitions and details. The result was an overburdened court that, by the late nineteenth century, was less and less able to cope with its civil caseload. Multiple court sessions and protracted lawsuits were common, and the court seldom took any action without repeated prompting.

The two patterns attest to both synchronic variations and diachronic changes in the Qing legal system. The synchronic variation came with uneven degrees of commercialization, social differentiation, and population density. The diachronic change came with long-term tendencies in those directions in many counties during the Qing. Together, the two patterns show that the system did work under certain conditions, and that it began to break down when conditions changed.

Magistrate handbooks revisited. If the observations above are substantially valid, are they also borne out by the magistrate and legal secretary handbooks that have for so long served as a major basis for our ideas about the Qing legal system? If so, how? And if not, how are we to understand the discrepancies? I have tried to test what I have found in the new case records against the old handbooks.

The handbooks in fact evince the same disjunctions between representation and practice that this chapter has argued characterized the entire legal system. To be sure, the handbooks were invariably packaged within moralistic declarations; reiterations of normative Confucian ideals were simply a standard part of legal discourse in the Qing. Nevertheless, as practical handbooks, they generally also contain specific instructions intended to guide the day-to-day actions of magistrates and legal secretaries. Those concrete instructions, it turns out, lend additional support to the points emphasized in this book. The discussion in Chapter Eight of how things looked from the magistrate's seat therefore serves also as a review and summary of the main arguments of the entire book.

Theoretical issues. What, finally, was the nature of the Qing legal system and how might it be characterized in the terms of contemporary Western scholarly discourse? Weber's dichotomy between arbitrary kadi justice on the one hand and rational modern Western law on the other remains influential in the theoretical literature, even as recent empirical research moved well beyond its confines.* It is easy to fall into the discursive trap of countering an argument with its opposite in a binary theoretical construction: the (inferior) difference of kadi justice would be countered by the (equivalent) sameness of rationality, and the absence of Western-standard civil law by its presence. It is a tendency that is evident in other subfields of Chinese history: the difference of economic stagnation or lack of democracy would be countered by the sameness of incipient capitalism or of a "public sphere" tantamount to incipient democracy (P. Huang 1991a, 1993a). What we need to do is to move beyond such simple juxtapositions and search for new theoretical conceptions. The final chapter reexamines Weber's original formulations and, building on his hints of a third category, "substantive rationality," attempts to work out a novel characterization that better captures the realities of the Qing legal system.

*Unger 1976 is a good illustration of such theoretical literature. Some outstanding examples of the recent scholarship are Brockman 1980; Alford 1984, 1986; Scogin 1990; Henderson and Tobert 1992; Shiga 1981, 1984; Fuma 1993; Zheng Qin 1988; and Zhang Jinfan 1994. For current scholarship, see the introductory discussion and the various contributions in Bernhardt and Huang 1994b.

All this, however, is to get well ahead of the main empirical story to be told in this book, for there is as yet an enormous evidentiary gap to be filled about the workings of community justice and official law, before we can attempt a new hypothesis about the structure and operative nature of the justice system as a whole and about the distinctive characteristics of what might be termed Chinese legal culture. The next chapter begins to close that gap with an overview of civil disputes in China and how the civil justice system operated to deal with them.

CHAPTER TWO

Defining Categories: Disputes and Lawsuits in North China Villages Before the Communist Revolution

T O   J U D G E   O N L Y   B Y   our standard village studies in English, which in general contain little or no information about lawsuits, one might think that villagers almost never engaged in litigation, and that except for criminal and administrative matters, state law mattered little in village society.* This widely held assumption, however, is contradicted by my county records for the Qing and Republican periods. It is also contradicted by the Mantetsu village surveys that paid systematic attention to disputes and lawsuits. For Shajing, Sibeichai, and Houjiaying villages, investigators documented a total of 41 disputes spanning the 1920's to the early 1940's, of which 18 went on to become lawsuits. Tables 1 and 2 tabulate those disputes and lawsuits by category.

To be sure, the Mantetsu ethnographic data contain only what was elicited by the investigators in three villages and can by no means be taken as a comprehensive representation of all varieties of civil cases. But the case files from the Shunyi county court for the 1910's to the 1930's (Table 3), and a complete register of cases received by that court for 1927, to be discussed below, afford a more complete picture, and those are on the whole consistent with the village data (Shunyi, of course, was the county of Shajing village). This fact should not be surprising, since rural residents were the principal users of the county court system and the majority of civil

---

* See, for example, Fei 1939; C. K. Yang 1959; Crook and Crook 1959; and Gamble 1963. Martin Yang's (1945: 157–72) discussion of village conflicts is the most detailed of the standard village ethnographies, perhaps because Taitou was exceptional for the deep fissures in the community between its Christian and non-Christian populations. Most of Yang's information pertains to those conflicts.

TABLE I

Disputes in Three North China Villages, 1920's–1940's

Category	Shajing	Sibeichai	Houjiaying	Total
Land				
Boundary	2		2	4
Sale	1	2	1	4
Rental		1		1
Debt	1		2	3
Marriage		2	1	3
Inheritance[a]	7	6		13
Succession		1		1
Old-age support		1		1
Administrative	2	1	3	6
Other	3		2	5
TOTAL	16	14	11	41

SOURCES: Shajing, KC, 1–2; Sibeichai, KC, 3; Houjiaying, KC, 5.

NOTE: The table includes only those disputes elicited by the questions of the investigators; it should not be seen as comprehensive. In fact these were the only villages of the six in these volumes where the matter was probed in any detail. In the other three, just three disputes (2 in Lengshuigou, Licheng county; 1 in Houxiazhai, Enxian, both Shandong province) and one lawsuit (in Wudian, Liangxiang, Hebei) were mentioned.

[a]All are cases of "household division": the dividing up of inherited family property among brothers to form separate households.

TABLE 2

Lawsuits in Three North China Villages

Category	Shajing	Sibeichai	Houjiaying	Total
Land				
Boundary	1			1
Sale		2	1	3
Debt			1	1
Marriage			1	1
Inheritance		2		2
Succession		1		1
Old-age support		1		1
Administrative	2	1	2	5
Intercommunity	1			1
Other			2	2
TOTAL	4	7	7	18

SOURCES: Same as Table 1.

lawsuits originated as village disputes. The resulting picture, though still by no means comprehensive, provides a broad-stroke characterization of the major categories of local civil lawsuits in North China during the Republican period.

Moreover, when we compare the Republican information with

TABLE 3

Case Files from Shunyi County, 1910's–1930's

Category	1910–19	1920–29	1930–39	Total
Land	5	15	22	42
Debt	7	9	7	23
Marriage	—	9	24	33
Inheritance	2	16	12	30
TOTAL	14	49	65	128

SOURCE: Shunyi xian dang'an.

TABLE 4

Case Files from Baxian, Baodi, and Dan-Xin Counties, 1760's–1900's

Category	Baxian	Baodi	Dan-Xin	Total
Land	100	23	125	248
Debt	96	51	51	198
Marriage	99	32	9	140
Inheritance	13	12	17	42
TOTAL	308	118	202	628

SOURCES: Baxian, Baodi, and Dan-Xin dang'an.
NOTE: Breakdowns by decade, outcomes, and other particulars are given in Appendix A.

data from the Qing, especially the case files from Baodi county, which neighbors Shunyi (Table 4), along with the court registers discussed below, we note a clear continuity between the two periods. The Republican code of 1929–30, to be sure, saw significant changes from the Qing, employing different terms, categories, and principles, particularly with respect to women's rights to property and divorce. Those changes in the code, as we will see, did have some practical effects on the local administration of justice, especially in the towns. Nevertheless, the content of civil lawsuits on the whole remained substantially the same in the Republican period as before. With the exceptions that will be noted, the lawsuits of both the Qing and the Republican period fall readily into the major categories used by Chinese archivists: land (*tudi*), debt (*zhaiwu*), marriage (*hunyin*), and inheritance-succession (*jicheng*; including old-age support, or *yang-shan*). Those categories give concrete substance to the term "civil" as it was used in Republican law, as well as to the category "minor matters involving family, marriage, and land," as it was used in Qing law.

It will be clear from the data on the courts that the content of village disputes also remained much the same from the Qing to the Republic. Major changes in this respect were to come only with the establishment of Communist rule in the villages. My account of village disputes in this chapter is therefore intended to provide the wider societal context for the court records at the heart of this study.

I begin below with narrative descriptions, first of family disputes, over household division and inheritance, marriage, succession, and old-age support; then of neighborhood disputes, especially over boundaries between cultivated and residential plots; and, finally, of contractual disputes, over debt obligations and land transactions. I will distinguish between the types of disputes that became lawsuits and those that did not. I will also distinguish civil matters from criminal and administrative matters, to delineate more clearly the scope covered by the terms "civil justice" and "civil law" as employed in this study. Throughout, the village information will be analyzed in conjunction with the county case records and the Republican and Qing codes, to bring out continuities as well as differences between the Qing and Republican periods.

Family Disputes and Lawsuits

Not surprisingly, a fair share of the disputes revealed by my materials took place within families, typically between brother and brother, less often between husband and wife, occasionally even between parent and child. Material matters were usually but not always at stake.

Inheritance: Household Division

According to the peasant informants interviewed by the Mantetsu investigators, differences between married brothers living together made up the single-most-frequent source of disputes in the villages. The usual solution to such disputes was household division. As one peasant put it: eight out of 10 families divided because of friction; the other two kept the differences "inside their hearts" and divided without dispute (KC, 1: 189; see also, e.g., KC, 1: 137, 153; KC, 3: 32; KC, 4: 359; KC, 5: 70–71). The 13 divisions of family property in Shajing and Sibeichai village accounted for more than a third of all the recorded disputes.

We do not have far to look for reasons. Villagers lived under the contradictory demands of an ideal emanating from elite society and the realities of day-to-day village social existence. That brothers should live together with their parents was the orthodox Confucian model, given legal sanction in a statute of the Qing code: "If sons or grandsons should divide up family property during the lifetimes of their parents or grandparents, they will be punished by 100 blows with the heavy bamboo stick" (No. 87). Under the influence of such a cultural ideal, almost every family made an attempt to stay together. Household division was seen as something to be avoided if possible, and mediators in such divisions normally attempted to reconcile the parties first (e.g., KC, 5: 424).

On the other hand, there was the harsh reality of different conjugal units living together in close quarters, often in dire financial straits. In the view of the male peasant informants, marriages were what most promoted frictions among brothers. Though they had grown up together and might be able to get along well, their wives came from outside the family and were apt not to get along. The differences between the sisters-in-law, in turn, supposedly carried over to the brothers. We might note that whatever the actual sources of fraternal conflict, the male informants made good sense in observing that strained financial circumstances, as in a bad harvest, tended to aggravate the frictions. Where the family did not have sufficient land to occupy all hands, so that one or more brothers had to hire out or engage in peddling, often resulting in unequal incomes or apparently unequal contributions to household support, tensions became especially severe. A lazy or ineffective brother or one who squandered money similarly made for conflict, the more so if the family was under financial pressure (KC, 1: 241, 251; KC, 5: 70–71, 424).

The social fact of frequent household divisions, even during the parents' lifetime, was reflected in the Qing code by the substatute that follows after the statute forbidding household division: "If the parents give their permission, then it may be allowed" (No. 87–1). In practice, so long as the parents went along, it was legal for brothers to divide up the family property while the parents were alive. Moreover, the implication was that, once the parents died, brothers were normally expected to divide up.

The Republican Civil Code of 1929–30 did away with the injunction against household division, but it is clear that the contradiction between the "traditional" elite cultural ideal and social practice persisted, especially in the villages. Even though the vast majority of married brothers split off into separate households, many during their parents' lives, villagers continued to speak of the undivided family as the ideal; no mention was made of the new code or the new ideology embodied by it in the interviews with the Japanese investigators.

The basic principle in household division was equal partition between brothers, explicitly stipulated by the Qing code (Substatute 88–1).* Despite the revision in the Republican Civil Code that granted daughters the same rights as sons (Art. 1138), the operative principle in the villages clearly remained the old one down to the 1940's. That principle applied to land and virtually all other forms of immovable property, including especially the family's house, as well as movable property like furniture, implements, and farm animals, excepting only items recognized as individual possessions, such as a woman's dowry and personal pocket money, a couple's bedroom furnishings, and personal clothing.†

The division process was of necessity intricate, complex, and fraught with the potential for conflict. The big item to be divided was generally the family's land, which frequently involved a multitude of small parcels fragmented over generations. Whereas large parcels could often be divided equally plot by plot, smaller parcels often needed to be appraised in some way to establish equivalencies between plots of differing size, quality, and accessibility (e.g., KC, 1: 290–92).

The division of the family's house involved similar difficulties. Where a household was relatively well-to-do and new housing was built with each marriage or with the birth of a child, the process was relatively simple. Often, however, household division had to be effected within the the family's old house. Rooms, hallways, the courtyard, and pigpens were among the spaces that had to be divided according to the principle of equal partition; here, too, equivalences between "apples and oranges" had to be established, and some sense of fairness and equity attained to avoid future conflict and disputes.

---

*This is not the place to try to trace out in detail the origins of the practice of equal division between brothers. As I have speculated elsewhere, the practice might be linked to a political-economic system forged in the formation of a unified Chinese empire in Qin-Han times and the state's decreeing of partible inheritance as a way to encourage early marriage and population growth (P. Huang 1990: 326–29).

†Fei 1939: 58–59 contains a useful categorization of the different kinds of properties involved. The pocket money (*yayaoqian*) a bride-to-be received from her relatives before leaving for her new marital home was considered entirely separate from the dowry (*jiazhuang*). The one was for public display, and the size of it a matter of public knowledge; the amount of the other would not be revealed even to the husband until the couple had lived together for some time (KC, 5: 509).

Single items such as a cart, a farm animal, a plow, and a water pump likewise had to be shared out meetly.

An elaborate set of customary practices evolved to minimize possible conflict during this process. Divisions were customarily overseen by several middlemen/mediators (called variously *zhongjianren, shuoheren, zhongbaoren, zhongshuoren*; e.g., KC, 1: 290–92, 319; 3: 93, 96, 102, 123), drawn from the larger common descent group and affinal kin, nonkin neighbors, and/or prominent members of the community.* Lengthy discussions were required to get brothers to agree about the division of even modest properties. A session of two full days was considered unusually short (KC, 3: 96).

After the parties to the division had reached some consensus over equivalencies (e.g., a cart for part of a parcel of land, a table or bench for a small farm tool), the agreed-upon equal batches of property were allocated by lot (e.g., KC, 3: 96; 1: 290–92). Once agreement was reached, a document (*fenjiadan*) was drawn up and witnessed by several kin and/or middlemen to avoid possible future disputes (see KC, 1: 290–92; 319, and KC, 3: 93, 95–6, 102, 123, for examples of actual fenjiadan).†

Of our 13 documented instances of household divisions, two were subsequently taken to court. In one, a stepbrother who had been adopted out to a maternal uncle returned to claim half his deceased father's property after the uncle became impoverished (KC, 3: 153–54). In the other, the only instance of its kind in these villages, a remarried widow with two daughters challenged customary village practice by filing suit against her brother-in-law for her daughters' right, newly defined by the Republican code, to inherit their father's half share in the grandfather's property (KC, 3: 155).

To judge by the data from county courts, lawsuits over household division were relatively rare. Just one among the 35 Baodi cases having to do with landed property or inheritance turned on household division and in highly unusual circumstances at that. Three brothers in their sixties had many years earlier gone through a division process but continued to live together while their mother was alive. After she died, a formal measurement was made of the land parcels that had been agreed on years before; a discrepancy turned up, and the brothers went to court (Baodi 104, 1867.8). More striking still,

---

*I prefer "common descent group" to "lineage," which is better reserved for descent groups that held substantial corporate property. Most village descent groups had few if any holdings in common (P. Huang 1990: 144; Ebrey and Watson 1986: 5).

† Wakefield 1992 contains large numbers of fenjiadan from this and other sources.

not one of the 72 land-related and inheritance cases from Shunyi county in the period 1916–34 involved the process of household division. "Household division" (*fenjia*), in fact, is not among the categories used by present-day Chinese archivists cataloguing Qing case records.

The Dan-Xin case records from nineteenth-century Taiwan tell the same story, showing only two suits among 142 cases related to land or inheritance (Table 4). In one case, a family had decided with the support of the descent-group elders against a household division between two brothers, the younger of whom was an opium addict. Instead, an agreement was reached for the older brother to pay the younger a monthly stipend for his support. When that brother sued for a division on the grounds that he had not been receiving his stipend, the magistrate rejected the plaint out of hand, declaring that "an elder brother should be treated with respect, in order to uphold the proper affection between brothers. You should not impetuously bring suit for a mere matter of a monthly stipend" (Dan-Xin 22524, 1891.2.23 [l-104]). In the other case, a family business appears to have been swallowed up by an uncle. When the heir brought suit, his plaint, too, was turned back by the magistrate, with an order for the descent group to handle the matter itself. The magistrate noted: "You should know that no good can come of brothers coming to court to fight one another" (Dan-Xin 22522, 1891.2.11 [l-102]).

In the Qing ideal, law was meant to uphold a social order based on familial hierarchy by punishing those who violated it, but it was not meant to interfere in the normal workings of such a hierarchy. Household division was seen as something that ought to be regulated by the descent group according to standard principles. To judge by our case files, the Qing courts did act on the principle of leaving household division as much as possible to resolution by kin-group mediation. Household divisions stemming from fraternal conflicts may have been the most frequent type of dispute in the villages, but they were not a major source of lawsuits in the county courts.

Marital Disputes

After fraternal conflicts leading to household division, husband-wife quarrels appear as one of the most frequent kinds of dispute in the village surveys. The Japanese investigators' informants attributed such disputes variously to laziness or extravagance on the part of the husband (KC, 1: 239), the unequal incomes of the natal and married families, the husband feeling put upon by an ugly wife, and so forth (KC, 4: 63). But few of these disputes ended up in the most drastic outcome of all—divorce—even in the Republican era.

Though relatively easy for men in the Qing, divorce was not much of an option for an unhappy wife. Without her husband's consent, it was well-nigh impossible. Qing law allowed a woman to divorce her husband only if the husband had deserted her for three years or more (Substatute 116–1), or forced her into adultery (Statute No. 367), or sold her to another (No. 102), or beaten her so severely that he broke a tooth or finger or toe or limb (No. 315). As for mistreatment by the parents-in-law, the wife would have had to have been beaten "without reasonable cause" (*feili*) so badly as to have been crippled or worse (No. 319). Of 32 marriage-related cases from nineteenth-century Baodi, just one involved a suit initiated by a woman for divorce, and that was for desertion: she had not heard from her husband for 13 years (Baodi 162, 1839.6.1 [m-7]).

Practically speaking, then, the disgruntled peasant wife's only real recourse was to return to her natal family. In the 32 Baodi cases, 13 were represented as involving "runaway" wives. Close examination of the actual records shows that six of those involved wives who had returned to their natal homes for extended stays but were charged by their husbands with having run away in order to make their actions appear criminal to the magistrate (e.g., Baodi 170, 1814.6 [m-16]; Baodi 166, 1837.5.22 [m-4]). In Republican Shunyi, similarly, 10 of the 33 marriage-related cases were represented as involving "runaway" wives. Of those, five actually involved wives who went back to stay at their natal homes against their husband's wishes.

In theory, women's rights to divorce were greatly broadened by the Republican Civil Code, now including adultery and ill-treatment as acceptable grounds (Art. 1052; see Bernhardt 1994). The villagers of Houjiaying noted one instance of a divorce suit initiated by a woman. Mrs. Hou's husband had left the village and gone off to work elsewhere some 10 years earlier. No word came from him during that time, and his whereabouts were unknown. Mrs. Hou finally left the home of her father-in-law, Hou Dingyi, and went back to her natal home to live. There she became pregnant by Li Baoshu. Her family then asked Hou, the father-in-law, to allow her to divorce his son so she could marry Li. When Hou refused, the family brought suit (KC, 5: 139–40).

The other two disputes from the three villages (from Sibeichai)

were both mutual consent cases that did not involve lawsuits. Zhao
Luohe's son had been married five years when his wife committed
adultery with another villager. Zhao went to the police about it, but
no criminal punishment was imposed. In the end, both families
agreed to a quiet divorce (KC, 3: 125–26). In the second case, Hao
Xiaodan and his wife simply did not get along. The two fought all the
time. They had no children, the marriage having apparently never
been consummated. In the end, after eight years of marriage, the two
divorced quietly, with the consent of both parties (ibid.).

The county case records from Shunyi, which included cases from
towns as well as villages, reflect a somewhat wider scope of change
in the area of divorce. Twelve of the 33 marriage-related cases involved divorce, and fully eight were initiated by the wives—for mistreatment (6), desertion (1), and bigamy (1). Nevertheless, the Republican reforms were slow to take effect in practice at the village level.
Greater changes would come only with the Communist Revolution,
when women's expanded rights to divorce would form the cutting
edge of legally initiated social change.

Succession

Succession was an issue when a household had no natural-born
son. Though village practice, which was codified in Qing law, called
for the adoption of an heir from one's patriline, beginning with the
closest relations (Substatute 78–1), when a property-owner failed to
establish an heir unequivocally during his lifetime, disputes easily
arose over succession.

The succession case in Sibeichai village well illustrates the problem: the eldest of a three-brother family had no natural-born heir,
and the two younger brothers each claimed the right for one of their
sons to succeed to his share of the family property. In this case, community mediators failed to work out a settlement, and the matter
went on to a lawsuit (KC, 3: 88).

The Baodi case records evidence of both this kind of dispute and
other kinds to which the practice of adopting heirs gave rise. We have
one case of four eligible brothers competing to have a son designated
the successor to their one son-less brother (Baodi 182, 1874.12.2
[i-12]). In another case, relations between a father and his adopted
heir deteriorated, leading to a property dispute ending in a lawsuit
(Baodi 182, 1859.9.10 [i-3]). In a third, a son who had been adopted

out became impoverished and sought to claim his natural father's property (Baodi 183, 1904.5 [i-8]).

Of the 30 inheritance-related cases from Shunyi, 12 involved succession arguments. Seven of these were between different claimants, three between the adoptive parent(s) and the adopted heir, and two between an adopted heir and other relatives.

A related and important issue, not illustrated in the village data, involved the property claims of widows. Five of the 12 Baodi cases and three of the 30 Shunyi cases involved property disputes between a widow and her husband's patrilineal relatives.

Old-Age Support

Old-age support was an issue closely related to succession and inheritance. According to one village informant, this was generally not an issue of dispute when there was only one son. With more than one son, there could be disputes over who was to bear what share of responsibility for parental old-age support. The example he gave was of brothers quarreling over how much of the burden of farming the parents' old-age maintenance land (*yanglaodi*) each was to shoulder (KC, 4: 189–90). When things worked as they should, sons shared equally in the maintenance of a parent or parents. In the case of the Sibeichai village head Hao Guoliang and his four brothers, for example, all contributed equally to the agreed-upon maintenance for the mother: two *shi* of maize and two shi of wheat a year, plus two *diao* (or strings of copper *cash*) per month. The agreement had been reached verbally, through the intermediation of the head of the descent group at the time of household division (KC, 3: 93). In another example, three brothers each cultivated one *mu* of the mother's old-age maintenance land, and she ate for five days in a row with each of the brothers (KC, 3: 79).

Both Qing and Republican law made the parents' old-age support from their sons a legal entitlement. Where the Qing code, characteristically, put the principle in negative terms of punishment—sons or grandsons who did not provide adequately for their parents were liable to punishment by 100 blows with the heavy stick (Statute 338)—the Republican Civil Code spoke in terms of the "right" of "lineal ascendants" to "maintenance" by their "lineal descendants" (Arts. 1114–1116). Regardless, the congruence between codified law and village customary practice added to the moral pressures within the community for children to fulfill their obligations to their aged parents.

The one recorded example in the village materials of a dispute over old-age support involved an impoverished widow and her married son. The mother, Mrs. Xu, wanted to sell outright the family's one mu of land, already pledged out in conditional sale. The son, Xu Fuyu, who was head of household, refused. The mother brought suit in the county court, charging that her son was not providing her with old-age support (KC, 3: 153). Three of the 12 inheritance cases from nineteenth-century Baodi and seven of the 30 cases from Republican Shunyi had to do with this issue. Widows were involved in four instances (2 in Baodi, 2 in Shunyi).

Neighborhood Disputes and Lawsuits

As might be expected, differences between neighbors were a common source of disputes. Arguments over boundaries between cultivated fields and residential plots were the most frequent, second only to household division among all categories of village disputes (Table 1; KC, 4: 359; see also KC, 1: 140, 189–90). In one of the cases, two people with adjoining plots argued over their precise demarcation (KC, 1: 240). In another, two neighbors fought over claims to the lumber from a tree that had been planted on one plot but grew and spread over the adjoining one (KC, 5: 154). In a third, two neighbors argued over the precise delineation of their land and whether the wall that one had built stood on the other's land (KC, 5: 270). In the fourth, an uncle sold his residential plot without consulting his nephew, a neighbor who held an easement right on a strip of the plot (KC, 1: 162–70); only the last went on to become a lawsuit. Ten of the 23 land-related cases from Baodi and eight of the 42 Shunyi cases involved boundary disputes between neighbors.

Contractual Disputes and Lawsuits

North China peasants were involved in a range of contractual relations with others, both inside and outside the village, that often came into dispute. The most common kinds of undertakings related to the lending and borrowing of money, and the purchase, sale, or rental of land. Though marital agreements were a form of contract in which almost all peasants were involved, they were not generally a major source of dispute, in the manner of other contractual relations or of family disputes after marriage.

Debt Obligations

Loans in the three surveyed villages fell into two main categories: informal loans for small amounts and short durations between kin and neighbors, generally without interest and without a middleman, a guarantor, or security; and formal loans with interest involving variously a middleman, a guarantor, and security, and often with written documentation.

Informal loans. According to village informants, informal loans were usually made to tide someone over, whether at the end of the year to clear debts or in the spring, after the fall harvest had been consumed, and new expenses were required for spring planting. In Lengshuigou village, by the estimate of one informant, almost all of the 270–80 poorer peasants (of a total of 350–70 households) and about 10 of the 60–70 middle-income peasants borrowed money in this way, the former generally for 10–30 yuan (in no case more than 50 yuan), and the latter for 10–100 yuan (KC, 4: 217–21; see also KC, 1: 38). Credit purchases from shops were also a common form of informal loans, as for example in Shajing village, though there were no such arrangements in Lengshuigou (KC, 4: 217–21; KC, 2: 197–201).

This picture is confirmed by the 51 debt-related cases for Baodi in the nineteenth century. Small loans of up to 30 diao were frequently made informally between kin, neighbors, and friends or acquaintances, simply on a verbal promise to repay, often in a matter of days. Larger loans were generally made with at least a middleman or guarantor.

Two instances of disputes over informal loans show up in the village material. In one, two relatives got into a brawl when one of them reneged on a promised loan of half a *dou* of grain. The fight got serious enough that the matter was taken to the police (KC, 5: 155). In the other, Hou Dingyi's son sold some muskmelon on credit to a long-term worker. The worker would not pay, the two got into a serious fight, and Hou Dingyi sued the man (ibid.).

To judge by the Baodi cases, informal loans could lead quite easily to disputes and litigation. Fully 24 of the 51 debt-related cases concerned such arrangements. To cite one example: Sun Jun loaned two nephews 10 diao on the promise that the money would be returned within a couple of weeks. When it was not returned, he went to collect the money. A fight ensued, ending in a suit (Baodi 186, 1830.11.10 [d-18]).

Litigation in Baodi also arose over purchases on credit. For example, Tang Guoxiang bought from his cousin Tang Wu 0.1 shi of sorghum (worth 1.6 diao) on credit on the first day of the sixth month, promising to repay him on the 20th. But, on the 12th, Wu demanded immediate payment ahead of time. Three days later, a fight broke out between the two, fueling tempers despite the small amount at stake, and led to a plaint from Guoxiang (Baodi 187, 1850.6.16 [d-47]). In all, 12 of the 24 informal loan cases in Baodi stemmed from disputes over credit purchases.

The Shunyi records evince similar patterns. Seven of the 23 debt-related cases concerned informal loans (five between kin, and two between friends/neighbors). For example, Wang Shaozhi loaned his nephew 20 yuan, at no interest, with no middleman, and without any security. The nephew did not repay the money. A fight ensued, and the matter ended in a lawsuit (Shunyi 2: 108, n.d. [d-8]). Though purchases made on informal credit were not the source of conflict they were in Baodi, this was the issue in two of the 23 Shunyi cases. Zhang Luozong, for example, purchased chickens worth 34 yuan from a peddler named Liu Qixiang on credit. Liu sued him for payment (Shunyi 3: 483, 1931.5.21 [d-19]).

The informality of such transactions, it seems, left much room for a breach of faith or at least misunderstandings. In many instances, to be sure, the goodwill shown by the lender would be repaid by the reciprocal good faith of kin, neighbor, or friend. But such harmony was predicated on the borrower's ability or willingness to repay and/or the lender's willingness to forgo repayment out of consideration for the other's difficulties. When a man was under subsistence pressures, he might feel that "face" with his kin and the community was a luxury he could not afford. Or he might simply think he could get away with not repaying, since the loan had been made so informally. Whatever the cause, the result was conflict of a sort that did not lend itself easily to resolution through mediation. Many creditors took it on themselves to try to collect rather than to go through a third party. Such direct contact between creditor and debtor increased the possibility of brawls and injury, which in turn would precipitate litigation.

Formal loans. Formal loans were generally for relatively large amounts, usually for wedding expenses or funerals, but on occasion also for heavy expenses like the purchase of a farm animal or even land. They were usually for longer durations than the tide-over small loans, either five months or 10, pegged to the spring or winter crop, or both. They invariably carried interest, usually at the rate of 2 or 3 percent a month. Cash loans of up to 100 yuan could be obtained with only a guarantor (*baozheng ren* or *baoren*) or a middleman, but sometimes had to be secured by land. For larger amounts lenders almost always required security. The borrower might pledge the right of cultivation (without actually transferring it) of his land, with a written document witnessed by a middleman. On the strength of that, the lender would typically grant him up to 50 percent of the land price. Or the borrower might pledge the title to his land, usually with the transfer of its use, by means of a conditional sale (*dian*), subject to redemption by the repayment of the loan. Again, there would be a written document, with witnesses. Conditional-sale loans would generally be for up to about 70 percent of the land price (KC, 4: 217–21; KC, 1: 38, 300; KC, 2: 197–201, 208–9; KC, 3: 319–23).

In contrast to informal loans, such formally contracted loans had a built-in mechanism for resolving conflict in the person of the middleman and/or guarantor. A would-be borrower generally sought the help of someone with whom he was well connected and who had the kind of substance and reputation that would give him credibility with the lender. In the event of nonpayment, that would be the person the lender turned to for help in collecting payment. Though a middleman's obligation was principally a moral one, a guarantor was expected to pay if the borrower defaulted (KC, 1: 210–11, 300).

According to village informants, one or two disputes a year over unpaid debts could be expected (KC, 1: 189–90; KC, 4: 11; KC, 5: 25), but in general the graduated steps for dispute resolution through the middleman/guarantor or through pledged security seem to have worked quite well to minimize lawsuits. The village material contains not one instance of a lawsuit over a formal loan.

This is not to say that there were no such suits. In fact, 13 of the 51 cases from nineteenth-century Baodi stemmed from formal loans. For example, Sun Dakua lent 10 diao to a certain Liu who was from another village and whom he did not know, with Zhang Kui as middleman. When Liu did not pay him back, Sun demanded payment from Zhang (Baodi 192, 1906.9 [d-45]). In another case, Zhao Lian had loaned Zhang Jingyu 98 diao, secured by land. Jingyu had been able to repay only eight diao. Bad feelings between them came to a head over some other, minor issue, and a fight broke out, ending in a lawsuit (Baodi 186, 1839.5.11 [d-21]).

Generally speaking, however, there were fewer lawsuits over formal loans than informal loans: 13 compared with 24 in the Baodi case files, and 3 compared with 7 in Shunyi. The two lawsuits over debt recorded in the village material, similarly, concerned informal and not formal loans.

Land Transactions

The commercialization of the rural economy in the Ming and Qing, and the acceleration of that process under the influence of the world economy in the twentieth century, led to greatly increased land buying and selling, as well as land leasing and renting (P. Huang 1985, 1990). It comes as no surprise to find a substantial number of disputes and lawsuits surrounding such transactions.

Conditional sales. As noted, a needy peasant would commonly try to avoid selling his land outright by executing a dian (a conditional sale for about 70 percent of the market value). Typically, this "dian-maker" (to use the term employed by the Republican Civil Code, Arts. 911–27) would agree to repay the conditional-sale price within a stipulated period of time, at which point he was to regain full title. Meanwhile, the "dian-holder," who may also be seen as the creditor, had the right to the use of the land, either to cultivate himself or to lease out to another, in many cases the dian-maker (for further details, see P. Huang 1990: 106–8). But often this arrangement merely delayed the day when the dian-maker had to give up his land altogether. Already under financial pressure when he pledged away his land, he generally saw his fortunes decline further with the loss of income from it. During the Qing, a customary practice evolved in which the dian-maker, seeing no prospect for ever redeeming his land, sold it outright to the dian-holder for the balance between the amount of the conditional-sale price and the full market value. By this practice, called zhaotie, the peasant ceded his title voluntarily, no matter how reluctantly.

Frequently, however, the end of a pledge period found the dian-maker neither able to repay the conditional-sale price nor willing to relinquish ownership completely. It was the rare borrower who would concede that he might never redeem his land. He would cling to what was left of the title for years, even decades, all the while refusing to sell outright to the dian-holder.* The result was a protracted impasse, in which both dian-holder and dian-maker retained partial claim to title over the land. The dian-holder could use the land but not sell it; the dian-maker could not use the land but could keep the dian-holder from exercising the rights of full ownership.

Qing law did not help resolve such impasses; indeed, its ambivalent stance on the issue was in large measure responsible for creating them. Though the law acknowledged the social reality of increasing land sales, it tried to hold to the longstanding policy of protecting the original owner's proprietary rights, taking the position that unless a sale was specified as irrevocable (*juemai*), which was rarely the case, the seller enjoyed the right to redeem the land indefinitely (Substatute 95 – 3). In this way, it encouraged a dian-maker to cling to his partial title for long periods of time. In 1753, the lawmakers added a substatute limiting redemption rights in such cases to 30 years (No. 95-7), but a time limit of such duration did little to remove the source of the disputes.

Inflation, which characterized much of the Qing period, aggravated the problem. As land prices rose during a pledge period, the fair price for the balance of the ownership came into question. A dian-maker could, with the law on his side, threaten to redeem unless the dian-holder paid him the inflated difference in price, called *zhaojia*. Sustained increases in price could lead to repeated demands for such payment. Land-transaction documents between 1659 and 1823 of the Shen lineage in Suzhou, for example, show frequent, multiple zhaojia payments for numerous parcels of land until 1730 (Hong Huanchun 1988: 99 – 144),† when the Qing code added the stipulation that only one zhaotie for a given dian transaction would be permitted (Substatute 95-3).

As for the dian-holder, he had good reason to resist redemption, since the value of the land and hence of the dian had risen above the original conditional-sale price. He might also wish to hang onto the dian in anticipation of further rises in value. Further, if he were to think in terms of purchasing complete title to the land, he might well try to insist on working with the prices prevailing at the time the dian was made, rather than the higher prices prevailing when it came due.

---

*The problem would have been exacerbated by the fact that many dian transactions were carried out sub rosa so the dian-holder could avoid taxes (Jing 1994: 70). A tax-evader was plainly not in a position to take a recalcitrant dian-maker to court.

† My thanks to Kathryn Bernhardt for sharing her notes on this material with me.

Even without rising land prices, the dian-holder generally developed a strong proprietary sense over the land with the passing of years. The dian-holder who cultivated the land himself for years and years came to take for granted his right to enjoy its use. And the dian-holder who leased out the land came to take for granted the rent he received.

Matters would come to a head when the dian-maker, or his heir, decided to try to recover full title, often many years after the initial dian agreement. The dian-holder, or his heir, or even his tenant, would be reluctant to relinquish the use of the land. The dian-maker, or his heir, on the other hand, would feel fully justified in insisting on redemption, backed as he was by the provisions of the code. Such conflicts were not easily resolved by middlemen or kin/community mediation mechanisms and therefore led frequently to lawsuits.

In Baodi, for example, Xin Wang's grandfather had conditionally sold his land to Li Xiang's grandfather. Two generations later, in the 1880's, the two men became involved in a lawsuit over their respective claims to the land (Baodi 106, 1882.2.18 [1-22]). In another, similar case in 1865, the family of Liu He and Liu Shun had rented a 10-mu plot from a landlord named Xiang for more than 45 years but found themselves now in a lawsuit with Zhao Yong, who claimed the right to redeem the land because his great-grandfather had owned it until 1788, when he sold it conditionally to the Xiang family (Baodi 104, 1865.5.22 [1-16]).

It is clear from the Shunyi records that such disputes over dian persisted into the Republican period, accounting for seven of the 42 land-related cases. For example, Wang Yongzeng's father Xiquan had conditionally sold three mu. Even though Wang redeemed the land by paying back the conditional-sale sum, in 1922 he found himself involved in a lawsuit with another claimant to whom the original dian-holder had pledged one of the three mu (Shunyi 2: 212, 1922.7.4 [1-8]).

The Republican Civil Code tried to remove some of the sources of these disputes by stipulating that where a period of time was specified in a dian agreement, the dian-maker would have only two years after the expiration of the term to exercise his right to redemption (Art. 923). But the fact was that many dian agreements had been made without specifying a clear time limit, and for those even the Republican code continued the Qing practice of allowing a 30-year redemption period (Art. 924). Thus, for example, in one

Shunyi agreement where no time period had been specified, the dian-maker and dian-holder found themselves in a dispute over their respective claims four years after the original transaction (Shunyi 3: 478, 1937.6.24 [l-19]).

The practice of conditional sales was very widespread in all three villages and was particularly common in highly commercialized and cotton-growing Sibeichai village, where in 1942, 70 of the 140 households had sold some land conditionally (KC, 3: appended table). Though no disputes over these parcels were recorded in the interviews conducted by the Japanese investigators, it is hard to believe that there were none.

Outright sales. Even unconditional sales and purchases of land were not always so legally straightforward. For a start, the imprecise ways in which land boundaries were delineated invited disputes. An owner and his heirs might operate by an impressionistic demarcation that would go unquestioned for years. At the time of sale, however, it was customary for a middleman, in the presence of the principals, to measure the land and ensure that it was as stipulated in the deed. For this purpose, he was usually armed with a stick (typically five-feet long) that conformed to the standard measure used in the locality (KC, 3: 161–62). Such measurements often confirmed the impressionistic demarcations. But they could also bring out gaps between what had been assumed in practice and what the deed specified. In Lengshuigou village, for example, Yang Rudong had his land measured when the neighboring plot of Li Wendou was sold. Yang, it turned out, had been using 0.4 mu less than he was entitled to by his deed and the formal measurement. In another, similar case, when Li Changhua sold 2.4 mu of land to Du Yannian, formal measurement showed that part of Li's land had been encroached upon by his neighbor Liu (KC, 4: 11).

Such differences easily led to disputes that, if not successfully mediated, turned into lawsuits. In Houjiaying in 1936, Hou Laoyin sold 15 mu of land to Hou Zhidong. Local people measured land in terms of *long* (or long, narrow mounds of earth separating fields), and four *long* were thought to make up one mu. When Laoying's 60-*long* plot was measured, however, it turned out to be substantially less than 15 mu. The two men compromised by Laoyin's giving up two more mu. But then Zhidong decided to bring suit in the county court (KC, 5: 286). Although the Baodi case records contain no examples of this kind of dispute, and the Shunyi records just one example, we might nevertheless speculate from the village information that they were a more widespread phenomenon.

A second source of disputes and lawsuits stemmed from the widespread practice in the villages of buying and selling land without registering the transaction in order to avoid taxes. In such instances, the buyers and sellers dealt in "white deeds" (*baiqi*), as distinguished from the official "red deeds" (*hongqi*) certified (and taxed) by the county government. In Sibeichai, Liu Shenglan's grandfather had purchased some land years before without registering it formally. Aware of this, his cousin Li Jun talked him into paying an ostensible 600-yuan fine, 400 of which Li pocketed himself. When Liu found out the truth behind his cousin's action, he was furious and sued him for blackmail (KC, 3: 215–16, 333). Here again, although our county records contain no examples of such disputes, we might speculate on the basis of the village data that they could well have existed.

A third source of disputes was breach of contract. In 1926 in Sibeichai village, Guo Mingyu contracted to buy 27 mu from Hao Laokai and sealed the purchase with a 200-yuan deposit, as documented and witnessed by the middleman Hao Changdong. Later Guo reneged on the deal, claiming he had lost the rest of the money to bandits, and demanded his deposit back. Hao sued to make Guo honor the contract to buy. The case went to the county court, where Hao lost; he then appealed to the superior court in Tianjin, where he finally won (KC, 3: 253).

The Shunyi county records reveal two other sources of disputes, distinctive to the locality. One concerned the bannerland the early Qing court had granted to its nobility and Manchu bannermen, a particularly common practice in this county near the capital. Most of this bannerland was later sold and became indistinguishable from private land (P. Huang 1985: 98–99). But when the Republican state, bent on laying claim to any bannerland still owned by the defunct Qing court and nobility, asserted ownership over bannerland in general, it threw into confusion the legitimate ownership of all of it. This issue accounts for three of the Shunyi cases. The other source of trouble here had to do with riverfront property, which was subject to the constant floods that inevitably left boundaries blurred and threw precise ownership into question.

Rent contracts. To judge by the Baodi and Shunyi case records, disputes between landlords and tenants over rent and related matters were an enduring and perhaps growing fact of life, accounting for 10 of the 42 land cases in Republican Shunyi, compared with four of 23 in Qing Baodi. Several of these turned on more than rent as such. For example, one sharecropping tenant of a big landlord tried to conceal a segment of the land he farmed. When the landlord confronted him about it, he and 10 other tenants apparently beat up the landlord, who then brought suit (Baodi 98, 1839.7.18 [l-11]). In another case, a sharecropper faced with a bad harvest sought compensation from the landlord for the seed he had advanced (Baodi 100, 1839.5.18 [l-12]). In still another, a group of peasant squatters brought some 450 mu of waterlogged land that had been unattended for years under cultivation and fabricated deeds to it. The owner sued to assert his rights to the land (Shunyi 2: 88, 1916.8.31[l-1]). In a fourth case, a new owner wanted to raise the rent or change the tenant on his land, but the existing tenant refused to yield, claiming permanent tenancy rights because his family had cultivated the land for generations. The landlord sued (Shunyi 3: 682, 1933.7 [l-26]).

In Shajing-Sibeichai-Houjiaying, we have just one recorded instance of a dispute involving rent. Wang Zanzhou, the biggest landlord in Sibeichai, wanted to terminate his agreement with his tenant Liu Yongxiang because of Liu's failure to pay rent on land he had conditionally sold to Wang and now rented back from him. The matter was mediated by the village head, Zhang Yueqing (KC, 3: 178–79). In another village (Houxiazhai), peasant informants spoke of a dispute between a small landlord and his tenant over a three-year agreement on the rent rate, set in cash. When grain prices rose, the landlord wanted to switch to rent in kind, but the tenant was set on staying with the agreed cash payment (KC, 4: 473–74).

Some of the Japanese investigators tried hard to elicit from their peasant informants further examples of conflicts between landlords and tenants. But even the two who were particularly insistent in their questioning (KC, 2: 89; KC, 4: 166) were unable to get any other hard information. Still, the village head of Sibeichai, Zhang Yueqing, did intimate that however disgruntled tenants might be, they tended to keep quiet lest they lose their rentals (KC, 3: 193); and one stalwart middle peasant of Shajing, Yang Ze, was at least open enough to explain that tenants could say little because landlords could pretty much do what they wanted (KC, 1: 141). Wartime inflation in the prices of agricultural commodities seems to have made farming a much coveted activity for a few years, and the land rental market very much a seller's market.

Other Disputes and Lawsuits

Six of the disputes in Shajing, Sibeichai, and Houjiaying grew out of the efforts of local governments of the Republican period to increase control over villages and to expand tax revenues by bureaucratizing village-level administration. As I have detailed elsewhere (P. Huang 1985: part 3, passim), those efforts, combined with the gradual weakening of community solidarity from social-economic changes, created power vacuums that permitted bullies and tyrants to insinuate themselves into positions of power. Each of the three villages had at least one such dispute, and five of the six disputes went on to become lawsuits.

One of the suits involved Shajing, where in 1939 a village tough named Fan Baoshan had stepped in as the township head when the legitimate community leaders refused to serve. Among other offenses, Fan stole railroad ties given to the village by the county authorities for his personal use and then tried to pin the blame on another villager. The natural community leadership managed to rally together to bring suit and have him removed. Fan was sentenced to two years' imprisonment (P. Huang 1985: 268; see also 41–42; KC, 1: 197–98, 200–201). In Sibeichai, similarly, community leaders had rallied to remove an abusive village head, Li Yanlin, in 1935. He was convicted of extorting money from the villagers (P. Huang 1985: 269–70; KC, 3: 50–51).* These two cases show that the formal court system could be, and sometimes was, efficacious in protecting villages against abusive political authority.

But two other cases tell us how limited that protection often was. For example, the self-same ruffian of Shajing village, Fan Baoshan, having served his prison sentence, was back in business by 1942. At the time of the Mantetsu investigations, he was trying, in collusion with a monk in town, to swallow up Shajing's 20 mu of temple land (P. Huang 1985: 41–42; KC, 1: 194–203). Similarly, when, in 1942, the courageous young teacher of Houjiaying village lodged a plaint against an ex-soldier, opium addict, and gambler named Qi, who in his capacity as the township head of Nijing was systematically ex-

---

* Wudian villagers likewise managed to remove their village head, Zhao Fenglin, in 1941 for embezzling 90 yuan of taxes (P. Huang 1985: 271; KC, 5: 408, 421).

torting money from the villagers, the suit failed because Qi managed to terrify all the villagers into silence. Young Liu received 50 lashes (under the provisions of the Qing code rather than of the Republican code) for filing false charges (P. Huang 1985, 273–74; KC, 5: 48, 50–51).

Other disputes stemmed from the levying of new taxes (the *tan-kuan*). In Houjiaying, one of the villagers, Hou Dingyi, had some years earlier charged that someone acting in the township's stead had collected a special levy from him and then denied having done so (KC, 5: 154–55). In the same village in 1927, the village head and his deputy, both from the Liu descent group, colluded with their wealthy kinsmen to conceal some 600–700 mu (of the village's total 3,300 mu) from taxation. Since the new taxes were levied on the village as a whole, the result was a heavier burden for the other villagers. The Hous got together to protest the action, led by Hou Xinru and Hou Yintang. In the end, they managed to have the Lius removed as village heads and their own kin installed in power (KC, 5: 38–39).

In nineteenth-century Baodi, rural administrative disputes concerned mainly the supravillage *xiangbao*, the lowest-level subcounty quasi-official under the Qing. The extant Baodi archival material contains over 300 cases concerned with the appointment and removal of xiangbao. As I have written elsewhere (P. Huang 1985: 50, 224–33), the xiangbao, situated on the meeting ground of the imperial state's bureaucratic apparatus with rural society, was subject to all the tugs of conflicting interest between state and rural community. The post was often seen as a thankless burden, to be avoided if at all possible. The Baodi cases detail many of the tensions involved: of nominated xiangbao seeking to avoid the proffered appointment, of their occasional abuse of rural society, and of bureaucratic pressures on them for tax collection and public security. The cases should be seen as the Qing equivalent of the Republican-period village-level administrative disputes and lawsuits outlined above.

In Republican Shunyi, along with the downward extension of bureaucratic authority, the locus of tensions in state-rural society relations shifted from the supra-village xiangbao down to the village head. The roughly 120 cases we have from the Shunyi archives concerned with the appointment and removal of village heads (Shunyi 3: 42, 50, 1929.1–12; 2: 281, 1925.4) strongly suggest that the state's efforts at bureaucratization and increased taxes severely aggravated those tensions. The proportion of men who sought to decline the "honor" of being village head exceeds the proportion who declined the xiangbao position in Baodi.

Contemporary Chinese archivists typically distinguish such cases from other civil cases. The Baxian cases, for example, are lumped under the general category of *neizheng* (internal administration). Dai Yanhui, the cataloguer of the Dan-Xin cases, similarly, placed them under the rubric "administrative" (*xingzheng*). This book will not attempt to analyze such administrative cases; they deserve a separate study.

Finally, five of the disputes recorded by the Japanese investigators do not fit comfortably into any one category. Only two of these miscellaneous disputes involved the villages as collectivities. One was a dispute between Shajing and the township authorities of Beifaxin village over the need for a road that the township officials wanted Shajing to construct. Shajing villagers, seeing no benefit to themselves, protested, and a meeting of the township officials and the leaders of Shajing and other villages was held to work out a settlement (KC, 1: 190). The other dispute, which went on to court (but was settled before a formal court session), involved conflicting claims between Shajing and neighboring Shimen village over eight mu of originally unused marshland lying between the two villages. The land belonged to Shimen, but it was Shajing villagers who planted it in reeds and sold the product. Shimen went to court to claim the property (KC, 1: 474–75).

Another dispute, this one in Houjiaying, is worth mentioning. There a new-style school was established in the 1920's and soon drew students away from the traditional school. The conflicts between the two led eventually to a lawsuit, illustrating the tensions attendant upon the limited "modernization" that was occurring in the villages in the Republican period (KC, 5: 154–55).

Criminal Justice

The village data also tell us something about criminal justice. The theft of crops and farm animals was one criminal offense with which almost all villagers had some experience, particularly during the disorderly Republican period. But when the thief was caught, the village usually dealt with the matter as it saw fit, without resorting to the formal criminal system. A poor homeless thief, often an opium or cocaine addict in this period, might be given a beating and released

(KC, 3: 50). A thief who was a fellow villager, as most such mis-creants were (KC, 4: 50, 356, 423; 5: 45, 444), or who was from a nearby village, might be fined, with the payment sometimes being made by his kin. He would then be released after he pledged not to steal again. The pledge might be in the form of a signed document or a ritual involving the offering of incense before the statue of Buddha (as in Sibeichai; KC, 3: 42, 206) or, in the case of children, the guar-antee of their kin that the offense would not be repeated. On occa-sion, the thief and his victim reached a financial settlement through the good offices of the village head and the offender's relatives (KC, 1: 120; 3: 42). Such occurrences, in any event, were almost never re-ported to the officials, and the thief was almost never handed over to the authorities by the village.

That petty thieves who stole the fruits of another's fields would be handled by the village communities themselves was actually an implicit principle of the Qing code. Where the Ming code stipulated simply that such a theft would be punished, the Qing code added: "If the value of the theft is one tael or greater, the offender shall receive 10 blows with the light bamboo; if two taels, 20 blows; the grade of punishment will increase by the tael, to reach a maximum of 60 blows and one year of banishment" (Statute 99). As Jing Junjian points out (1994: 47–48), since most thefts of crops did not come close to one tael's worth, what the Qing annotation did, in effect, was to keep such petty cases outside the formal court system.

More serious offenses, like murder and robbery, were to be handled by the authorities. That was true of the Republican period no less than of the Qing. The Qing, especially, required that all seri-ous offenses be reported upward through the judicial hierarchy, from the county to the prefecture to the province. Capital cases had to move on up to the central government, and that has resulted in the several hundred thousand surviving records in the Board of Punish-ment archives for the Qing (P. Huang 1982; see also Huang 1985: 47–49).

At the village level, where the majority of the population lived, however, such offenses were relatively rare. In the three Mantetsu-surveyed villages, for instance, there was not one murder within memory. The only case involving a loss of life was the suicide of a daughter-in-law in Houjiaying, over a bitter relationship with her mother-in-law (about which more in Chap. 3). There was no inci-dence at all of robbery that resulted in a report to the authorities.

To be sure, banditry was a problem afflicting many villages during the warlord years.* But Shajing, Sibeichai, and Houjiaying seem on the whole to have been free of such disruptions until the outbreak of the Sino-Japanese war. Then Sibeichai had the worst of it, subjected so often to the predations of bandits that the long-time village head, Zhang Yueqing, declined to continue to occupy that hot seat (KC, 3: 49–50). Still, those forced encounters did not put the peasants in contact with the official legal system; to the contrary, they reminded everyone of the ineffectiveness of the formal system and of the security vacuum at the village level.† In Sibeichai, Zhang Yueqing did what he could, in "High Noon" fashion with the help of his son and agricultural worker, to fight off 15 bandits (P. Huang 1985: 269). The state's security apparatus played no role at all.

Village informants spoke of only two instances of criminal litigation in the three villages. One was the previously mentioned suit in Sibeichai that Liu Shenglan brought against his blackmailing cousin Li Jun (KC, 3: 215–16). The other, also mentioned earlier, was the suit that Hou Dingyi of Houjiaying brought against his neighbor's hired laborer in the wake of his son's fight with the man (KC, 4: 154).

To judge by the ethnographic evidence, then, the criminal justice system figured relatively little in the lives of villagers. Most village "crimes" were dealt with informally by the community itself, without involving outside authorities. When peasants did come in contact with the formal legal system, it was more often with its civil rather than its criminal arm.

Village Lawsuits and County Court Records

As I noted at the outset, county court cases closely reflect village disputes and lawsuits. Local courts in the Republican period were required to maintain a running register of outstanding cases, new cases received, and cases disposed of, divided into civil and criminal categories. The monthly reports sent up the judicial ladder were based on those registers. The Shunyi register of 1927 lists each of the 101 new civil cases received that year by the names of the liti-

---

*Wudian, located on a strategic highway, suffered the ravages of a defeated army during the Zhihli-Fengtian war, in 1924 (P. Huang 1985: 270), and relatively out-of-the-way Houxiazhai, the scourge of a bandit gang in 1918 (KC, 4: 410).

†Houxiazhai, for example, resorted to organizing Red Spears for community self-defense. Lengshuigou took similar steps, establishing a corps of 80 men to keep round-the-clock watch against a small band of six or seven bandits (P. Huang 1985: 262–63; see also 244–45).

TABLE 5

New Civil Cases Received by the Shunyi County Court, 1927

Category	Number	Category	Number
Land	39	Marriage	7
Boundaries, etc.	29	Inheritance,	
Rent	3	succession	4
Conditional sale,		Old-age support	2
redemption	2	Compensation	3
Crops	5	Other[a]	15
House	11	TOTAL	101
Debt	20		

SOURCE: *Minshi anjian yuebao biao,* 1927.

[a] These miscellaneous cases involved mainly the kinds of disputes that one might expect to find more among town residents than villagers: disputes over association fees, sugar price, a contract involving a salt shop, and so on.

TABLE 6

Major Categories of Civil Lawsuits in Three North China Villages and in the Shunyi County Court, Republican Period

Category	Shunyi county		Three villages	
	Number	Percent of total (N=101)	Number	Percent of total (N=13)[a]
Land	50	49.5%	4	30.8%
Debt	20	19.8	1	7.7
Marriage	7	6.9	1	7.7
Inheritance-succession (including old-age support)	6	6.0	4	30.8
TOTAL	83	82.2%	10	77.0%

SOURCES: See Tables 2 and 5.

[a] This total differs from the one in Table 2. It excludes the five administrative cases shown there because that class of case was not included in the 1927 Shunyi register.

gants and a two-character capsule description of the type of dispute. Table 5 gives a breakdown of the cases by the major categories used in the register.

The results are as we might expect from the village information and the county case files. Disputes concerned with land (including houses), debt, marriage and inheritance-succession (including old-age support)—the four major categories used by contemporary archivists and adopted for this study—triggered the great majority of lawsuits in Shunyi, just as they did in our three villages. All told, they account for 82 percent of the 1927 civil suits. Table 6 shows the comparable figures for the villages.

TABLE 7

Proportion of Civil and Criminal Cases in Dan-Xin and Baodi, 1833–1894

County	Civil	Criminal	Total
Dan-Xin, 1833–94			
Number	202[a]	361	563
Percent	36%	64%	100%
Baodi, 1833–81			
Number	209[b]	367	576[c]
Percent	37%	63%	100%

SOURCES: Dan-Xin dang'an, as categorized by Dai Yanhui; Baodi 329: *Cisong anjian bu*, 1833–35, 1861–81.

[a]Cases related to land, debt, marriage, and inheritance; excludes seven files missing from the microfilm copy and five files that were not lawsuits.

[b]Cases explicitly identified by the titles in the registers as having to do with land, debt, marriage, and inheritance. 31 of these also involved a physical assault or fight (*ou* or *dou'ou*).

[c]Excludes 78 cases pertaining to the appointment and duties of *xiangbao* and *paitou*, and 274 cases that involved a physical assault or fight without identifying the cause. Presumably a substantial but indeterminable number of the latter also involved disputes over land, debt, marriage, or inheritance.

Available data from the Qing period suggest the same pattern. The 25 extant annual registers of disposed cases reported by Baodi county for the years 1833–36 and 1861–81 list a total of 209 cases in which the issue at dispute can be explicitly identified as related to land, debt, marriage, or inheritance (Table 7). Similarly, 202 of the 214 Danshui-Xinzhu cases categorized as "civil" fall into those categories. There can be no question about the predominance of these issues among civil lawsuits.

Table 7 also shows that civil disputes accounted for something over a third of the county courts' caseload of civil and criminal cases in the nineteenth century. Judging by the data in Table 8, the Republican years may have seen an increase in the share of civil litigation—to the point where it came to approach the totals of criminal suits as reported by 255 local courts across China in 1936 and to exceed the totals reported from five selected counties over the years 1918–44.

To sum up, three facts emerge from what fragmentary data we have on the county courts: first, that under both the Qing and the Republic, civil lawsuits involved mainly disputes over land, debt, marriage, and inheritance (including succession and old-age support); second, that civil suits might have accounted for one-third of all (civil plus criminal) county court cases during the period 1750–1900; and, third, that civil suits might have become more prominent under the Republic, rising to one-half of all county court cases by the 1930's.

TABLE 8

Proportion of Civil and Criminal Cases in "China" and Five Selected
Counties, 1918–1944

Area	Civil	Criminal	Total
China, 1936[a]			
Number	94,259	104,006	198,265
Percent	48%	52%	100%
Counties, 1918–44[b]			
Number	2,700	2,432	5,132
Percent	53%	47%	100%

SOURCES: China, *Sifa tongji 1936*, 2: 1–8; 3: 30–40. For the counties, see Table 19.

[a]The numbers are for cases of "first instance" reported by 255 local (or first-instance) courts (*difang fayuan*); 236 of these were county courts, and the others were the local courts of the principal cities (i.e., 17 of the 19 provincial capitals and Beiping and Shanghai cities). The civil total also includes 12 civil cases of first instance reported by superior courts (*gaodeng fayuan*).

[b]Songjiang, 1918, 1924; Shunyi, 1927, 1930; Linhai, 1928, 1929; Suixian, 1935, 1936; Ningdu, 1940, 1944.

In the previous chapter I noted how greatly the Qing authorities' attempt to trivialize so-called "minor matters" has influenced past scholarship on civil law in the late imperial era. Ideally, in practice as in law, squabbles over "small" things like inheritance or marriage were to be settled by the local residents themselves, and if some of these disputes did happen to intrude upon the official system, they were to be disposed of by the local magistrate without further ado. The Qing code did not provide for the kind of higher review to which all "weighty matters" were subjected. Magistrates needed only to send up a monthly register listing the cases handled (Substatute 334-4); higher levels of the bureaucracy were otherwise not to be troubled. As if to underscore the triviality of these matters, the Qing practice was to limit the days on which plaints could be filed: until the late eighteenth century, to the third, sixth, and ninth days of each 10-day period of the month, and only outside the busy farming season lasting from the fourth through the seventh months; thereafter, despite mounting complaints about burdensome caseloads, to the third and eighth days of each 10-day period of the month (Ch'ü T'ung-tsu 1962: 274, n. 13).*

But in fact, though the Qing pretended otherwise, this chapter has shown that civil cases constituted a significant proportion of the local courts' caseloads. Indeed, to judge by our ethnographic data, for

* Ch'ü indicates that the number of filing days was not reduced until the nineteenth century. But it is clear from Wang Huizu 1796, 2: 9, for example, that the 3–8 practice started earlier. Magistrates, their secretaries, and the yamen staff, of course, were not restricted to these days in their work on the cases.

the majority of the population of any given locale, "civil" matters were of more important and regular concern than criminal matters. Nearly all households were affected in the normal course of their lives by issues of property, debt, marriage, and inheritance; relatively few were ever involved with serious crimes. And a magistrate's relations with the local society probably depended more on his handling of civil cases than criminal ones, even though his relations with his superiors (and hence his career opportunities) depended more on his handling of "weighty" criminal cases. Far from being trivial, civil cases of the types detailed in this chapter were in fact an integrally important aspect of the regular operations of the local courts.

CHAPTER THREE

Informal Justice: Mediation in North China Villages Before the Communist Revolution

T HE WORKINGS OF community/kin mediation have not received much attention in past scholarship. K. C. Hsiao's "Compromise in Imperial China" (1979) is to my knowledge the most thorough treatment of the subject to date, but it is limited by the nature of the sources he uses—mainly local gazetteers, with no ethnographic evidence. As a result, he discusses mostly larger scale conflicts and disputes, like interlineage and interethnic feuds, peasant tax resistance, and irrigation controversies. The study contains little information on disputes among peasants occurring in the normal course of village life.

Like the previous chapter, this one draws on the Mantetsu surveys of Shajing, Sibeichai, and Houjiaying, supplemented by less detailed but still useful information on other villages. These materials contain extended general discussions about the personnel, methods, procedures, and principles involved in mediation. They also contain specific details about the mediation process in the 41 disputes and 18 resulting lawsuits recalled for the Japanese investigators (Table 9). The majority of those mediated resolutions (26 in all) concerned intravillage disputes, precisely the area where our existing literature is the weakest. They fall mainly into two types. One involved middlemen as mediators of the first resort, usually in disputes stemming from contractual obligations. The other involved descent group and/or community leaders as mediators, usually in family and neighborhood disputes. As in the preceding chapter, whenever the ethnographic information seems to me to be applicable only to the Republican period, I will so note; otherwise, my analysis will focus on basic

TABLE 9

Outcomes of Disputes and Lawsuits
in Three North China Villages, 1920's–1940's

Category	Shajing	Sibeichai	Houjiaying	Total
Disputes	16	14	11	41
Mediated	11	5	3	19
Outcome unknown	1	0	1	2
Other	0	2[a]	0	2
TOTAL	12	7	4	23
Lawsuits	4	7	7	18
Mediated	3	3	1	7
Adjudicated	1	4	4	9
Outcome unknown	0	0	2	2
TOTAL	4	7	7	18

SOURCES: KC, 1–2, 3, 5.
[a]Divorce by mutual consent.

characteristics of village-level informal justice that seem to me to apply to both the Qing and the Republican period. This chapter builds on information in the preceding chapter and its demonstration of the essential continuity in village-level justice until the coming of Communist rule.

Contracts and Transactions: The Middleman

As we have seen, almost all villagers were involved in one way or another in contractual relations (including marriage contracting), and those transactions gave rise to a fair share of disputes. They also entailed different forms of mediation and dispute resolution from those employed in settling run-of-the-mill squabbles among family members and neighbors, generally centering around the figure of the middleman.

Formal Loans

Formal loans are the area that perhaps best illustrates the role the middleman (zhongren) played in village society. Typically this may be just someone who was in a position by personal relationship or reputation to facilitate a transaction—hence the common terms "introducer" (jieshaoren) or "person talking into agreement" (shuoheren). Once the transaction took place, that person's most important function was to mediate in the event of a dispute. If the borrower was unable to pay, it was up to the middleman to try to work out some kind of a compromise: he might arrange for an extension, for one harvest (five months) or two (10 months; KC, 4: 222), or another loan to pay off the outstanding one, tantamount to an extension (see also KC, 2: 195–96), or he might pay the outstanding interest himself to obtain an extension on the principal for the borrower (KC, 2: 215).

On occasion, the middleman was also a guarantor (*zhongbaoren* or just *baoren*), though that was relatively rare. In such instances, he was usually a close kinsman of the borrower and someone whom the lender was willing to trust. In the event of a default, he was expected to pay in the borrower's stead (KC, 1: 210–211, 300). Du Xiang of Shajing village, for example, had to sell 10 mu of land to make good on the 300-yuan loan his relative took out to start a business (KC, 2: 260).

When loans were secured by land, there was usually no need for a guarantor (KC, 2: 212, 215), and the middleman's role was chiefly that of a peacemaker. In the event of nonpayment, he might try first to get an extension or to arrange for the borrower to work off the loan (KC, 3: 319). But if the lender was insistent and the borrower simply could not pay, then his task, in the case of loans secured by cultivation rights, was to see to it that the lender actually got to cultivate the land (KC, 2: 250). Where the contract involved a conditional sale (dian), his task was to act as the go-between for the rest of the transaction, in which the lender would acquire complete title to the land by paying the balance between the conditional-sale price and the full land price. Fu Ju in Shajing, for example, arranged for Zhang Yongren, who had purchased a plot conditionally from He Changjiang, to pay a balance of 20 yuan to He for complete title to the land (KC, 2: 211).

The role of the middleman stopped some distance short of a paid brokering profession. According to Shajing villagers, for small contracts involving less than 100 yuan, middlemen were generally not remunerated at all for their services. For loans larger than that, they might receive a gift from the borrower, say, five catties of white flour, or some cabbage, or some wheat-flour buns (*bobo*), but this was not obligatory. They were never paid in money (KC, 2: 212).

The use of middlemen as mediators in formal loans appears to have helped minimize conflict. Our ethnographic data contain not one record of a dispute over a formal loan that was not resolved by the middleman. None went on to kin/community mediation or a lawsuit. The two instances of debt disputes that required community/ kin mediation both concerned informal loans worked out directly between the two parties. We noted the same pattern earlier in our examination of the kinds of cases that went to court—that despite the expectation that informal loans would not be conflict-prone, contracted as they generally were among close relatives or friends, for small amounts and short durations, in both the Qing and the Republican period, they triggered many more lawsuits than the arrangements worked out through middlemen. The comparatively low incidence of suits over formal loans attests to the importance of the middleman institution as a method of resolving disputes.

Land Rentals

In land-rental contracts, the middleman was usually someone who was at once close to the tenant and had some credibility with the landlord, though he could also be just someone known to both by reputation (KC, 3: 188). If there was a written contract, as was often the case with vegetable plots (*yuandi*), which were usually rented for a number of years at a time, his name would appear in the written document (*zupi*; KC, 2: 94–95). If the contract was a verbal one, as was generally true of year-to-year rentals, he would be the acknowledged facilitator and witness for the agreement. In the event the agreed-on rent was not paid, it was up to him to mediate. He might press the tenant for payment. If the tenant could not pay, he might ask the landlord for an extension to the following year. Failing that, he might look for other solutions to avoid conflict (KC, 3: 188). When, in 1941, Liu Yongxiang of Sibeichai could not pay his rent to his landlord, Wang, the middleman, Zhang Yueqing, arranged for another villager, Zhao Luoyou, to guarantee Liu's rent for the next year, promising to pay in Liu's stead if Liu did not. On that basis, Liu got to continue his rental (KC, 3: 178–79).

In Houxiazhai village in Enxian county, Shandong, the small landlord Liu Shicun and his tenant Ma Chang had contracted in 1941 for a three-year rental of 16 mu at a cash price of six yuan a mu, with Ma Ruiyuan as the middleman. But prices on agricultural produce rose rapidly thereafter, and the majority of village rental contracts were switched to in-kind arrangements. Liu wanted his agreement switched like the others, since at the fixed price of six yuan he would be receiving less in value every year. But his tenant held out for sticking to the original arrangement. The dispute was mediated by Ma Ruiyuan, the middleman for the original contract, who worked out the following compromise: tenant Ma would pay in cash in the second of the three years and then in kind in the third year (KC, 4: 473–74).

These middlemen of rental contracts, like their counterparts in negotiating loans, should not be equated with brokers of a modern commercial society. They were potential mediators at least as much as they were facilitators of business transactions, and they were usually not paid a fee for their services (KC, 3: 188). Zhang Yueqing of Sibeichai is a good example: serving as middleman for rental contracts was just one of his many unremunerated services to the community as its leading member. He had served as village head for 12 years and was one of the community's principal mediators for disputes. His middleman work was predicated on his reputation as a peacemaker, not as a broker of business agreements.

Where mediatory services were not needed, rental transactions often took place without middlemen. In Shajing village, for example, the land-rental market at the time of the Mantetsu investigations was very much a seller's market, and standard practice called for the payment of rent in advance; there was thus no question of nonpayment and no need for mediation. Likewise, where the landlord knew the tenant personally, as was often the case, he had no need for an "introducer"; the two would simply work out the rental terms themselves (KC, 2: 92).

Land Sales and Purchases

With a one-time transaction like a land sale, the middleman's responsibilities terminated with the conclusion of the transaction. His functions as mediator were therefore much more limited than with land-rental and formal loan contracts, which came with obligations over a period of time. Still, he filled an important role in seeing to a conflict-free contract. In a land sale, he would ideally make sure that customary practices had been observed: if one brother was selling, he would make sure that the other brother(s) had been consulted. And if the parents were alive, he would make sure that they approved of the sale, even if they were of advanced age and the selling son was the official head of household. If there was a widowed mother, she too needed to approve of the sale. (Otherwise there could be a lawsuit, and prospective mediators as well as the court would likely side with the mother.) He should, finally, make sure that the neighbors on all sides of the field would not object to the sale. If differences arose during the course of the transaction, it was up to him to mediate. If the seller or the buyer changed his mind over the agreed-on price or the transaction itself during the process, or if the two had different understandings of an agreement, it was up to the middleman to act as peacemaker (KC, 1: 83).

If the transaction went forward, it was up to the middleman to measure the land formally in the presence of both buyer and seller. On that day, or a few days later when the sales document was drawn up, the buyer would host a meal to mark the conclusion of the transaction.* The intent was to thank the middleman for his facilitative and mediatory services (KC, 1: 40).

These middlemen to land sales, once again, were not professionals making a living off their occupation as brokers, but rather villagers who were principally employed in other pursuits. They generally did not charge a fee for their services; payment was made only in the symbolic form of a gift or a meal. Fu Ju of Shajing, for example, had served as the middleman in four or five land-sale transactions in the year preceding the investigations, but he had not been paid for any of them. He made his living mainly from peddling, of firewood in 1940, and of pork, vegetables, and fruit earlier. Peddling gave him the necessary contacts and information for serving as the middleman in land transactions (KC, 2: 20). His middleman work was not so much a "job" born of a modern market society as a service function in a partially commercialized and tight-knit peasant community.

Marriages

Marriages in these villages typically took place in two-steps: first the engagement (*dingqin*), with an exchange of the "small cards" (*xiaotie*), conveyed by a go-between, and then the actual marriage, with the delivery of the groom's "big card" (*datie*) or "take as wife card" (*qutie*) to the bride, again conveyed by the go-between. The wedding ceremony usually followed two or three days later (KC, 3: 100).

The entire process seems to me best understood as a symbolic

---

* Note here how custom took into account the fact that the sale of land was generally a sad loss for the seller, and the contrast with our own practice of making the seller responsible for the sales commission.

transaction or exchange, and not as a purely economic deal.* It had non-businesslike aspects as well as businesslike ones. To be sure, betrothal gifts and dowries were discussed in detail and haggled over by the two parties.† But the process cannot, should not, be reduced to a simple commercial transaction like a purchase or sale. Indeed, a disregard of the ceremonial niceties and reduction of the entire process to a mere economic exchange would have been considered crass and could break down the whole arrangement (KC, 1: 266–67).

The go-between was a part of the symbolic-exchange process. His or her role was to facilitate the reaching of the agreement to marry and to minimize the chances for conflict. To pay this go-between (male or female) outright would have been uncouth. In the surveyed villages, custom called for treating the person to "snacks" (*dianxin*) of about two to three yuan's worth at the time of the engagement (after the delivery of the small cards) and a full meal after the delivery of the big card—both more tokens of appreciation than actual remuneration. Relatively well-to-do (owning 40 mu) Liu Shenglan of Sibeichai, for example, spent 50 yuan for a banquet for his relatives and the go-between on the day of the delivery of the big card. But his go-between was not otherwise paid (KC, 3: 110; see also KC, 1: 266–67, 279–80).

This middleperson was often a relative or neighbor of one of the parties (though not necessarily so)—another reason for observing symbolic niceties. The marriage of the Shajing villager Yang Yongyuan's daughter, for example, was arranged by his fellow villager Du Xiang for the nephew of his eldest daughter-in-law (KC, 1: 279–80). And the marriage of the Sibeichai villager Hao Zhuazi's son was arranged by his relative, who was the maternal uncle of the bride (KC, 3: 100). In Lengshuigou village near Jinan in Shandong, the marriage of Li Yongxiang's son Xingjun was arranged by the wife of a fellow villager, unrelated, who came from the same village as the bride-to-be (KC, 4: 123–24). The function of such kin and neighbor serving as go-betweens was clearly understood to be a favor, not a paid service.

---

*Bourdieu 1977: 4–9 contains a useful discussion of the difference between exchanges in which the fiction of a gift had to be maintained and the purely commercial exchange of simple "economism."

†In Shajing village in 1941, the average cost of a marriage for a middle peasant family was about 200–300 yuan apiece for the bride and the groom, and about 1,000–2,000 yuan apiece for the "rich." For the poor, the cost was about 100 yuan, and the whole was borne by the groom's family (KC, 1: 267).

The go-between's responsibility ended with the wedding, seen as the conclusion of the marriage contract. Disputes between the couple after marriage were considered family affairs, to be mediated by kin or neighbors. They take us outside the realm of mediation by middlemen into the other major type of mediation.

Community and Kin-Group Mediators

In family and neighborhood disputes where there were no middlemen to turn to as mediators of first resort, villagers typically looked to a third party for help in resolving the conflict, and specifically to someone with a solid reputation in the community for this kind of service. It was a system of informal justice that had much flexibility and was easily adapted to other situations.

Individuals who served frequently as mediators were readily identifiable in every village. They were generally middle-aged or older men of substance, often the leading members of their descent group and of the community. In Shajing village, for example, the seven mediators named by the informants in 1942 were Li Ruyuan, age sixty-five, who owned 76 mu and was the village's doctor; Zhou Shutang, age unreported but old enough to have served as village head in 1925–26, who owned 33.5 mu and rented another 14 mu; Yang Yuan, forty-four, who owned 40 mu and a jewelry shop in town with five employees, and had served as village head after Zhou Shutang; Zhang Rui, forty-two, who as owner (with his father Wentong) of 130 mu of land was the wealthiest person in the village and the current deputy village head; Zhao Shaoting, fifty-six, who owned 16 mu, rented another 30, and hired a half-year laborer; Yang Yongcai, sixty, who owned 18 mu and also earned 100 yuan a year for watching after the village temple; and Chong Wenqi, forty-nine, who owned a cake shop (KC, 1: 96–97, appended chart; 2: 12–13, 17–18, 23, 31–32, 38, 52–56). Three of the seven (Li Ruyuan, Yang Yuan, and Zhang Rui) were among the 10 active "association heads" (*huishou*) who made up the village's informal governing council (P. Huang 1985: 237–240; KC, 1: 100, 124). Two (Li Ruyuan and Yang Yongcai) were the senior members and heads of their descent groups (KC, 1: appended chart).*

---

* Yang Yuan, though junior to Yang Yongcai, was the senior member of his generation. Zhang Rui routinely acted in the stead of his aged (80) father Wentong, though Wentong remained the head of the household. The other four headed the only households of their patrilines in the village.

One Lengshuigou villager named advanced age with moral uprightness (*niangao youde*) and a reputation for trustworthiness (*you xinyong*) as the important qualifications for mediators, citing as examples the *baojia* heads (of the Qing and under Japanese rule); the village heads (of the twentieth century);* the heads of descent groups; and the local schoolteacher. After them came relatives and kin. Another Lengshuigou informant named advanced age, sizable landed property, and fairness as the qualifications, but went on to say that a younger person who "understood things well" might also qualify (KC, 4: 11–12, 358, 359). In Shajing, one informant identified Zhao Tingkui, just thirty-eight years old in 1942 but an association head, as one of the people serving as mediators. But Zhao Shaoting of the same village, an established mediator himself, observed that Tingkui, like Yang Ze and Yang Zheng (the village head Yang Yuan's brothers), though able, was really still too young and lacked experience (KC, 1: 139; 189).

In Sibeichai village, the two men who appeared most frequently as mediators were Zhang Yueqing, who had served for a total of 12 years as village head, and Hao Guoliang, the current head. In Houjiaying village, one man had stood out for some years as "the well-do'er of the village" (*yixiang shanshi*). It was said that whenever Hou Yongfu mediated a dispute, "big problems became small problems, and small problems became non-problems" (*dashi hua xiao, xiaoshi hua liao*). After Hou died, things reverted to the more common situation, with six or seven men frequently serving as mediators, and no one towering above the others in reputation (KC, 5: 154; see also KC, 4: 358).

When individuals or groups from different villages were involved, the system adapted itself readily, with the same basic approach. Thus, in Zhou Shutang's dispute over land boundaries with a Zhang of neighboring Wangquan village, he enlisted the help of Li Ruyuan and Du Xiang (an association head close to Zhou and known for his ability to write, but not one of the common mediators). They, in turn, brought in Wangquan village's Mr. Liu, known for his work in mediation. Together the three worked to resolve the dispute (KC, 1: 140). In the dispute arising over Shimen's swampy land that Shajing villagers had planted in reeds, the two parties turned for help to leaders from four other villages (KC, 1: 474–75). Finally, in the Shajing vil-

---

* The village head system was instituted in these villages during the first years of the twentieth century (P. Huang 1985: 240–44).

lagers' dispute with the village tough Fan Baoshan over his fraudulent claims to their temple land, the village leaders even enlisted on
an ad hoc basis the aid of the Japanese investigators, who were better
connected than they with the county authorities.

In instances of household division, the mediators were typically
drawn from not just the acknowledged leading members of the community and kin but also other villagers, often neighbors affected by
the change. Even if not particularly effective as mediators, they made
necessary witnesses. Thus, in Shajing village, the division between
Yang Puzeng and Yang Shaozeng involved two kin and one nonkin
middleman (zhongbaoren), and that among Du Chun's four sons,
one kin and three nonkin (KC, 1: 291, 292). Where the family was a
prominent one, as in the case of Yang Yuan, Yang Zheng, and Yang
Ze, the division document was witnessed by three kin and nine nonkin, including almost all of the respected mediators of the community (KC, 1: 255–56, 292). In Sibeichai, a village leader joined members of the Hao descent group in mediating the division among Hao
Goucheng and his three brothers, but two other Hao family divisions,
among Guoliang and his four brothers and between Zhuazi and his
brother, were handled by the descent group without outside help. Interestingly, six kin oversaw the last, in which just two brothers were
involved, twice as many as participated in what one would think to
be the more complex five-way division (KC, 3: 69, 95–96, 102).

The division among Hao Goucheng and his three brothers illustrates the process. In addition to three senior members of the Hao
descent group as mediator-witnesses (zhongjianren), the assistance of
the village head Zhang Yueqing was enlisted. In this case, the relationship among the brothers was said to be comparatively good and
therefore only two days of discussions were required to reach agreement. Two items, the water pump and the cart, would continue to be
held in common. All the other family properties—36 mu of land, the
house, and the furniture—were parceled out into four equal shares.
Each brother then drew a slip of paper from a teacup held high by
Zhang Yueqing to see who was to get what (KC, 3: 95–96).

To forestall future arguments, the division agreement was given
all of the moral and legal weight the descent group and the community could bring to bear. The discussions were detailed and concrete,
and involved the participation of all concerned. Once agreement was
reached and the distribution settled by drawing lots, a formal document was drawn up, spelling out the properties divided, and was

signed by the brothers and witnessed by the middlemen. It was a process that left little room for later challenges and disputes. That was why household division, though the principal source of disputes in the villages, was not a major category of lawsuits (Chap. 2).

Principles and Methods of Mediation

As the above examples suggest, the informal justice system was concerned above all with maintaining peaceful relations among kin and neighbors in close-knit communities. Its main method was compromise, though generally within a frame set by law and by the community's sense of right and wrong. Where legal or normative standards seemed irrelevant to a dispute, as was often the case with family or neighborhood squabbles, then the mediators would be guided almost exclusively by the aim of making peace through compromise.

The Primacy of Compromise

Let us begin with the case in Houjiaying village of Hou Dingyi's dispute with his neighbor over the tree that was planted on Hou's plot but whose branches spread across the boundary to his neighbor's land. Both parties claimed the lumber from the tree. The decision, as mediated by the village's leading "well-do'er" Hou Yongfu, gave the wood from the top branches to Dingyi, and the wood from the stems and lower branches to his neighbor. The "settlement" came with some concession from Dingyi, since the lower branches were bigger and thicker than the higher ones. Asked why he compromised willingly, Dingyi said it was because his neighbor was poor. What is more, he did not want to incur the man's wrath, lest he seek revenge against Dingyi by breaking into or setting fire to his house (KC, 5: 154).

In this example, we can see that there was little concern with the law of the state (guofa). No attempt was made to analyze the matter in terms of property rights. Nor was there much attention to what might be called the moral principles (li or tianli) of right and wrong. The operative principle was renqing: the kinds of courtesies and considerations that help to maintain peaceable day-to-day human relations. It was the aspect of renqing that gave rise to the permutated meanings in which the term came to mean something close to *guanxi*, or personal connections that can be used and exploited, even given and exchanged like a gift—as in the expresssions *songge renqing,* "give a favor," or *zuoge renqing,* "do a favor." In this case, they had to do with compassionate concession to a poorer neighbor as well as the very practical calculation of avoiding harm to oneself.

The competing claims of two impoverished stepbrothers of Sibeichai provide another illustration of the primacy of compromise. One of the brothers, Xu Xiaomao, had opted 10 years earlier to go live with his maternal uncle (*jiujiu*) in another village. The uncle had some property, and the understanding was that Xiaomao would become his heir. But then the uncle lost all his property, and on his death, the now-destitute Xiaomao returned to his natal village to try to eke out a living. Since he and his stepbrother Dehe had never formally undergone household division, he claimed one-half of the family's property. Dehe felt that Xiaomao, having adopted himself out, had relinquished any claim to the property.

The four village mediators who intervened (including the ubiquitous Zhang Yueqing) were of no mind to hairsplit over who had what legally defensible claim, but simply set about finding the best compromise solution to the real human problem before them. Xiaomao, who had a larger family than Dehe but did not farm, was to receive most of the old house: four rooms (*jian*) out of six. The other two rooms would be torn down, and Dehe would build a new house. But the land, six mu, was to remain undivided and to be farmed exclusively by Dehe (KC, 3: 153–54).

The four village heads who mediated in the land dispute between Shajing and Shimen likewise did not concern themselves with the legal bases of the respective claims of the two parties but looked instead for a compromise that both sides could accept as fair: the settlement called for the two villages to split the proceeds from the sale of the reeds (KC, 2: 474).

In one case, mediation followed a failed resort to the formal legal system. This was the dispute between Xu Fuyu of Sibeichai and his widowed mother over the disposition of the family's land. The mother, who had a reputation as a spendthrift, had demanded to sell the family's (already conditionally sold) land outright. The son, who was known as honest and hardworking, refused. In retaliation and to get her way, she brought suit against him, ostensibly for not providing her with food for proper old-age support. The county court, on learning the truth of the matter, rejected the mother's suit as groundless. But the real human problem of conflict between mother and son remained. It was a matter of concern for community justice, even if no longer for the state's courts. It was up to the members of the common descent group and the village head to mediate some kind of a solution. Though they thought the mother in the wrong to demand the sale of the land, they settled on arranging for the widow and her son and his family to live separately as the only way to put an end to the conflict (KC, 3: 153).

The Influence of Law on Community Mediation

Important as the informal justice system of kin/community mediation was, in most disputes there at least loomed the possibility of a lawsuit. Consequently, formal law wielded some influence, even if not an active voice, over the mediation process. Congruence between formal law and customary practice, as for example in the principle of equal division among sons, helped to minimize conflict, as has been seen. Conversely, disjunction between formal law and customary practice, as for example over the degree of alienability of landed property, made for frequent disputes (Chap. 2). The point here is not that law did not matter, but rather that the primary concern of informal justice was peacemaking, not law enforcement.

If a dispute became a lawsuit, as happened in the case discussed above of the dispute between Xu Xiaomao and his stepbrother Dehe, community mediators had little choice but to consider what was laid down by the law. Xiaomao, unwilling to let the matter rest with community mediation, decided shortly after the settlement was made to file a lawsuit for half the land. This time the mediators had to take into account the prospect that the court would find for equal division. They prevailed on the two men to work out a compromise between the original agreement and what they thought would be the likely ruling of the court: Dehe had to concede to Xiaomao two of the six mu of land. He got to keep more of the land because he had earlier conceded a larger portion of the house. To forestall future conflict, the stepbrothers were persuaded to execute a formal division document. Though the matter was settled without a formal court judgment, there could be no mistaking the influence of official law in the final mediated settlement.

We have another, similar example from Sibeichai in a dispute between Hao Luoke and his widowed sister-in-law over the family property. The widow had returned to her natal home with her two daughters on her husband's death, and remarried soon after. By established village custom and the old Qing code, neither she nor her daughters had any claim to the family's land in those circumstances. But the widow brought suit under the new provisions of the Republican Code recognizing the right of daughters to inherit their father's property. She argued that the family's 50 mu of land should be partitioned between Hao Luoke and his deceased brother, with her daughters as the latter's rightful heirs. As in the other case, once she filed suit, the mediators—the village head, Hao Guoliang, and two others—had to take into account the likely judgment of the court. What they worked out was a compromise between the community's customary practice (as well as the old code) and the new code. Failing to persuade Hao Luoke to entertain any thought of giving half the family's land to his nieces, which seemed to him an outrageous and unjust demand, flouting both long-standing village custom and centuries-old Qing law, they got him to agree to provide dowries for the two girls on behalf of his deceased brother. That arrangement fell within the boundaries of what was traditionally acceptable and also made Hao look good. The actual agreement worked out called for Hao to pay 1,000 yuan in cash, the value of about 10 mu of land. Though this amounted to far less than a full half share of the family's land (in fact only about a quarter share), it was represented as a household division, complete with a written document. Hao was persuaded to go along with that representation to forestall any future claims from his sister-in-law or nieces (KC, 3: 155, 338–39).

Right and Wrong

The last section shows how formal law could figure prominently in informal mediation, once disputes entered into that intermediate space between the formal and informal justice systems (on which more in Chap. 5). On the other hand, even in those situations, informal justice clearly did not act in any purely legalistic manner, as a formal court might have done. Its primary concern was not to adjudicate the right and wrong of a case according to law, but to make peace through compromise. Nevertheless, the right and wrong of things was generally an important part of the peasants' commonsense approach to village conflicts. Thus, compromise was the chosen path in the dispute between Hou Dingyi and his neighbor over the tree, between Xu Xiaomao and Xu Dehe over the means of subsistence, and between Shajing and Shimen over the reeds precisely because both parties seemed more or less equally in the right. On the other hand, the community would not give the widow Xu her way over her son because her demand to sell the land was seen to be wrong. In that instance, the compromise worked out sought to pacify both parties by arranging for them to live separately.

Indeed, the communities did not shy from standing up to defend what they thought was right. As has been seen, Sibeichai villagers filed suit successfully in 1935 to obtain the removal of the abusive village head Li Yanlin. And Shajing villagers took the bully Fan Baoshan to court in 1939 and got him removed. When Fan Baoshan returned in 1942 and conspired with the head monk of the Cheng-huang temple to take over Shajing's 20 mu of temple land, the villagers appealed to the Japanese investigators for help. Hatada Takashi, one of the principal investigators (who went on to become a major historian), first collected the relevant facts and documentation, and then, in good mediator style, arranged a meeting for all concerned, to which he invited the county authorities. Presented with incontrovertible evidence, including the village's receipts for tax payments on the land dating back to 1915, the county authorities berated the town monk for his unfounded claims. The monk had to sign on the spot a document renouncing all claims to the land and pledging not to make any more trouble (KC, 1: 194–203; P. Huang 1985: 41–42).

Mediation, then, was not always a mere matter of compromise between two sides. In instances when right and wrong were unequivocal, mediation could as well be a method of vindication, to result in a clear-cut "victory" for the party in the right. In those situations, the difference from court adjudication was that there would be some face-saving for the loser by representing the matter as a mediation rather than a vindication. Justice would be done, but the offender would be left with the symbolic space for keeping his "face" more or less intact.

Compromise, Morality, and Law in Informal Justice

Much as the Qing officials pretended that law mattered little in informal justice, it clearly did figure in in important ways. At the same time, as the foregoing analysis should make clear, the actual operation of that system differed substantially from its idealized Confucian representation. To see informal justice as guided only by tianli and renqing is to oversimplify, for qingli did not have quite the same meanings lent it by Confucian idealization. In the actual operation of village justice, renqing took on above all the more practical meaning of maintaining peaceful human relations, and li the less lofty meaning of common-sense right and wrong, as conveyed by the popular usage of the term daoli. Villagers were concerned above all with working out compromises for the sake of maintaining amiable relations among people who had to live in close proximity to one another in insular groupings.

The complex interworkings of law, compromise, and common-sense right and wrong can be illustrated in some detail with the example of a dispute in Shajing village between Li Zhuyuan and his nephew Guang'en over easement rights. Zhuyuan's house was west of Guang'en's and adjacent to the road. To get to his house from the road, Guang'en needed to go through Zhuyuan's yard. The household division leading to this situation dated back some 60 years, and the arrangement had worked well until Zhuyuan decided to sell his land. It turned out that though Guang'en's copy of the original agreement stipulated his right to use the path running through Zhuyuan's yard, Zhuyuan's copy did not specifically stipulate his obligation to allow Guang'en such access.

By custom, in the Republican period as in the Qing, Zhuyuan had to allow his neighbors on all four sides first refusal in the sale. They therefore had to be consulted before he sold his plot. Custom also called for their witnessing the deed of sale. But the letter of the law was out of sync with social practice. Neither the Qing code nor the Republican code required a land-seller to seek the permission of the adjoining landowners. That gave Zhuyuan the opening he needed to go ahead and sell the plot without consulting Guang'en or his other neighbors. Zhuyuan apparently also concealed the easement problem from the buyer, Zhao Wenyou, who had recently come to live in the village. Instead of having the village head witness the transaction as middleman and registering the transaction through him, as was usual in such cases, Zhuyuan found an out-of-town middleman and registered the transaction with the town government in Renhe (zhen). He could do so legally because he had a legitimate household division document proving ownership and a legitimate deed of sale. In this way, he obtained a price of 100 yuan for the plot, higher than he might have obtained from a more conventional sale, with the easement obligation attached.

From the point of view of village custom, or the villagers' common-sense notions of right and wrong, Li Zhuyuan was clearly in the wrong. The first three mediators—Zhou Shutang, Zhao Shaoting, and Yang Yongcai—therefore took the position that Li Zhuyuan should buy back the easement path from Zhao and give it to Guang'en. They persuaded Zhuyuan to agree to concede "20 to 30 yuan" of the 100 yuan sales price for the purpose.

But the new owner, Zhao, wanted to build his house over the easement path, not north of it as he would have to do if he turned it over to Guang'en. He thought he had acted well within the boundaries of the law, having bought the land fair and square. He saw no reason why he should have to make concessions for something he had not been told about. He therefore refused to give up the easement path unless he was paid 100 yuan—the price he paid for the entire plot—for the path.

In response to this turn of events, community members next tried to make peace by appealing to the magnanimity of Li Ruyuan, the senior and leading member of the Li descent group. Ruyuan offered a strip of his own plot, north of Guang'en's, to Guang'en for free. Though less convenient than the path through Zhuyuan's plot to the west, the strip would allow Guang'en access to the crossroad north of Ruyuan's plot. Ruyuan went so far as to offer to have a formal deed of sale drawn up, so that there could be no dispute in the future from his heirs over Guang'en's ownership of the strip. In the villagers' eyes, Ruyuan's was exemplary behavior based on renqing, for the sake of maintaining amiable relations among members of his kin.

But Guang'en was not willing to settle for less convenient access, since he was entirely in the right by the standards of village custom. Things once more reached an impasse. Matters came to a head when Zhao began constructing his house on the right-of-way. A fight broke out between him and Guang'en, and a furious Zhao rushed off to the county seat to file suit to enforce his claim. With that action, he took the dispute out of the strictly informal realm into the formal realm, or at least into the intermediate space between the two.

Convinced though the community mediators were that Guang'en was in the right, they feared that the court would find for Zhao according to the letter of the law. They therefore sought to work out a compromise between what they considered just and what they thought would happen if a court were to adjudicate the matter. They persuaded Zhuyuan to increase what he had agreed to pay Zhao, from the original figure of "20 to 30 yuan" to "30 to 40 yuan." At the same time, they got Zhao to agree to lower his demand from 100 yuan to 50. Ten yuan, however, still separated the two parties.

The mediators now turned to the Mantetsu investigators for

help. The latter, who were studying the workings of community mediation in this matter, decided to try to settle the dispute. In the compromise-working spirit of the community's justice system, they offered to provide out-of-pocket the 10-yuan difference to bring the two sides to agreement. At that, Zhao accepted the settlement, on the strength of the investigators' "face" (*mianzi*), he said. The lawsuit was withdrawn—or, perhaps, was never even filed, since it was rumored that in the heat of the moment Zhao had gone to court when it was closed, on a Sunday (KC, 1: 162–70).

We can see from this example how the triad of state law, the community's sense of right and wrong, and compromise to maintain peace all operated together. Obviously, it would be wrong to assume that state law did not matter; once the lawsuit was filed, or even just threatened, the formal system in effect set the negotiating baseline from which the compromise had to be worked out. It would also be wrong to assume that right and wrong did not matter. Quite plainly, the village mediators believed Guang'en was in the right and Zhuyuan in the wrong. But that was just as plainly not the sole principle guiding their actions. What mattered most was the community's concern to avoid litigation and maintain peaceable relations among kin and neighbors. That was what guided the series of efforts at peacemaking compromise that succeeded in producing the final resolution.

Abuses of Informal Justice

Our consideration of informal justice, finally, must not overlook the abuses that came with it. Mediated compromise worked best in instances of disputes among people of roughly equivalent status and power; it could do little in the way of righting injustices against the powerless by the powerful. The emphasis on mediated compromise, in fact, could serve to excuse or cover up gross injustices.

There is one particularly graphic example of such injustice among my Shunyi court cases. In 1927, seventeen-year-old Liu Changjiangtou raped Lu Shenglan's seven-year-old daughter. The little girl died of the injuries inflicted on her, as revealed in a coroner's report, and the girl's father brought formal charges. Young Liu quickly went into hiding to avoid arrest, while his father, Cungui, a wealthy and powerful man, set to work to get him off. Though we do not have the full details of what the father did, the result was to have this criminal case treated as if it were a mere civil dispute, by the procedures operative in the Qing and in 1927 yet to be fully replaced by the new procedures of Republican law. First the village head and several association heads, representing themselves as "mediators" in the dispute, filed a petition with the county court claiming that they had looked into matters and found that "Lu Shenglan and Liu Cungui each stuck to his version of events, each had his reasons, and neither was sufficient to establish whether what allegedly happened really happened." Next, the plaintiff, Lu Shenglan, was somehow persuaded to file a petition to close the case. In his petition, Lu stated that a group of 10 prominent local mediators (including Zhou Shutang of our Shajing village), had arranged for him and Liu Cungui "to meet face to face and observe the appropriate courtesies" (*jianmian fuli*), and that both wished now to end the lawsuit. "On the matter of the death of my daughter," Lu stated in his petition, "now that the middlemen have talked us into agreement [*jingzhong shuohe*], there are no further difficulties [*bing wu jiuge*]." Then the magistrate, who had also been appropriately persuaded, went along with the whole cover-up, writing on the petition, in the style of old Qing practice, the incredible comment, "permission granted to close the case."* Thus did the powerful employ the principles, procedures, and language of informal justice to cover up a crime of rape-murder (Shunyi 2: 485, 1927.6.6).

Those same principles and procedures could also provide the opportunity for official extortion, as evidenced in a suicide case from Houjiaying village in the early 1940's. Hou Zhenxiang's daughter-in-law had married into his household at the age of 17 *sui*. She got along well with him, but not with his wife, her mother-in-law, who was something of a shrew. The tensions came to a head three years later (in the summer of 1942). The young woman regularly worked four days a week for someone in the village to gather straw, for 0.8 yuan a day (a pay rate that reflected the price inflation of the later years of the war in this area) and apparently would keep the earnings herself (as was rural custom with respect to a wife's earnings outside of the household). She would return to her natal home to visit on her off days. This one time she left without having been paid. The father-in-law got the money in her stead and took it to her. Since he did not have the exact change, he gave her a full four yuan. Furious, Hou's wife insisted that he go and get the change. (Another version has it

*The procedures on this manner of resolution of civil lawsuits are discussed in more detail in Chap. 5.

that she insisted that he bring the daughter-in-law back to help with the sorghum harvest.) Instead of getting the money, however, Hou simply complained to his in-laws about his wife's unreasonable outburst. In the meantime, the wife decided to go get the money herself. Angry words were exchanged with the in-laws; the young woman became extremely upset; and after she returned to her marital home later that night, she apparently killed herself by jumping into the well (KC, 5: 49–50; see also 40).

The police came to investigate and questioned everyone to determine whether the young woman had been mistreated. Fearful of criminal prosecution, Hou enlisted the aid of the leading mediators of the community in an effort to smooth things over. They arranged for him to pay 500 yuan to the local bully in power (and opium addict and gambler), the town head (*zhenzhang*), Qi; about 200 yuan in gifts to the deceased girl's family; 30 yuan to the coroner who came to examine the body; 20 yuan in drinks to entertain him and others; plus expenses for the girl's funeral and banquets. Added to all this was the interest on loans he took out to meet these outlays—1,000 yuan, which he borrowed from Qi at 6 percent interest a month, through the "good offices" of the *bao* head, who was Qi's underling, and miscellaneous amounts from relatives and friends. In the end, he had to sell 20 of his 40 mu of land to repay these loans. His expenses totaled about 2,400 yuan in all, the kind of sum that lent substance to the horror tales about astronomical legal fees. The entire "settlement" was driven by the town head Qi's demands and Hou's fear of trouble. The possible injustices behind the young woman's suicide received no attention at all. What the mediators did in working out the settlement was in effect to facilitate the extortionist actions of the bully Qi (KC, 5: 40, 49–50, 53–54).

Informal Justice and Power Relations

The two examples above underscore the fact that informal justice, like all aspects of village life, operated within a context of power relations. To be sure, most communities were composed of roughly equivalent peasants, making the kinds of gross imbalances of power reflected in these cases relatively rare. Men like Liu Cungui, who had the wealth and power to bend the county magistrate, the village head, and prominent local mediators, as well as the plaintiff, to his will were rather exceptional in the North China countryside. Still, this case serves to remind us of the limits of informal justice: it could not easily right a wrong done by the powerful against the powerless.

The Houjiaying case, similarly, reminds us of the scope for abuse by the powerful, in this case by subcounty officials rather than the local elite. I have written elsewhere at some length about the spread of the phenomenon of local bullies and tyrants insinuating themselves into subcounty government in the Republican period, because of the vacuums in power created by the twin pressures of state intrusion (especially increased taxation) and community fragmentation (especially the breakdown of the old social bonds; P. Huang 1985: chaps. 14 and 15). The town head Qi is an extreme example of that type of figure.

But even if we remove figures like Qi and Liu Cungui, and concern ourselves with the relatively cohesive village community of mainly middle and poor peasants, it is clear that there were still great gaps in relative power and status among different village groups. The daughter-in-law was truly the lowest person on the totem pole: an outsider to the village community, a junior to her parents-in-law, and a mere woman before her father-in-law and husband.

The suicide of the young daughter-in-law in Houjiaying is a particularly poignant reminder that an absence of formal litigation should not be equated with the absence of conflict, or the potential for conflict. One cannot in fact find any instance of the proverbial mistreated daughter-in-law appearing in her own right in either the court records or the Mantetsu data on disputes. In the Qing, she had to be represented by her natal family, generally her father, or not at all. In the Republic, though in principle she was entitled to bring suit in her own name, there were tremendous social and practical constraints to overcome for her to do so. In both periods, as we saw in the preceding chapter, unhappily wed wives could and often did return to their natal families. If that resort was somehow barred to them, they had little choice but to submit to their subordinate position in their marital families.

Just as civil lawsuits need to be seen in the larger context of disputes that did not end up in court, so too mediated disputes need to be understood in the context of social conflicts that did not become open disputes resolvable through the workings of informal justice. Kin and community mediation was in fact generally open only to the stalwart members of the community, mainly male heads of households. It worked best with people who were roughly equal in power

and status: as for example between squabbling brothers and neighbors, lenders and creditors, buyers and sellers of land. And it worked
mainly to produce compromises in disputes in which there was no
clear-cut right and wrong. It was not intended to be a system that
would protect the underprivileged against the powerful. Social inferiors, like the married-in daughter-in-law, stood implicitly outside the
system. Compromise-seeking mediation between a daughter-in-law
(unrepresented by her natal family) and her parents-in-law and husband was simply unheard of in the villages surveyed.

An entire worldview stood in the way of any such mediation.
Thus, when the Mantetsu investigators, their "consciousness" raised
by the suicide of the young woman, sought to ask in some detail about
the condition of daughters-in-law in Houjiaying village (something
they had not probed in any of the other surveyed villages), informants
simply dismissed the issue. Take, for example, this exchange between the investigator Hayakawa Tamotsu and one informant:

Q: The relationship between the son's wife and her mother-in-law is
probably not so good, as is common?
A: It's fine.
Q: Doesn't the son usually favor the wife and slight the mother?
A: Such cases are rare. (KC, 5: 453)

Later, another investigator persisted with a different informant:

Q: Do your daughter-in-law and your wife ever disagree over something?
A: No.
Q: Why?
A: Because women cannot decide things. Since I am the one who makes
the decisions, there is no question of a difference of opinion.
Q: What if there were?
A: That doesn't happen. Since the parents are still around, the daughter-
in-law is not supposed to express her own opinion. So there is no difference
of views. (KC, 5: 474)

Typically, male peasant informants insisted that relations between
daughters-in-law and their husbands' parents were just fine (KC, 4:
140; 5: 107, 474). There could be no disputes, hence no need for
mediation.

This sanguine picture might have gone unchallenged had it not
been for the suicide incident. The case serves to remind us just
how conflict-ridden the mother-in-law/daughter-in-law relationship
could be. It was not the absence of conflict but rather the great imbalance in power relations that snuffed out open dispute and formal

litigation. It was only in the years after 1949, when daughters-in-law gained greater independence in the home through their earnings, that these frictions came out in the open to become one of the leading categories of village disputes. The tensions were greatest between the young brides who in the mid-1980's came to earn their paychecks from the rural industrial enterprises directly (rather than in the earlier system of earning collective workpoints that were paid to the head of household) and mothers-in-law who had had to live under the old relations themselves and expected similar kinds of relations in their old age (P. Huang 1990: 298–301).

Though we do not have similarly illustrative details for hired agricultural workers, their status was in many ways not unlike that of the daughters-in-law. As I have written in detail elsewhere (P. Huang 1985: 199–201, 214–16; see also 88–99), the hired worker was very much at the bottom of rural society. To be forced into a condition of having to sell all of one's land and hire out to another was the dreaded fate for any peasant under subsistence presssures. The majority of hired workers generally had to leave their home villages, go on the road, and hire out wherever they could (KC, 2: 52–54; see also KC, 4: 188–89). As mere sojourners, these wage-workers were not considered full-fledged members of the community with the kinds of rights to dispute resolution through mediation conferred by its informal justice system. What is more, they did not have the recourse open to a daughter-in-law of returning to their natal families. Those reasons, not the absence of conflict, I would speculate, account for the lack of any evidence on mediated disputes between managerial farmers/rich peasants and their hired workers.

In fact, most agricultural laborers had to live with their lot. Unlike the other middlemen we have discussed, the middlemen in employer and wage-worker agreements did not generally serve any mediatory function. Their role ended with introducing or "talking into agreement" employer and wage-worker. What happened between them thereafter was not their concern. If the worker turned out to be lazy or damaged something, the "introducer" (or "bring-person"; *lairen*) was not usually called in. Differences would be settled directly between employer and worker (KC, 2: 49, 47).

As is well known, until the second half of the eighteenth century, agricultural workers were classed by Qing law as "worker-serfs" (*gugongren*), outside of and below "commoners" (*fanren*), though not quite of the lowest status group, "mean people" (*jianmin*). Legally, they were seen as a kind of indentured servant (signatories to a written contract, effective for a number of years), something like a subordinate member of the employer's household; the employer was commonly referred to as the head of household (*jiazhang*) vis-à-vis the worker. Eventually, however, the spreading practice of managerial farmers and rich peasants hiring other peasants as workers brought the law to the acknowledgment that wage-workers were often in fact equal commoners who "normally sit and eat with their employers, and address them as equals, and are not differentiated from them as serfs are from masters" (P. Huang 1985: 98; see also Jing 1981: 18–23). Nevertheless, as the lone case we have (among 628) of a laborer's complaint illustrates, the Qing code never quite reached the point of including the employer–wage-worker agreement as a form of contract involving obligations to be honored by both sides, as it did with respect to land and debt transactions and marital contracts. In this isolated case, from Baodi in 1832, Jin Wende filed a plaint against his employer, Yang Fugui, charging that he had beaten him, thrown him out, and refused to pay him the wages due him for three years' work. The facts were clear enough and were not disputed by Yang. But the code did not give the magistrate any basis for ordering Yang to pay Jin his wages.* He therefore turned the case away, though he was moved to comment, in an appeal to Yang's sense of compassion, that one should not drive away "an impoverished man from afar" who had "lived a hard life working for three years" (Baodi 188, 1832.7.9 [d-2]).

Tenants, of course, had it better under Qing law to the extent that they were not considered a special subcommoner category like the "worker-serfs." In 1727 a substatute was even added to the code specifically forbidding gentry landlords from privately punishing their tenants (No. 312-3). In the ethnographic information from the early 1940's, as noted, we have a clear example of a middleman mediating a dispute between a landlord and a tenant over whether rent should be paid in kind instead of cash to take account of the inflation in agricultural produce. That suggests a fairly equal relationship. It would be a mistake, however, to project that kind of relationship to all landlord-tenant relations. In Sibeichai, a single absentee landlord, Wang Zanzhou, towered above the community, with 304.5 mu of leased-out land, plus another 80 mu to which he held conditional

---

*Unless he chose to treat the matter as a debt obligation under Statute 149, which even if it had occurred to him, he would probably have rejected as too far-fetched.

title, out of a total of 2,054 mu of cultivated land in the village. He alone accounted for 28 percent of all the rented land (P. Huang 1985: 177). To hear him tell it, he had no problems with his tenants. But as the village head, Zhang Yueqing, explained, that was just how things looked on the surface; tenants did not complain because if they showed any dissatisfaction, they would lose their rental (in what was clearly a seller's market; KC, 3: 193). In Shajing village, similarly, the middle peasant Yang Ze ventured that since the landlord could pretty much do as he pleased, the tenant was not really entitled to an opinion (KC, 1: 141). The rental market there, as mentioned, so favored the landlord at the time that contracts standardly called for the payment of all rents in advance.

What, finally, have we learned about the nature and operation of informal justice? To begin with, it seems to me that village conflict and justice can be schematized into a three-tiered structure of suppressed conflict, open disputes, and formal lawsuits, each corresponding to a different mode of conflict resolution: domination/subordination, mediation, and litigation. Not all conflicts erupted into open disputes that were then handled by mediation. Where gross inequities in power and status existed, domination/subordination could serve to snuff out open disputes; informal justice could do little to right legal or moral wrongs against the powerless. Where the disagreements were between relative equals, mediation succeeded famously in heading off lawsuits; only a minority of open disputes proceeded on to court.

For all the informal justice system's flexibility in the name of good order and peace, it abided by certain principles. Community consensus about right and wrong counted, and so to some extent did the formal justice system; second-guessing a possible court decision often affected the shape of an agreement. But the guiding concern of informal justice was above all peacemaking compromise, which set it apart both from Confucian idealization and from the formal justice system, to which we now turn.

CHAPTER FOUR

Formal Justice: Codified Law and Magisterial Adjudication in the Qing

IN FORMAL LAW AS IN informal justice, we find a substantial disjunction between official representation and actual practice. As I have argued, the Qing state put a face on its legal system that has prompted two misimpressions: first, that the system dealt hardly at all with civil matters; and second, that when magistrates did deal with those matters, they mostly did so either as arbitrary administrators or as compromise-working mediators, not as judges adjudicating according to codified law.

The arbitrary administrator image is reinforced by the official representation of the magistrate as the local embodiment of the emperor. By the ideology of the state, the emperor's authority was total. He was the source of all laws. Until 1740, in fact, his edicts were normally incorporated into the code as substatutes.* The magistrate, as the emperor's local representative, supposedly wielded similarly absolute power over his childlike subjects as their "father-mother official." At the local as at the central level, there was no check on absolute governmental power by "civil society" or by autonomous judicial, legislative, and executive branches.

Philip Kuhn's excellent book *Soulstealers* (1990) has dramatically spotlighted the arbitrary authority of the emperor and his agents. It shows how the Qianlong Emperor's unfounded suspicion of sedition, following a spate of queue-clipping incidents in 1768, compelled local magistrates to employ severe torture to extract confessions from innocent suspects. Readers of Kuhn's book will likely find unforget-

---

*Under the new code promulgated by the Qianlong Emperor in 1740, all imperial edicts would be published instead in a separate volume (Zheng Qin 1992: 61).

table the bone-crushing ankle press (*jiagun*), so widely and indiscriminately used by his account.* Some will surely take away also an impression of unchecked arbitrary authority through every administrative level.

The image of the magistrate as compromise-working mediator, on the other hand, is reinforced by his assigned role in Qing juridical theory. Chinese legal theory did not presume, as modern Western formalist legal theory does, that the "truth" established in the courtroom, though not necessarily the actual truth, is ideally the best possible approximation of or substitution for it. It was therefore in theory not up to the magistrate to adjudicate, to decide himself the truth of the matter. His role in criminal cases ideally was instead to get the real perpetrator to confess and thereby reveal the substantive truth (Shiga 1975: 120–24). That was the logic behind the practice of requiring confessions.

By extension, that logic would have the magistrate in a civil dispute merely facilitating the revelation of the substantive truth by the litigating parties and, on that basis, to help work out a voluntary settlement between them. Just as, in theory, a criminal case was not concluded until the perpetrator confessed, so a civil case could not (in theory) be closed until the litigants pledged to accept the judgment of the court. In principle, in civil cases, as in criminal cases, the magistrate did not adjudicate.

Thus, Shiga Shūzō, who has made great contributions to the study of Chinese legal principles, subscribes to the prevailing image of the magistrate's role in civil cases as chiefly that of a mediator. Given only sparse and unspecific stipulations, the magistrates did not act "like an umpire officiating a game" according to given rules, but rather like a paternalistic compromise-worker engaged in "didactic conciliation." Their adjudication, if it could be called that, "was [therefore] strongly colored by mediation" (Shiga 1981: 76, 94, 96).

In our Western frame of reference, the implication of such constructions is that, in civil matters at least, there was really no "law" or "rights" to speak of. If magistrates enjoyed absolute power, there could be no legal rights independent of the will of the ruler. If mag-

---

* Let me note, for readers whose image of Chinese justice may be shaped by this part of Kuhn's story, that the Qing code explicitly restricted the ankle press to "cases of robbery and homicide," and cautioned that it be used only "with careful consideration" (*zhuoyong*; substatute No. 1-1). In fact, as Xue Yunsheng (1820–1901) stated in his note to the substatute, by the late nineteenth century, the ankle press was "never used, even in connection with cases of homicide and robbery."

istrates acted as mediators, it would make little sense to speak of a consistent body of law or of judges acting to protect the rights of individuals. And if compromise was the guiding principle in magistrates' actions, there could be no genuine adjudication.

In this chapter I will demonstrate that the system did not operate this way at all, that magistrates in fact hardly ever engaged in mediation. My case files from Baxian, Baodi, and Dan-Xin tell the story. In 170 of the 221 cases that reached a formal court session,* or 77 percent, magistrates adjudicated unequivocally according to the Qing code for one or other of the litigating parties. This pattern held across all three counties. The Baxian court ruled unequivocally in 69 of 98 cases, the Baodi court in 38 of 45, and the Dan-Xin courts in 63 of 78. I categorize these as "one-winner" cases.

The bulk of the "no-winner" cases were likewise adjudicated by the code: 22 of 33. Fully 87 percent of all cases, in other words, were quite clearly resolved by law. And well over half of the others (17, or 8 percent) were put over for further investigation, sent back to the kin group for settlement, and so on. This leaves only 11 cases (or 5 percent of the total), then, in which magistrates can be truly said to have acted as arbitrators, to work out binding compromises between the conflicting claims and interests of the litigants, usually on the basis of extralegal principles.†

These numbers, of course, say nothing about the kinds of legal principles and statutes the magistrates applied in their adjudication. For that, we must break these cases down by category and look at the governing code provisions, mainly in the "Household Law" section of the code, from Statute 75 to 156. We begin with the major cause of complaint, disputes over land.

Land Cases

The great majority of land cases fall under just four statutes and their accompanying substatutes, three of them (Statutes 93, 95, and 149) from the "book" on "Household Law." As Table 10 shows, Statute 93, "Fraudulently Selling [Another's] Land or House" (*daomai tianzhai*), accounted for 31 of the 74 one-winner land cases; No. 95, "Conditional Sales or Purchase of Land or House" (*dianmai tianzhai*), six cases; and No. 149, "Charging Interest at Forbidden Rates" (*weijin*

---

* Cases that did not reach a formal court session are discussed in the next chapter.
† All the data in this chapter are summed up in the Appendix tables.

TABLE 10

One-winner Land Cases in Baxian, Baodi, and Dan-Xin

Category	Baxian	Baodi	Dan-Xin	Total
Main statutes				
No. 93	10	3	18	31
No. 312	0	0	14	14
No. 95	3	0	3	6
No. 149	3	1	2	6
False accusations (No. 336)	5	2	7	14
Other statutes	1	1	0	2
Extralegal ruling	1	0	0	1
TOTAL	23	7	44	74

quli), another six cases. No. 312, "Using Might to Forcibly Control or Tie Up Other People" (*weili zhifu ren*), which contains the code's only stipulation with regard to rent payments, accounted for 14 cases. In addition, as with all categories of cases, a substantial number of defendants were cleared under Statute 336 as targets of false accusations: 14 cases. In all, these five statutes accounted for fully 71 of the 74 cases, or 96 percent.

All four of the statutes begin with the Qing code's characteristically negative approach, first prohibiting violations of what was considered legal and proper, and then spelling out specific grades of punishment for specific violations. The positive principle was not explicitly stated at all. But there can be no mistaking the intended principle; and the substatutes, most of which originated in memorials from officials dealing with actual cases and problems, sometimes provide concrete, if sparse, illustrations of its application.

"Fraudulently Selling Another's Land or House." Statute 93 sets down the punishments for fraudulently selling, exchanging, pretending ownership to, faking prices or ownership deeds, or encroaching on or occupying another's land or house: for one mu or less of land or one room's width or less of house, 50 lashes with the light bamboo, to increase by one grade every five mu of land and every three rooms' width of house, up to a maximum of 80 blows with the heavy stick and two years of imprisonment. The code writers felt no need to go further here—there is no abstract discussion of "rights over things" or of "ownership," or of "immovables" vs. "movables"; or any attempt to deal with the great varieties of ownerships and conditions, as a modern civil code in the European continental tradition (as opposed to the Anglo-American common-law tradition) might do.

Nevertheless, the courts well understood the intent of this law and abided by its principle: to sustain and protect the legitimate ownership of land or houses.

The 31 one-winner land cases that came under this statute all involved some form of encroachment on another's property and an appeal for the court's aid in enforcing an ownership "right." Tao Yuheng, for example, filed a complaint that Mrs. Jin was cutting down the pine trees on the land her husband (now deceased) had sold to him 12 years earlier. The magistrate, on verifying the sales document, ruled simply that the trees belonged to Tao and not to Mrs. Jin (Baxian 6:1:711, 1767.12 [l-1]). Similarly, Tian Younian successfully pressed his suit against his neighbor Tian Fulu and son Yongheng across the road, who had piled dirt in front of their house onto the road, causing traffic to go through Younian's fields. The magistrate, on verifying the facts, ordered Fulu and Yongheng to remove their dirt from the road (Baodi 105, 1884.2.20 [l-8]).

In Danshui, to cite a third example, Xu Tianding complained that a Mrs. Xu, née Chen, of his lineage was trying to lease a piece of the Xu lineage land to a new tenant. Mrs. Xu's segment of the lineage, it turned out, had at one time had charge of the lineage land, but had been forced in its poverty to sell the land conditionally. It was Xu Tianding's segment of the lineage that had ultimately redeemed the land and taken charge of it, leasing it out to a tenant. The court ruled that the land should continue to be leased out to the old tenant, not the new one desired by Mrs. Xu (Dan-Xin 22405, 1870.3.9 [l-42]).

The scope of Statute 93 was extended by a substatute (No. 93–34) forbidding descendants from fraudulently selling ancestral burial or charitable land. Once again, the approach of the Qing code was simply to stipulate different grades of punishment for different degrees of violation, depending on the amount of land involved without stating the obvious intention: to preserve the integrity of lineage property. Among the three cases of this sort in the records was a Baxian suit filed by Tian Zishan and his brothers against Tian Zihua, the son of their paternal uncle, who had cut down a fir tree on their lineage's ancestral gravesite for lumber. The court ordered Zihua to return the lumber (Baxian 6:1:720, 1769.11 [l-4]; see also Baodi 102, 1861.2.27 [l-2]; and Dan-Xin 22703, 1877.7.3 [l-109]).

As these examples suggest, the provision for punishment was honored mostly in the breach. Though the threat of caning was always there, it was rarely used in suits involving these "minor matters." In fact, as we will see, the local courts were often surprisingly lenient in this respect, considering that the code made no qualification in its stipulations.

The Qing code's approach in this domain, as in others—to imply by negative example the positive principle—may only confirm for some the notion that this was strictly a criminal or penal code. As it was applied by the courts, however, the implied civil principle was in fact consistently upheld.

"Using Might to Forcibly Control or Tie Up Other People." The original intent of Statute 312, it would seem, was to safeguard people against abusive treatment by the powerful and to reserve the right of punishment to the state. The statute forbade any "private family" (*sijia*) use of punishment or incarceration, and stipulated different sentences for different degrees of such private coercion. Substatute 312–3 was added in 1727, to specifically forbid gentry-landlords from abusing their tenants. Almost as an afterthought, the substatute then went on to stipulate also that "evil and truculent" tenants who were delinquent in rent payments would be punished (by 80 blows with the heavy stick), and their owed rent paid to the landlord.

This was the code's only reference to rent payments and tenant obligations to landlords. Considering the central importance of landlord-tenant relations to the entire agrarian social-economic order, the code might seem surprisingly perfunctory on the issue. Yet, once again, the guiding principle was obvious: the law would enforce the tenant's obligation to pay and, by implication, uphold the landlord's right to collect rents. Whatever the state's original intent, this provision emerged as the crucial one in practice.

Take, for example, the case of Mrs. Guo, who filed a plaint in Danshui charging that her tenants Wu Congqing et al. would not pay the rent they owed her on 11 *jia* of land. It turned out that Wu and the others had leased the property when it was just wasteland and had had to build embankments and ponds. Both parties had in consequence agreed to a reduced rent for the first three years. But then Wu and his fellows wanted to continue to pay rent at the reduced rate. The magistrate, on verifying the terms of the agreement, ordered them to make good on the rents due Mrs. Guo (Dan-Xin 22102, 1868.6.18 [1-2]). The Dan-Xin records alone show 12 one-winner cases where the court found for landlord plaintiffs seeking to collect back rent.

Still, magistrates occasionally did act to protect tenants from abuses by landlords, in the original spirit of the statute. In Xinzhu, for example, a local Military Inspector (*xunjian*), Xu Qifen, tried to bump an old tenant for another, ostensibly because the middleman in the original transaction had decided to withdraw his sponsorship (*bao*). The magistrate leaned entirely toward the inspector at first, but, on learning the facts, ruled that the tenant, Huang Yizhi, should continue to rent the land, albeit at a higher rent rate (Dan-Xin 22431, 1887.1.24 [1-68]). This is one of two cases in which the courts prevented a tenant's ouster. But in the main, as with the cases involving landownership rights, the courts' concern in these various disputes, though ostensibly to punish offenders, had the practical consequence of protecting the landlord's "right" to collect rent.

"Conditional Sales or Purchase of Land or House." Statute 95 begins with a stipulation about taxes: a person who conditionally purchased land or a house and did not pay the required tax would be punished by 50 lashes with the light bamboo. Other negatives followed: reselling land or a house that had already been conditionally sold would be treated the same as theft. And any dian-holder who refused to allow the dian-maker to redeem his conditionally sold land when the term came due would be punished by 40 lashes with the light bamboo. In other words, the law should and would uphold all legitimate agreements.

The substatutes specified that if a transaction was specified as an irrevocable sale (*juemai*), then no redemption would be allowed. If not, then redemption would be allowed, presumably for an indefinite period (No. 95-3). In 1753, a substatute was added to limit the period of redemption henceforth to 30 years (No. 95-7).

Although the weight of the law was very much behind the seller's right of redemption, many peasants desperate enough to sell their land conditionally were not able to redeem their land and were forced into a *zhaotie* transaction (selling the land outright to the dian-holder for the balance between the original conditional sale price and the market value). To prevent abuse, the law stipulated that only one zhaotie transaction would be allowed (Substatute 95-3).

Six of our 74 one-winner land cases fell under one or another provision of this statute. In one case, from Baxian, the county government ordered the sale of some land it had confiscated from a temple engaged in illegal activities. But that land, as it happened, had earlier been sold conditionally (*dang* instead of *dian* in this county) by the temple to a number of parties. The dian-holders thus petitioned for repayment of the original dian-price. The magistrate found their conditional purchases legitimate and ruled that they be paid from the proceeds of the sale (Baxian 6:1:722, 1770.7 [l-5]). Two other cases, also from Baxian, involved peasants who, unable to redeem their land, had been forced into a zhaotie transaction and now attempted to assert some claim to it: one by encamping on the land and cutting down its trees for sale, another by attempting to extort additional payments. In both cases, the magistrates found for the new owners (Baxian 6:2:1415, 1797.1; 6:2:1416, 1797.6 [l-15, l-16]).

"Charging Interest at Forbidden Rates." Cases involving claims of debt related to landownership or transactions were sometimes classified by archivists under "land," even though they could more appropriately fall under "debt." For the six such cases in my 74 one-winner land group, the relevant statute is No. 149. It defined forbidden interest rates as in excess of 3 percent per month and prohibited total interest that amounted to more than the original principal. It also forbade the forcible seizure of a man's property, or his wife, concubine, or children, to satisfy a debt. Here, as with the statute forbidding private punishments, the state represented itself as the protector of the underdog. But bracketed between these provisions was a paragraph stipulating the punishments for defaulting debtors: 10 lashes for a three-month-long default on five taels, with increasingly harsh penalties according to the length of time and the amount of the debt, up to a maximum of 60 blows with the heavy stick. As it happened, courts found much more occasion to rely on the message of this tucked-in provision: that legitimate debts would be enforced in legitimate ways.

For example, Chu Kun had loaned Duan Kui money two years earlier. Duan had paid off part of the loan in cash and, to repay the rest, turned over to Chu cultivation rights on two plots of land he rented. Thereafter, Chu paid the rent on the plots. Now Duan wanted the plots back, but Chu maintained that the 215 diao (copper *cash*) Duan owed him was in effect a deposit for the rental rights on the land. The magistrate concurred, ruling that Duan had willingly conceded the rental rights to Chu (Baodi, 104, 1862.2.10 [l-3]).

Similarly, Huang A'ai had agreed to use, for four years, one-third of the rent on land he owned to repay the loan he received from Huang Junxiang. But he did not pay up. Junxiang, having tolerated the situation for 20 years, finally brought suit in 1874. The magistrate, on verifying the facts, ruled that A'ai must pay Junxiang the four years' rent, starting that year (Dan-Xin 22302, 1874.3.18 [l-36]).

Again, in these cases, as in most of the civil cases, we find the courts reluctant to mete out punishment, despite the wording of the statute. Even though the Qing code did not make as clear-cut a distinction between criminal and civil cases as the later Republican code did, the local courts plainly took a largely nonpenal approach to "minor matters" of civil disputes.

"False Accusations." Statute 336 sought to deter false accusations (*wugao*) by subjecting the accuser to a harsher punishment than his target would have received: two grades more severe than the law provided in the case of relatively light crimes punishable by lashes with the light bamboo, and three grades for more serious crimes.

All categories of cases examined in this study contain substantial numbers in which the court, on investigation, dismissed the plaintiff's accusation as false or unfounded. To cite two examples among the 14 of this sort, Fei Tinghui accused Du Xuezhu of cutting down more than 20 trees on his ancestral grave land. Looking into the matter, the magistrate learned that Fei's grandfather had sold all his land to Du's family 29 years before, with the sales documents specifying that "not an inch of earth" was to be retained, and that Fei had nonetheless tried again and again to extort additional payments from Du. Satisfied that when Du refused to go along, Fei had concocted the false charge to make trouble for him, the magistrate sentenced Fei to 20 lashes with the light bamboo and ordered him to pledge in writing not to cause any more trouble (Baxian 6:2:1423, 1797.4 [l-19]).*

More flagrant still was Zhou Fulai's plaint charging that his paternal first cousin Fushun was trying to occupy 10 mu of his land. It turned out that Fulai's father had sold the land conditionally some years back, and that when he was unable to redeem it, Fushun's father had stepped in to pay the redemption money in his stead. Then, later, Fulai's father sold title to Fushun's father outright, for the balance between the redemption price and the value of the land. It was a legitimate transaction, and Fulai's accusation mere mischief-making. On learning all the facts, the magistrate sentenced Fulai to 30 blows with the heavy stick, or one grade more severe than for the offense he accused Fushun of. Fulai was, as usual, also required to file a pledge accepting the court's ruling (Baodi 194, 1839.2.23 [l-1]).

---

* Note that in this case the magistrate merely gave Fei the same penalty as a guilty Du would have got. The minimum penalty for encroaching on another's property was set at 50 lashes (Statute 93), but adjusted by the standard factor of 0.4 (a practice instituted after the Kangxi period, 1662–1722; see Xue Yunsheng's annotation to Statute 1) brings it down to 20 lashes.

As these examples show, magistrates were readier to use physical punishments in false accusation cases than in other kinds of civil disputes, though usually not to the full severity called for by the letter of the code. The local courts, understandably, wished to check any abuse of the system, lest the courts become impossibly overburdened.

Other statutes or extralegal judgments. Two of the three other one-winner land cases involved other statutes. One, from Baxian, fell under those dealing with markets (Nos. 152–56). The other, from Baodi, was based on Statute 99, "Eating Without Permission the Melons or Fruits of Another's Field or Garden" (*shanshi tianyuan guaguo*).

Considering the official Qing disdain for commerce, it is somewhat surprising to find an entire chapter of the Household Law "book" devoted to Markets (*shichan*). The key statutes for our purposes are Nos. 153 and 154. The first forbade government regulatory agencies (for commerce on land and on water, the *yahang* and the *butou*) from manipulating the price of goods, "making what is dear cheap or what is cheap dear." The second extended the prohibition to "peddlers and vendors" (*fanyu zhi tu*), who might act in collusion with these agencies "to sell cheap goods dear or buy dear goods cheap."

The case in point: Wang Tai'an charged that his nephew Wang Yuanchen would not let him sell his land to Liu Zuohan. As custom demanded, Tai'an had given his nephew the chance to match Liu's purchase offer. But Yuanchen wanted to buy the land at a lower price, insisting that this was his due based on the customary right of first refusal of neighbors and kin in a land sale. The magistrate tried to honor both principles while ruling in effect for the plaintiff: Tai'an should sell his land to Yuanchen, but Yuanchen must pay the price Liu was prepared to pay (Baixan 6:1:723, 1770.10 [l-6]; see also P. Huang 1985: 266–67).

Statute 99 further concretized the implicit principle of property rights embodied in the prohibitions against encroaching on the land or houses of others. It stated that eating without permission, discarding, or destroying the produce on someone else's field would be treated as theft. This Baodi case grew out of a fight between Chu Kun and his neighbor Chu Fusheng, resulting in minor injuries to Fusheng and his eighty-year(sui)-old father. It was Chu Kun who brought suit, charging that Fusheng would not let him have access to his own fields through his (Fusheng's) land. What actually happened, the magistrate learned, was that Chu Kun had rolled his cart through Fusheng's planted fields and damaged his crops—a fact attested to by two community leaders. The magistrate ordered Chu Kun "never again to drive his cart through the other's fields and damage his crops" (Baodi 104, 1869.8.10 [l-4]).

In only one of these land cases did the magistrate hand down a ruling that fell outside the scope of the code. This involved Meng Yongshun's claim to 400 trees that he had bought six years earlier, in 1816, from the Xingu Temple, through its resident monk, Dehuai. He had paid a deposit of 12.5 taels on a purchase of 320 taels, and had a contract to show for it. But Dehuai stalled after the transaction and would not let Meng cut down the trees. After Dehuai died, the new monk in charge, Guangyu, flatly refused to acknowledge the agreement, contract or no contract. Meng sued, asking the court to uphold his right to the trees.

In this instance, the magistrate went directly counter to the principle of upholding legitimate commercial transactions implicit in the code. He did not deny the facts, and indeed acknowledged in his judgment that a contract had been executed in 1816, and that the plaintiff Meng had paid a deposit on the purchase. But he then went on to note, simply, "Now that Monk Guangyu has just taken charge of this temple, he should of course protect all of the trees of the temple's grounds in order to add to the impressiveness of its appearance, and may not presume to cut them down. As for Meng Yongshun's contract [yue] to buy the trees, whether it is genuine or not, it is hereby canceled at this court. The deposit that Dehuai received from Meng Yongshun is canceled by Dehuai's death." Meng was required to file a pledge not to "bother" Guangyu any further (Baxian 6:3:2631, 1822.11 [l-22]).

This case reminds us of the arbitrary discretion a magistrate could wield. But the fact that it is the only instance of its sort among my 74 land cases argues for the view that the use of such administrative latitude was exceptional rather than representative. All of the other 73 one-winner land cases, as we have seen, were clear-cut rulings based on explicit stipulations or implicit principles of the code.

It is important to note, before we turn to the next group of cases, that my ordering by statute is based almost wholly on my own interpretation of what laws obtained, not on the texts of the magistrates' judgments. In civil cases, as Mark Allee (1994) has noted, judges seldom made specific references to the code. But this fact does not mean that the code played no role in magisterial adjudication. It is simply that, since magistrates were not required to report their judgments in civil cases to upper levels for review, merely to send along monthly registers of the cases filed, they were effectively writing for the benefit of the litigants alone. Indeed, in most instances, the judgments were pronounced on the spot at the court session before the prostrated litigants. Since in the official ideology of the state, the magistrate's position before the subjects in his charge was meant to be that of the all-knowing father and mother, there was no reason for him to call on the code to justify his authority. It would in fact have been inappropriate to cite specific statutes in the common run of cases.

Only in exceptional circumstances would a magistrate feel obliged to make specific reference to the code. As we will see shortly, he would explain himself when the suit involved another county, and he had to send his judgment on to his colleague in that court; and similarly, with a litigant(s) who was a learned or powerful person and therefore to be addressed as more or less an equal. In those kinds of situations, magistrates did take some pains to justify their rulings, in the manner of their reports on criminal cases. My argument here is simply that even in the absence of specific citations, a close reading of magisterial judgments in conjunction with the code leaves no doubt about their basis in law. The relevant statutes are implicit but obvious in virtually all these judgments.

Debt Cases

"Charging Interest at Forbidden Rates." The majority of one-winner debt cases fell under Statute 149, already discussed above. Though the original intention, as noted, might have been to protect the underdog against usurious interest rates (and to represent the state as the champion of the little people), the second paragraph, specifying punishments for defaultors, came to be the important one in practice. Table 11 shows that in 27 of my 49 one-winner debt cases the court upheld one or the other litigant's right to be repaid for a legitimate debt.

For example, Xu Zizhong had borrowed 18,000 *wen* (equal at the time to 12.94 silver taels, as noted in the records) from Guo Yucheng through Zhu Gui as middleman. When the loan came due, Xu ran

TABLE 11

One-winner Debt Cases

Category	Baxian	Baodi	Dan-Xin	Total
Main statutes				
No. 149	15	5	7	27
Nos. 152–56	0	2	2	4
No. 344	2	0	0	2
False accusations (No. 336)	4	6	2	12
Other statutes	1	1	0	2
Extralegal ruling	1	1	0	2
TOTAL	23	15	11	49

away to avoid paying it off. Zhu Gui and others found him and brought him to court. The magistrate ordered the defendant held pending payment of the debt (Baxian 6:1:1062, 1789.2.23 [d-4]).

Under Statute 149, Xu's offense was punishable by 10 lashes with the light bamboo (for a debt of five to 50 taels that had lapsed three months; one added grade for each month over three months, up to a maximum of 40 lashes with the light bamboo). At the downward adjusted rate of 0.4 (in effect, as mentioned, since the Kangxi reign), he was under threat of just four lashes. But in this instance, as with most of the civil cases in my study, the court was clearly more concerned with enforcing payment than imposing the light punishment stipulated by the code.

In a Baodi case, similarly, Li Luzhan had bought on credit 10 *diao*'s worth of pork at Liu Xijiu's shop, incurring, with interest, a debt of 12 diao. Li refused to pay. The two men got into a fight, and Liu sued. The magistrate reprimanded both for fighting, but ordered Li to pay off his debt within five days (Baodi 187, 1838.8.29 [d-4]).

In one instance, a magistrate acted under the part of the statute that prohibited the forcible removal of another's property to satisfy a debt. In Baxian, the deceased husband of the plaintiff, Mrs. Zhou, had borrowed 10 taels with Monk Xiong acting as middleman. The husband later repaid eight of the 10 taels. After Zhou's death, Xiong tried to collect the balance from the widow Zhou, and when that failed, he took some of her clothing and furniture as compensatory security. The magistrate ordered Xiong to return the removed goods (Baxian 6:4:2554, 1852.11.21 [d-21]).

"Markets." Where debt cases involved market sales and purchases, they could fall under Statutes 152–56 in the chapter on markets. As discussed above, though concerned mainly with the ad-

ministrative regulation of commerce, this subsection did take a posture on fair market prices. It also forbade tampering with officially set weights and measures and using private ones (Statute 155); and declared that anyone who manufactured goods that were not durable and genuine (*laogu zhengshi*) or who sold cloth or silk that was "unwoven, thin, short, or narrow" would be punished by 50 lashes with the light bamboo (No. 156).

Four of the debt cases were concerned with one or another type of abuse of market transactions. One case had to do with a coal peddler who sold 26 *dan* of coal to one buyer and then promised it to another, causing the two buyers to get into a fight. On verifying the facts, the magistrate ordered the peddler to turn the coal over to the first buyer (Dan-Xin 23404, 1876.7 [d-3]). In another example, Zhang Cai sold Lei Er a mule on credit, but on discovering that Lei Er did not have the money to pay for it, he had taken the animal back and sold it. The two men argued, fought, and came to court. The magistrate found for Zhang Cai; Lei Er got off with a reprimand and a caution: "If you should cause trouble again, you will be severely punished" (Baodi 186, 1849.9.10 [d-6]).

Official corruption. When debt cases involved officials, magistrates could take their guidance from Statute 344, which set out the penalties for "Officials and Clerks Accepting Bribes" (*guanli shoucai*). One substatute (No. 344–3) dealt specifically with extortions from the common people, punishable according to the amount extorted. Two of my 49 debt cases were of this sort. In one, five runners incurred a bill of 7,000 wen at Zhao Jianpei's restaurant, but paid only 1,000 wen. Then, a year later, in 1790, another group of runners consumed 13,000 wen's worth and refused to pay at all. This time Zhao brought suit against both, whereupon the first group of runners paid up, while the second ran off. The magistrate ordered their arrest (Baxian 6:1:1069, 1790.11.5 [d-7]; see also Baxian 6:1:1076, 1794.5.4 [d-10]).

"False Accusations." As with the land cases, some of the charges against defaultors turned out to be fraudulent, violating Statute 336. In one flagrant example, Yu Zaiyin's father had rented Liu Zejian's land on a share-crop basis, paying 40 taels rent deposit. He then accumulated a substantial debt to Liu. When his father died, Yu Zaiyin paid off the debt with 40 taels, four oxen, and two big wooden chests. But Liu Zejian's son, Chaoxiu, concocted a false loan contract and tried to extort 95 taels from Yu. When Yu refused to pay, Liu brought

suit, charging Yu with failure to repay a debt. The magistrate, on verifying the facts, declared the accusation fraudulent, voided the fake contract on the spot, and required both parties to pledge their acceptance of the closing of the suit (Baxian 6:3:4623, 1821.10 [d-17]). False charges accounted for almost a quarter of the debt cases.

Consistent with the relatively light punishments stipulated for debt-related offenses, the local courts tended to treat debt-related false accusations rather leniently. In the example above, no punishment was imposed. Of the 12 false accusers, only five were punished: two with the light bamboo (for an unspecified but presumably relatively few number of lashes), and three with still lighter punishment (one with face slaps [zhangze] and two with unspecified "light punishment" [boze]). The others were not punished at all, even where the amount at issue was much larger than 50 taels.

Other statutes and extralegal principles. Together, the four code sections discussed accounted for 45 of the 49 one-winner debt cases. Some of these cases were precipitated by a physical fight. But usually the parties had done little injury to each other, and the magistrate would merely wave the matter off with some pat phrase like "the minor wound has now healed" (suo shou weishang quanyu) and concentrate on the real issue at stake. There were instances, of course, where an injury was severe enough to overshadow the original cause of the dispute, placing it under Statutes 302ff covering "fighting" (dou'ou) and assault and battery. Very rarely was a minor physical fight itself the main issue. In the only example of this sort from my cases, Zheng Zhaoxiang was taken to court for beating up the butcher Zhang Fuliang and his son Xi'er, injuring both, ostensibly because they owed him a day's pay for some work he had done for them. It turned out Zheng was a ne'er-do-well who was always getting into some kind of trouble. Fortunately for Zheng, the court decided the injury to the Zhangs was minor and heeded his elderly father's petition to be allowed to apologize to everyone in his son's stead. The magistrate let Zheng off after requiring him to file a pledge that he would not misbehave again (Baodi 189, 1830.6.8 [d-1]).

As indicated in Table 11, in only two instances do we find magistrates appealing to extralegal principles in their adjudication of debt cases. In the first, a year-laborer Jin Wende (from Zhangqiu in Shandong) filed a plaint with the Baodi court stating that he had worked for Yang Fugui for three years, only to be beaten and thrown out without the one tael and 2,000 wen he was owed in back pay. The injury report noted that Jin had a scar on his left forehead.

One relevant statute for this case would have been No. 312, forbidding the private administration of punishment. But the important issue here clearly had not so much to do with Jin's having been beaten as with the back wages owed him and his dismissal. On those issues, the code offered little guidance. Nowhere did it stipulate or imply anything about an employer's obligation to pay an agricultural worker wages. The magistrate could perhaps have found for Jin under Statute 149, but to extend the obligation to pay a debt to wages owed would have been something of a stretch. The statutes under markets also did not apply readily, since nowhere in the code was labor treated as a "good" that was bought and sold.

What the magistrate did was to appeal to the compassion of the employer, writing: "To drive away an impoverished man from afar who has lived a hard life working for three years does not seem a kindly thing to do. . . . If Jin Wende has not done anything inappropriate to his station, you should keep him and avoid a lawsuit." Yang agreed to keep Jin on. Nothing was said of the wages owed to Jin or of Jin's beating (Baodi 189, 1830.7.8 [d-2]). This case suggests that when the substance of a dispute fell outside the scope of the code, there was more room for magisterial discretion and here, at least, an appeal to extralegal morality or compassion.

In the other case, the plaintiff Na Yutu charged that Wu Dayong, the brother of his deceased concubine, owed him some 10,000 wen for monies she had earned from needlework and turned over to him. The dispute had earlier been mediated by community and kin, who arranged for Wu to pay Na 35 taels. Wu did not pay, and Na brought suit. The court in this case decided simply to uphold the mediated settlement. Wu complied with the court's order to pay but countered that Na's entire claim was fabricated, and that he was paying only out of consideration of Na's poverty. The magistrate seems to have been convinced by Wu and, before turning the money over to Na, commented in writing: "If you should again fabricate charges and bring suit, the court will definitely deal with you severely" (Baxian 6:2:2412, 1797.7.21 [d-13]). He nevertheless preferred in his verdict to go with the earlier mediated settlement.

Marriage Cases

As Table 12 indicates, the bulk of the marriage (*hunyin*) cases fall mainly under three groups of statutes: Nos. 101 to 117 in the "book" on "Household Law," concerned mainly with the marriage contract;

TABLE 12

One-winner Marriage Cases

Category	Baxian	Baodi	Total
Main statutes			
Nos. 101–17	2	5	7
No. 275	7	1	8
Nos. 366–67	4	3	7
False accusations (No. 336)	6	1	7
Other statutes	1	1	2
Extralegal ruling	0	0	0
TOTAL	20	11	31

NOTE: Because a large proportion of "illicit sex" cases involved adultery and therefore related to marriage, Chinese archivists have tended to lump the two together (*hunyin jianqing*). That was substantially the practice of the cataloguers of the Baxian and Baodi archives. One of the four Baxian cases shown under Statutes 366–67, for example, was in fact an attempted rape case (Baxian 6: 3:8635, 1821.7.28 [m-23]). Dai Yanhui, the cataloguer of the Dan-Xin archives, however, applied modern legal categories and separated out marriage-related cases from adultery and rape, placing the former under "civil" (*minshi*), and the latter under "criminal" (*xingshi*). See the note to Appendix Table A.2. The distinction in Qing law between "minor" and "weighty" approximated but was not as exact as the civil/criminal distinction. Dai's scheme, it so happens, left no one-winner marriage cases.

No. 275, "Abduction and Abduction for Sale of People" (*lüren lüemai ren*), concerned in part with the buying and selling of women into marriage; and No. 366–67 "Engaging in Illicit Sexual Relations" (*fanjian*), concerned in part with adultery. The latter two groups shade over from the civil into the criminal and from the "minor" into the "weighty."*

The marriage contract. The statutes in the marriage chapter account for 17 of the 82 statutes in the code's "book" on Household Law. The first (No. 101) began by prohibiting false representations in a marrige contract and went on to stipulate the various requirements for a legitimate contract (e.g., parental permission, a match-maker, a written document). Following statutes specifically prohibited various kinds of violations of a marriage contract, such as pawning or hiring out to another as wife or concubine one's own wife or concubine (No. 102); forcibly abducting another's wife (or concubine) or daughter to be one's own wife or concubine (No. 112); and forcibly abducting and selling another's wife (or concubine) or daughter to a third person as wife or concubine (Substatute 112-1).† Statute 116 specified under what conditions a husband could divorce a wife and

* My case files contain no one-winner marriage cases for Dan-Xin because Dai Yanhui catalogued them all under "criminal" cases.

† In due course, we will see that Statute 112 is to be distinguished from No. 275; and that No. 102 overlaps with No. 367 to a certain extent.

what kinds of actions on her part constituted the punishable violations of the marriage contract. Substatute 116-2 spelled out two of
the very limited number of conditions under which a woman could
nullify her marriage: if, five years after the contracted date, the man
did not marry her, for no good reason; and if a husband deserted his
wife and did not return for three years.

The Qing code here departed from the approach it took to other
sorts of contracts. Where a few simple stipulations about punishable
violations were deemed sufficient notice to the courts that legitimate land and loan contracts were to be upheld, when it came to
marriage, the code became more specific and elaborate over time,
perhaps because of the greater frequency of cases and universal applicability of the provisions, and perhaps because, in the official posture
of the state, marriage was not beneath its concerns in quite the same
way as market transactions.

All together, seven of the 31 one-winner marriage cases from
Baxian and Baodi fell under one or another of these 17 statutes. Statute 101, for example, was the relevant one when Zu Zheng'an sued
Liang Guotai, the father of his betrothed, for breaching their marriage contract and not going through with his daughter's marriage to
him. The magistrate ordered Liang to return the betrothal gift (*caili*)
of 10,000 wen and further fined him 2,000 wen (Baxian 6:1:1736,
1780.10.14 [m-3]).

In an unusual case of tug-of-war, a county runner Ma Yongcai
forcibly abducted a widow, née Qi, to make her his concubine. The
widow's father, Qi Yongxiang, then recaptured her and wed her to
someone else, with all the proper procedures. Ma brought suit, charging Qi with the forcible abduction of his concubine. The magistrate,
after ordering the xiangbao to investigate and verify the facts, upheld
the new marriage contract and ordered that the woman Qi be turned
over to her new husband. Ma was found guilty of abducting another
to be his concubine (Statute 112) and was punished with 200 lashes
with the light bamboo (Baodi 170, 1887. 10 [m-14]).

Another aggrieved parent, Chen He, in the same county in 1837,
filed a plaint claiming that a local bandit, Kou Fusheng, and his
daughter had "seduced" his daughter-in-law into their house and
would not let her return home to him. In fact, the girl (16 sui) had
fled from a place where she had been mistreated by her in-laws and
her husband (who beat her and verbally abused her when she would
not do heavy farmwork) and was in hiding at her grandmother's

house. She had only spent a night with Kou and his daughter before going to her grandmother's. The magistrate upheld the marriage contract in his ruling: he ordered the girl to go back to her marital home. But he also reprimanded Chen He for his false charges and required both Chen and his son to file a pledge to the effect that they would not again mistreat the woman (Baodi 166, 1837.5.22 [m-3]).

Two of the seven cases involved divorce, and one of these was on the petition of the woman. Tian Fa's adopted son Tian Rui had gone to the northeast to work and left his wife, née Xu, with his father. Tian Fa did not hear from Rui for 13 years. He had even gone to the northeast to look for his son but could not find him. From Tian Fa's point of view, the daughter-in-law was a burden to maintain, and she was as eager as he to have the marriage nullified so as to have a chance to remarry. Tian Rui was the first to petition the magistrate, asking him to nullify the marriage and permit Xu to go home to her natal village and remarry. But the magistrate, unwilling to take the father-in-law's word for it, would not act without verification that Xu indeed had no wish to remain wed to Tian Rui. Xu herself then petitioned the court, stating that since she could not make a living, it was difficult for her to "preserve her chastity" (*shoujie*), and that she did in fact wish to remarry for the sake of a livelihood. At this, the magistrate granted his permission, in accordance with Substatute 116-2 (Baodi 162, 1839.6.1 [m-6]).

"Abduction and Abduction for Sale of People." This statute, No. 275, part of the chapter on "Theft and Robbery," began with a general stricture against the abduction (*lüe*) or abduction for sale (*lüemai*) of "commoners" (*liangren*) to become slaves (*nubi*), then went on specifically to forbid the sale of wives into slavery. These were serious criminal offenses, punishable by 100 blows with the heavy stick and banishment to a distance of 3,000 *li* (1 li = 0.3 mile). As Ch'ü T'ung-tsu (1961) and Jing Junjian (1981) have demonstrated, the Qing code was very much preoccupied with maintaining what was seen as the proper social order, which is to say, to preserving the distinction between superiors and inferiors, between elders and juniors, between people of status (degree-holders) and commoners, and effectively between all recognized social groups and the lowest of the low, the so-called mean people. An inferior who committed an offense against a superior was subject to more severe punishment than an equal against an equal, and the reverse to less severe punishment. From its concern with violations of the social hierarchy, Statute 275

went on to forbid the abduction of girls or women in general, whether commoner or slave, and whether to become wives or slaves.

To cite two of the eight cases that fell under this statute, Long Jiuchuan, under the pretense of finding a husband for Chen Wenzhi's servant girl Chunxiang, took her off and hid her for nine months. When Chen found out what had happened, he brought suit. The magistrate ordered that the girl be returned, and that Long wear the cangue for a month as punishment (Baxian 6:1:1742, 1781.9.30 [m-5]). In the other case, Xu Tianyi had given his daughter Chungu to Zheng Wenke as a child-bride. Later, however, Zheng sold Chungu to Mrs. Chen as a slave for 12,000 wen. On learning of the sale, Xu brought suit. Zheng had really committed a double offense, punishable under either Statute 275 for selling a commoner into slavery or under Statute 102 for selling his wife. The magistrate ordered that Chungu be returned to her father, Xu Tianyi, and that Zheng be held in prison pending a decision on his punishment (Baxian 6:1:1732, 1780.3.14 [m-2]).

*"Engaging in Illicit Sexual Relations."** The Qing code considered adultery by a woman a serious crime, on the same level as the other infractions grouped under Statutes 366–75, titled "Engaging in Illicit Sexual Relations" (fanjian): rape, incest, and the sexual abuse of the common people by officials. Only two of these statutes are of concern here: Nos. 366 and 367. The first prohibited all "illicit sexual relations" (jian), whether by a man or a woman, and whether by consent, under false pretenses, or by force. The punishment was increased (from 80 blows with the heavy stick to 90 blows) if the woman involved was married. An adulteress was to receive the same sentence as her paramour even if she was seduced under false pretenses. She would be considered innocent only if it was clearly a case of forcible rape.

The second statute, No. 367, made a husband who abetted in his wife's adultery also guilty of a criminal offense. By extension, a father who abetted in his daughter's illicit sexual relations was similarly punishable. And, by further extension, anyone who bought or sold a formal termination of a woman's marriage contract, whether to acquire her for himself or to sell her to another, was criminally liable. This statute also forbade husbands (or adoptive fathers) from forcing their wives (or adoptive daughters) into illicit sexual relations. Such

---

*See Sommer 1994 for a study on how the Qing state conceptualized and dealt with illicit sex.

offenses would be punished by 100 blows with the heavy stick, and the woman would be granted a divorce and returned to her parents.

Here we note a clear overlap with marriage statutes. In the eyes of the Qing, illicit sex on the part of a married woman was really a double offense: she both violated what the law considered acceptable sex and violated her marriage contract. Incest (Statute 368) or illicit sex between "mean people" and "commoners" (No. 373) similarly violated both acceptable sex and the social order.

The courts acted, first of all, to uphold legitimate marriage contracts and punish violators. A lower-degree holder (*jiansheng*), Wang Xixian, was brought up on charges for buying the termination of Chen's marriage so he could make her his concubine. Chen's husband had apparently sold her for 28,000 wen because he was ill. The case came to the attention of the court when Wang's mother, unable to get along with Chen, decided to have her sent away to her relatives. En route, Chen's background came to the attention of the patrol guards. In this instance, perhaps because Wang was a degree holder, the magistrate made specific reference to the code, noting that Wang had engaged in the illegal "buying of the termination of a woman's marriage" (*maixiu weilü*), and that by rights he should be punished (but that the court would act leniently in this instance). Since the woman's husband had engaged in the illegal "sale of the termination of a woman's marriage," she was not to be returned to him but to be sent back to her relatives (Baxian 6:1:1731, 1779.11.29 [m-1]).

When the husband and/or parents willingly abetted in a woman's adultery, there was usually no clear-cut division between victim and offender. All parties were guilty. To illustrate the working of the law on this issue, therefore, we have to turn to a no-winner case. In Baodi, Sun Keyong, a poor peddler, and his parents-in-law, the Xins, allowed Keyong's wife to carry on with wealthy Zhang Fu in return for various payments and favors. The arrangement went on for three years, until Zhang Fu refused their demands and angered them. At that point, Sun Keyong brought suit, charging that Zhang Fu was engaged in adulterous relations with his wife. The magistrate learned the truth on investigation and sentenced Zhang Fu to 30 blows with the heavy stick for adultery, Sun Keyong and his parents-in-law to 40 slaps (zhangze) for abetting adultery, and the woman herself to 40 slaps for adultery. Everyone involved was required to file a pledge not to engage any further in the offense (Baodi 166, 1839.1.23 [m-5]).

"False Accusations." As usual, the courts confronted a healthy

number of fraudulent charges in these cases—something over a fifth in the Baodi-Baxian group. Malice was not necessarily a motive, as previous examples may suggest. For example, twenty-four-year-old Gao Suo'er had fallen in love with her family's day-laborer, Luo Bai, and run off with him. Fearful that her family would bring suit against Luo, the young couple tried to force the family's hand by filing charges first, claiming that Suo'er had been legitimately married to Luo, and that the parents, upset by his poverty, were now trying to annul the marriage. On verifying the facts, the court ordered that Luo be held in prison and Suo'er returned to her father. In the eyes of Qing law, there could be no legitimate marriage without parental permission (Baodi 171, 1894.12 [m-15]).

Other statutes. Both of our "other" examples, initially cases of "illicit sexual relations," ended up turning mainly on the issue of "fighting" (dou'ou), bringing Statutes 302–23 into play. One illustration will do. Liu Yitai had harbored a runaway wife. When the husband came to look for her, Li Shitang, an outsider from Shandong, told him where she was, and the husband succeeded in taking the woman back. In anger, Liu Yitai, with several others, beat Li up, breaking his leg. The magistrate sentenced Liu to a month in the cangue and ordered him to pay Li 200 diao in damages (Baodi 169, 1865.5 [m-11]).

As Table 12 shows, none of the 31 one-winner marriage cases was adjudicated by an extralegal principle. To some extent, we might lay this fact to the Qing code's specificity on marital matters. Compared with modern European civil codes, of course, it was very terse even in those matters, just less so than it was in respect to most others.

Inheritance Cases

By Qing times, the principle of equal division among sons had long since been established in both law and social custom. And we saw in Chapter Three, thanks to well-established community practices for resolving disputes over the process, very few cases made it to court. By and large, problems arose only when a property owner had no natural sons. The question of inheritance then became closely tied to the issue of succession to the family line. As Table 13 indicates, only one statute need concern us here.

"Violating the Law in Establishing an Heir." Characteristically again, this statute, No. 78 (li dizi weifa), begins by stipulating the

TABLE 13

One-winner Inheritance Cases

Category	Baxian	Baodi	Dan-Xin	Total
Main statute: No. 78	3	3	3	9
False accusations (No. 336)	0	0	5	5
Other statutes	0	2	0	2
Extralegal ruling	0	0	0	0
TOTAL	3	5	8	16

punishment for violating the law of succession: 80 blows with the heavy stick. The positive principles of what constituted acceptable practice are then elaborated in substatutes. In the choice of a successor, one was to turn first to the sons of one's brothers, then to lesser relations. If there were no eligible successors among one's relations, then one could turn to someone of the same surname. Any natural son born after a legal successor had been named was to share equally in inheritance with him (Substatute 78-1).

The code was strict in its view that only someone of the same surname could be made a successor. Substatute 78-4 specifically stated that a son adopted from a family of a different surname did not have the same status as a legal successor. He might be given some property, but he had no legal claim to succeed to the family line and inherit the family property.

As for the property rights of a son-less widow, the code placed much emphasis on whether she "maintained her chastity" to her deceased husband. If she did so, she would be given charge of the property, pending the establishment of a rightful successor. If she remarried, however, her deceased husband's property, as well as her dowry, would be disposed of according to the wishes of the deceased husband's family (Substatute 78-2).

There are particularly interesting cases among the nine one-winner cases falling under the provisions of Statute 78 and its various substatutes. One turned on the succession rights of an adopted son. Li Chunyou had adopted a boy of another descent group and named him Li Maofu. He later had a natural son, named Maochang. Li Chunyou subsequently arranged for a wife for Maofu and also gave him 50 taels, plus an ox and some grain, and sent him back to his natal family. Nevertheless, when Li Chunyou died, Maofu brought suit in an attempt to get half of the inheritance. The court ruled against him, in accordance with Substatutes 78-1 and 78-4 (Baxian 6: 3:9755, 1839.10 [i-3]).

In the other case, from Xinzhu, the third of four lines of the Wu family had no son and decided to make Wu Tianze, from the second line, its successor. Tianze was later sent away to the mainland for education, and his grandmother managed the property for him. She managed it so poorly that before she died, she had been forced to sell the land conditionally. When Tianze returned, he was confronted with the first and fourth lines' claim that, under the grandmother's will, they were to inherit the third line's properties in equal shares with him, and that accordingly he should receive only one-third of the property. Tianze sued. The magistrate verified that he had indeed been established as the legal successor to the third line, and ruled that the entire property should go to him (Dan-Xin 22705, 1879.3.6 [i-11]).

"False Accusations." Once more, we find a large proportion of claims dismissed as fraudulent—five of 16 or close to a third. Among them was another contest between lineage lines over a son-less line's property. With no son of its own to inherit, the third line of the Zheng family decided to make Zheng Bangchao, the legal heir of the second line, its successor. The dispute came from Zheng Bangshi, the younger of two brothers of the fifth line, who succeeded only to their own line. In the hope of expanding that inheritance, Banshi claimed that he had been adopted by the second line when he was very young and was therefore entitled to half of its property. The magistrate rejected the claim as untrue and pronounced Bangchao the legitimately established successor to both the second and the third line of the Zheng family. Bangshi, because of his young age, was only reprimanded and required to pledge his acceptance of the court's ruling (Dan-Xin 22615, 1893.7.4 [i-15]).

Other statutes. At his death, the husband of Mrs. Wang had left 2.5 mu of land to each of his two sons by a previous marriage and five mu to her as old-age-support land (*yanglaodi*). The elder son had subsequently died, leaving his 2.5 mu to his own son. The widow Wang lived with this grand-stepson. The difficulty came from the wife of the second son, Wang Tong, who brought suit to claim both her young nephew's 2.5 mu and the widow Wang's five mu of old-age-support land. The court found for the widow and the grand-stepson with whom she lived (Baodi 100, 1850.3.15 [i-2]). The plaintiff in this case in fact had no legal leg to stand on. Though by law, the two sons (and their offspring) were entitled to equal shares in inheritance (Sub-statute 88–1), the widow was entitled to old-age support, under Statute 338, which put things characteristically in penal terms: son(s) or grandson(s) who did not provide adequately for their elders would be punished by 100 blows with the heavy stick. That principle, however, takes us into the realm of old-age support (yangshan) for parents, which Chinese archivists often group separately from inheritance and succession cases.

As with the marriage cases, none of the 16 inheritance cases was decided on extralegal grounds. Once again, the relative specificity of the law, as well as the strength and clarity of social mores, left little room for magisterial discretion. There could be little question where the law and social custom stood with respect to disputes like those cited above.

The Use of Compromise

It remains for us to consider the resort to face-saving compromises in magisterial adjudication. If Qing magistrates, even when they ruled for one or the other party, typically also imposed compromises in the interest of "harmony," it may be argued that, in the final analysis, they were indeed more mediators and administrators than judges.

In illustration, let me cite three examples. Tao Yuheng, the plaintiff in a Baxian case, had purchased the widow Jin's husband's land outright, but the impoverished widow now claimed that she still had rights over the 40 pine trees on the land. The magistrate verified that the sales document did not contain any clause preserving ownership of the trees and therefore found for the plaintiff. However, in consideration of Mrs. Jin's poverty, he also ordered Tao to give her 5,000 wen to help her in her livelihood (Baxian 6:1:711, 1767.12 [1-1]).

Similarly, the Danshui court took account of the defendant's poverty even as it ruled for the plaintiff. The widow Chen and her daughter rented Zeng Yuntan's house (for nine yuan a year) but were too poor to pay. Zeng first applied the deposit of 10 yuan to the rent and then, when the widow fell several months in arrears, asked her to move out. When she refused to do so, Zeng filed suit, charging that the Chens were noisy and engaged in prostitution. Zeng, who was clearly wealthy and powerful, managed to get a runner to report to the magistrate in his favor, and also some 40 neighbors to petition on his behalf. The magistrate found the charge of prostitution a fabrication, but also noted that Zeng was entitled to evict a renter who did not pay rent. He therefore found for the plaintiff and ordered the Chens to move out. At the same time, however, he ordered that Zeng be gracious and give up the several months' back rent (Dan-Xin 22103, 1876.9.26 [1-3]).

Finally, to return to one of our earlier examples, though the magistrate found for the plaintiffs in the case of the runaway daughter-in-law and ordered her to go back to her husband's family, he also exacted a pledge from her husband and his parents that they would never mistreat her again.

In rulings like these, courts clearly went beyond what a strict application of the law would decree. But it is just as clear that these were only face-saving or kindly concessions, after unequivocal judgments about the right or wrong of one or the other party. In any event, such compromise settlements are to be found in only a very small number of the one-winner rulings: just 11 in a total of 170 cases (Appendix tables A.5–A.7). In most of these, the magistrate appeared to be motivated mainly by compassion for the underprivileged, not a concern to preserve the losing side's face.

If that is true, then these cases stand out as exceptional in another way, for in operation, the courts tended on the whole to interpret the "qing" in the stock phrase *zhenqing zhuoli* ("consider the *qing* and consult the "li") more in the sense of *qingshi*, or the actual facts, than in the sense of *renqing*, or (Confucian) compassion, and the "li" more in terms of *daoli*, or common-sense reason, than in terms of Confucian *tianli*, or the moral principle of the universe. For example, we find repeated examples of magistrates using the expression *chaqing lichu*, or investigate the facts and circumstances and resolve by reason. Many chose also to speak of a plaintiff's version of events in terms of *kongqing*, in which the "qing" clearly refers to facts rather than compassion. The highly moralistic connotations of tianli and renqing, I would insist once again, mattered more in Confucian representations of the legal system than in its actual operation. For all the Confucian view of what ought to be, daoli or common-sense reason, *shiqing* or what really happened, and *lüli* or statutes and substatutes were the three real guides in what was. Among the three, law was paramount. The Confucian scholars who compiled model cases and rescripts most likely saw the common and mundane as unworthy of special illustration, and therefore concentrated on difficult cases in which magistrates had to find guides other than those stipulated in the code. From our point of view, however, it is the common and mundane that tell us the most about actual legal practice during the Qing.

No-Winner Cases

The magistrate as judge. Even when court adjudication resulted in no simple ruling for one party or the other (i.e., no-winner cases, in my terms), the magistrate usually made his decision according to the law: 22 in a total of 33 cases (Appendix tables A.5–A.7). For example, a tenant, Tan Delong, brought suit against his landlord, Liu Chang'an, for forcibly taking away his ox. There was a history of hard feeling between them, it seems. Tan had earlier asked Liu for a piece of land on which to bury his mother, and Liu had subsequently accused him of stealing land from him. That dispute had been settled by mediation: Tan paid Liu for the land. This new dispute arose because Tan had at some later point borrowed money from Liu but had not paid up when the loan came due. Liu had therefore taken away the ox. Tan was obligated to repay Liu, by Statute 149, but Liu was wrong to forcibly remove Tan's property in his effort to collect payment, also by Statute 149. The magistrate ruled accordingly: Tan was to repay all the money he owed Liu, and Liu was to return the ox to him (Baxian 6:1:745, 1775.4 [l-10]).

In a trickier case from the same county (Baxian), Chen Wannian married a woman surnamed Wang, then went away to seek work, leaving her in the care of his father, Chen De. When Chen De did not hear from his son for two years, he decided to betrothe the daughter-in-law to Liao Enfeng, for a price of 21,000 wen. Soon after, Liao was killed in a flood, and his elder brother married the woman off to Dong San of Liangshan county, for 38,000 wen. At this point, Chen Wannian returned. Fearful that his son would be upset at him for what he had done, Chen De decided his best out was to file false charges against Dong San, claiming that he had abducted the woman. Wannian believed his father and pressed a second suit against Dong in his own Liangshan county, but then left again for Shaanxi, where he was now employed. The court uncovered the facts on investigation and ruled as follows. Chen De had falsely accused Dong San of abduction and by rights ought to receive 80 blows with the heavy stick. But in consideration of his ready admission of guilt and his poverty, the punishment would be reduced to two months in a cangue, followed by 30 blows with the heavy stick. Chen Wannian, having been deceived into filing charges, did not deserve to be punished. As for Dong and his wife, strictly speaking their marriage should be nullified (because, by the letter of the law, which required desertion for three years, the woman was still legally married to Wannian). But given that Dong had married the woman in good faith and by proper procedures, that she was now pregnant with his child, and that Chen Wannian had not even troubled to show up for the court session, the magistrate ruled that Dong would not be required to give up the woman in divorce (*liyi*). All these circumstances and judgments were spelled out in detail by the Baxian magistrate, complete with references to the code, because in this instance he had to transmit his ruling to his colleague in Liangshan county (Baxian 6:1:1760, 1784.3.19 [m-9]).

As a last example, Chen Qi filed a plaint charging that Zhang Deren had tried to extract a loan from his brother Xiu's wife and beat her when she refused. Zhang claimed, in his own defense, that he had loaned Xiu money, but that Xiu had gone off to hide, leaving his wife to deal with him. The magistrate noted on the original plaint his skepticism of Chen Qi's version of events, and also that the woman had not come to court to have her injury examined, per standard procedure. Then, at the court session with everyone convened, he satisfied himself that none of the parties could document their claim of a debt. Accordingly, he ordered that all be reprimanded and required to pledge not to cause any further trouble (Baodi 190, 1861.8.18 [d-8]).

The magistrate as arbitrator. As I noted at the outset, in only 11 of the no-winner cases did magistrates act as arbitrators to work out compromises between two disputing parties with equally legitimate claims. In these court rulings, the question of who was legally in the right played little role, and the magistrates operated much as community mediators might have done when faced with two sets of conflicting claims and interests, except, of course, that their rulings were binding.

Two cases will illustrate the point. Zhu Guangji, a merchant from Yunyang county, had loaned Zheng Lao'er of Baxian 16,000 wen. When the loan came due, Zheng Lao'er hid from Zhu and would not repay the money. At this point, Lao'er's paternal first cousin Zheng Yangyi agreed to "guarantee" (*danbao*), simply on his word, that the debt would be repaid within three to five days. Yangyi's intent was to get after Lao'er to honor his obligation. But then Lao'er suddenly died. He apparently had neither property nor heirs, and Yangyi was not willing to make good on an informal "guarantee" that was not legally binding. Zhu brought suit. As a compromise, the magistrate ordered Yangyi to pay Zhu a return-home fee of 2,000 wen (Baxian 6: 4:2552, 1852.11.19 [d-20]).

In Baodi, Zhang Yu had two sons by his first wife, and three more by his second, née Hu. After his death, the widow lived with Yu's brother Mo. It seems she might have had an affair and borne a child, who apparently died at birth. Mo was in any case eager to drive her out of the family—to send her packing back to her brother and strip her of any claims to her husband's property. The dispute had been mediated by community and kin leaders, who suggested that Zhang Yu's property be divided into six equal shares, one each for the five sons and the sixth for the widow as old-age support. Dissatisfied with the settlement, Zhang Mo brought suit, charging that his widowed sister-in-law had not maintained her chastity and had killed the child she bore at birth. The widow, however, insisted that she had not had an affair, that she did not know how she became pregnant, and that the child had died of natural causes. Zhang Mo named the supposed lover, Tian Youquan, but could not corroborate his charges. The magistrate decided at the court session simply to uphold the original settlement proposed by the community and kin mediators (Baodi 162, 1845.3 [m-8]).

In cases like these, one can reasonably argue that the magistrate's role was more administrative than adjudicatory, that he was more a mediator than a judge applying the law. But such cases were clearly rare, constituting a mere 5 percent of the 221 cases heard by the courts in formal session. Moreover, both of the magistrates here, as was generally true of such rulings, operated within the legal framework set by the code; magisterial discretion did not contravene the law but rather occurred in the open spaces left by the code. Even as arbitrators, in other words, the magistrates were no mere compromise workers acting without any regard for the law.

The Code in Light of Legal Practice

The great majority of our case records, then, bring to light easy-to-miss practical civil stipulations in the code. They are easy to miss because they are packaged in administrative and/or penal terms, and often occur as appendages to administrative and penal stipulations. They become clear only when we look beneath the surface layers of the code.

I do not want to rehearse the Qing code's chief characteristics here; they have all been relatively well analyzed in the existing literature and are beyond dispute. It is enough to note, once again, that this was a code that was administrative and penal in its approach, and that was at once Legalist and Confucian in its inspiration and avowed ideology. The volume by Bodde and Morris (1967) seems to me still the most judicious summary of these multiple aspects of the code.

What the literature has not done is to see the code in conjunction with the actual operations of the legal system, especially with respect to civil matters. Bodde and Morris certainly broached the issue and attempted in preliminary ways to grapple with it through model cases, but without access to the files of local courts, they could not do more. With those court records in hand, it becomes clear that operationally the most important parts of the Qing code consisted in the later adjustments and additions that were made as practical responses to changing social realities. Those passages were often buried in the middle or end of a statute, or in an insignificant-appearing substatute tucked into a long series of substatutes. Moreover, they are daunting in their very numbers. Substatutes alone increased from the original 449 in the Shunzhi reign (1644–61), to 824 in early Yongzheng (1723–35), 1,045 in early Qianlong (1736–95), 1,603 in early Jiaqing (1796–1820), and 1,892 in early Tongzhi (1862–74; Zheng Qin 1993: 71). They totaled 1,907 by the time of Xue Yunsheng's compilation (used throughout this study) of ca. 1900. The result was something of a hodge-podge: a text still replete with hollow principles and anachronistic stipulations, supplemented with a host of new key provisions introduced for the most part at inconspicuous places, often under well-stretched extensions of original concepts or even misleading headings.

The code, then, should be read as a text comprising multiple layers formed over time from a variety of influences. There is the original bureaucratic and Legalist inspiration and approach, from the inception of the imperial law code, with their concerns for administration and penalties. There is also the Confucianization that followed, with its concerns for maintenance of the existing social hierarchy and moralistic and compassionate representations of the state. There are finally the adaptations of the code to practical reality over time, occurring principally through the addition of substatutes, sometimes in clear contradiction to the original intent of the code. Earlier scholarship was understandably drawn to the more prominent and external layers; what civil case records bring into focus is the easy-to-miss third layer.

Take household division, for example. The relevant statute, No. 87, read: "When the grandparents and parents are alive, if the sons and grandsons establish a separate household and divide up the property, [they will be punished by] 100 blows with the heavy stick." That was the stated Confucian ideal. Yet we know that household division during the parents' lifetime was in fact very common, and a substatute was tacked on in concession to this social reality: "If the parents permit the division, then it will be allowed" (No. 87-1). That should be taken as the practical intent of the code. As for the crucial operative principle of equal division among sons, it appears only in the middle of a substatute of the next statute, ostensibly dealing with "Inferiors and Juniors Using Money Without Permission" (No. 88-1). But as we have seen, there was actually little litigation surrounding that principle, because it was so very well established in customary practice. For all practical purposes, then, the main issue that brought the courts into play was succession rights in families with no natural-born sons. Statute 78 clearly spelled out how such a successor should be chosen, and substatute 78-1 addressed the problematic eventuality of the birth of a son after a legitimate successor had been chosen. Magistrates adjudicated accordingly.

On debt, similarly, we must not let the packaging of the statute "Charging Interest at Forbidden Rates" (No. 149) mislead us into thinking that its only, or anyway main, thrust was constraining usurious interest rates. In fact, lawsuits about such violations were relatively rare. Far more important in practice was the provision that brought the courts to uphold legitimate debts, which lurked behind the penalties for defaulting that were buried in the middle of the second paragraph: "Those who violate an agreement and do not repay private debts, in excess of five taels, for three months, will be punished with 10 lashes with the light bamboo." It was the positive civil principle implicit in this penal stipulation that dominated the magistrates' approach to debt.

On conditional sales and purchases of land, to recapitulate with another example, the code began with administrative stipulations about tax. The important operative principle—that the law would uphold legitimate transactions and punish those who violated them— appears only later, packaged within stipulations about punishments for violations.

On markets, finally, the code began with an administrative and haughty attitude, interested only in stipulating that private concerns must not attempt to usurp state prerogatives in the regulation of commerce. Beyond that, commerce was presumably too lowly a subject for lofty Confucian attention. Nevertheless, as we have seen, the final statute of the subsection (No. 156), in two simple sentences, articulated what amounted to a principle of fair market practice. And that statute, not the earlier and more prominent ones, was what really mattered in legal practice.

That the Qing code encompassed a substantial body of stipulations about civil matters seems to me beyond argument. That body of civil laws, to be sure, did not include formalistic discussions of abstract principles, in the manner some might consider necessary to a "rational" code. Nor did it proceed from the premise of rights that were independent of the will of the ruler. Rather, it was born of the practical adaptations of a state concerned first and foremost with control through punishment and administration. But it was no less consistent and important for all that. Those who would dismiss Qing civil law out of hand as falling short of some abstract standard of civil law might do well to remember the role that autocratic power played in the origins of the continental (as opposed to the Anglo-American common-law) tradition.

Once the way in which operative civil principles were embodied in the code is properly understood, it becomes clear that there was a striking consistency between codified law and magisterial adjudication. We must not be misled by the exterior packaging and the penal or administrative approach of given statutes into dismissing their relevance for civil adjudication. The key to understanding the relationship between formal code and legal practice in the Qing is to see the one in conjunction with the other.

That we should find magistrates consistently conforming their rulings to the code should really not be surprising. Despite the official construction that these men enjoyed absolute administrative power as local representatives of the emperor, they were in practice functionaries working at the bottom of a bureaucratic hierarchy with elaborately articulated rules and review procedures. The magistrate's position must not be equated with the emperor's. One stood at the apex of the bureaucratic system, as the source of all power, answerable only to the symbolic checks of tradition and morality. The other functioned at the bottom of that system, his actions subject to regular review by upper levels and his much vaunted discretionary authority in fact severely constrained by bureaucratic regulations. Even with civil cases, which he did not have to report on in detail, he faced the possibility of appeals to the higher levels. Under those conditions, his safest course of action was to follow the code closely.

Similarly, though magistrates were in theory not supposed to decide on their own what the truth was, they routinely did so in both criminal cases and civil cases. In criminal cases, it was usually after they were satisfied in their own mind of the accused's guilt that they had him tortured into confession. In civil cases, having formed their own opinion, they would rely on the intimidating presence of the court, always with an implied threat of punishment, to induce the litigants to file pledges of willing acceptance of that opinion. The great majority of cases heard by the magistrates, as has been seen, resulted in unequivocal judgments for one or another party. Despite the moral ideal that magistrates did not adjudicate, they in practice routinely made legal judgments and acted on them.

This fact also should not be surprising. The magistrate was subject to the pressure of being evaluated for his performance on the basis of whether or not he disposed of civil cases expeditiously. Large numbers and proportions of unresolved civil cases were a matter of considerable concern to upper-level authorities. Under those conditions, most magistrates sought to dispose of civil disputes in a single court session, with the litigants prostrated before the bench. That was hardly a time frame and a setting conducive to compromise working. Adjudicatory judgments were unavoidable, official constructions to the contrary.

Finally, despite the official ideology of absolute power for the emperor and his administrators, and consequently of no "rights" in the sense of rights guaranteed by law independent of administrative will, local courts regularly and consistently upheld property and contractual rights. And large numbers of litigants, including peasant and common town residents, went to court to assert or protect those rights. Legal practice, as well as the practical consequences of the law, in other words, gave protection to rights, despite the official construction of absolute administrative authority.

All this is not to say that official constructions did not matter, and that the Qing legal system should be understood only in terms of its actual practice. As will be seen in Chapter Seven, litigant and magistrate choices and actions are really understandable only in terms of a legal structure made up of paradoxical representation and practice. The Qing legal system in fact cannot be understood in terms simply of either its representation or its practice, but rather only of the two in combination. That combined structure was what set the parameters of choice for the actors involved in the system. For the purposes of this chapter, however, my concern has been to correct the misimpressions of earlier scholarship derived from Qing representations and establish the fact that the formal legal system of the Qing did deal frequently and consistently with civil matters, in accordance with the law.

CHAPTER FIVE

Between Informal Mediation and Formal Adjudication: The Third Realm of Qing Justice

To CLARIFY HOW civil justice worked in the Qing, we need to look not only at the informal justice of community and kin mediation and the formal justice of court adjudication, but also at the intermediate realm where the two met and interacted. A large proportion of disputes that entered into the formal system with the filing of a plaint were settled before they got a formal court hearing. In this middle phase, there was something of an institutionalized dialogue between the formal and informal systems, to make up a realm of semiformal justice that has not been examined by past scholarship. This chapter delineates that intermediate space and points to some of its major characteristics.

This semiformal justice system may be seen in fact as a particularly good illustration of a larger intermediate sphere in the Qing political system as a whole. In modern society, we are accustomed to a state of immense infrastructural scope. In the Qing, however, much was left to informal governance, by communities and kin groups, and a great deal of the work of government was undertaken through collaboration with the unofficial leaders of society. Indeed, for the majority of the population, contact with the state occurred largely in this third realm (as elaborated in P. Huang 1993b). From this point of view, each of the three parts of the justice system provides concrete illustrations for the corresponding parts of the larger political system: the formal legal system for official government, the informal justice system for unofficial societal self-government, and the semiformal justice system for the part-state part-society intermediate sphere where the two met and collaborated.

The Three Stages in a Qing Lawsuit

Civil lawsuits in the Qing were pursued in three distinct stages. The first extended from the filing of a plaint to the magistrate's initial response. Next came the stage before the formal court session, during which there was usually a good deal of interaction between the court and the litigants and their would-be informal mediators. The final stage was the formal court session, at which some definitive judgment was usually rendered.* The three stages marked, respectively, the first actions of the formal system, the subsequent interaction between the formal and informal systems, and the final action of the formal system. The interval between the first and final stage tended to range from a few days to a few months, but could sometimes be as long as several years, especially in the overburdened late-nineteenth-century Danshui and Xinzhu court.

We know for certain that 126 of the 628 cases in this study were successfully mediated out of court after the trigger of a formal filing. If, as we might reasonably suppose, something in the neighborhood of half of the 264 plaints whose final disposition is not documented (for reasons that we will take up in due course) were also mediated ahead of a court hearing, it is clear that for peasants who got so far as pressing a civil suit, the "probabilities" of a semiformal resolution were greater than for a formal one. The process of third-realm justice accounted for perhaps 258 cases, compared with 221 adjudicated by the courts (Appendix A, Table A.3).

The Initial Stage

Would-be litigants coming to the yamen were screened first of all through regulations governing the filing of a plaint. The required forms generally came printed with the conditions under which the court would not accept a suit. Some of these stipulations were uniform across the counties (all of the courts, for instance, required proof of injury in assault and battery cases and a list of stolen items for robberies), and a few were unique to one county, reflecting the particular concerns of that court (Dan-Xin's form, for instance, stated

---

*Usually but not always. Some cases lagged on after they were heard for lack of a definitive court ruling, and others were reopened by further plaints, which meant that they had to go through all or parts of these stages again. Both phenomena were particularly frequent in Danshui-Xinzhu for reasons to be considered in the next chapter.

that clerks and runners could not have others file suit on their behalf). But neither the one nor the other was the rule. For example,
both the Baxian form and the Baodi form stipulated that marriage
suits required the matchmaker's name and the date of the marriage,
illicit sex cases "definite proof," and land and credit cases the appropriate supporting documents. Both also stipulated that degree holders and women must be represented by proxy, that previous judgments must be reported honestly, and that the petitioner could name
only a certain number of witnesses (three) and defendants (three in
Baxian, five in Baodi). But the Baodi form did not give printed notice,
as the Baxian and Dan-Xin forms did, that a scribe who deliberately
altered the content or text of the plaint and a person who made a false
accusation would be punished. All three courts required that forms
be filled out just so, showing the name of the petitioner and the seal
of the scribe, and with no more than one character entered per square
and no more than one line per column.

Plaints were generally limited to one standard form sheet, con-
sisting of a grid with squares for just a few hundred characters: 288
(12 lines of 24 squares) in Baodi, 320 (16 lines of 20 squares) plus a
head line (wider and not squared) in Dan-Xin, and 325 (13 lines of
25 squares) in Baxian. In this space, plaintiffs were expected to give
only a concrete and straightforward account of the case. They were
not expected to provide legal arguments or to cite the code.

On receipt of a plaint, the magistrate might decline to accept the
case. He might reject the plaint for lack of documentation, particularly in respect to loan and land contracts, noting the fact on the form
and finishing off with a firm "permission not granted" (*buzhun*; e.g.,
Dan-Xin 23405, 1876.9 [d-4]). Or he might find the plaintiff's assertions clearly untrue. Again he would so note, sometimes giving his
reasoning, and end with "Permission not granted," or, alternatively,
a less definitive comment, such as "It will be hard to grant permission to accept [this plaint]" (*ai nan zhun li*; e.g., Dan-Xin 22519,
1887.7.1 [l-99]; 22520, 1887.10 [l-100]). Finally, the magistrate might
decide that the matter was more appropriately handled by the lineage, the community, or a middleman. This happened especially in
disputes among close kin over household division or informal loans.
In those cases, he might simply reject the lawsuit outright (Dan-Xin
23417, 1884.12 [d-16], 23312, 1887.1 [d-35], 22522, 1888.2.11 [l-102],
22524, 1888.2.23 [l-104]; Baxian 6:3:9761, 1850.10 [i-18]). Ten of my
628 cases were turned back in this manner.

A magistrate might accept a plaint as worthy of consideration but decide that the matter was too minor for him to handle personally and remand the case to lesser lights—the xiangbao or one of the ya-men's own runners, acting in concert with the xiangbao (and/or the original middleman in land or credit disputes).* In this event, he might simply instruct his surrogate to look into the matter (chaqing) and use his best judgment to resolve it (binggong lichu; e.g., Baodi 104, 1862.2.10 [l-3]). Or he might express an opinion about how he wanted the matter settled, as for example: "Look into the com-plaint. If it is indeed the truth, then [do such and such]" (Baodi 190, 1861.6.25 [d-5]).

In delegating such matters to an underling, the magistrate was in fact violating the Qing code. In 1765, a substatute had been added stipulating that the magistrate "may not order the *xiangbao* to settle minor matters [*xishi*], but must adjudge them himself [*qin jia pou-duan*]" (No. 334–8). The intent of the provision was probably to check xiangbao and runner abuse. Initially, it seems to have suc-cessfully curbed the practice: not a single instance is to be found in the mid-eighteenth to mid-nineteenth-century Baxian cases. But the mounting caseloads of the local courts, from population growth and commercialization, led to increasing violations of the substatute. Thus, among the 118 Baodi cases, mainly of the second half of the nineteenth century, we find six in which the magistrate chose not to handle the plaint himself and instead ordered runners and/or the xiangbao to investigate and settle the matter on their own authority. And in the more heavily burdened Danshui-Xinzhu court of the late nineteenth century, the figure climbed to 31. Tellingly, not one of these cases was ever resolved, or at least is not shown to have been in the records. They account for fully 36 percent of the incomplete case files (Appendix A, Table A.3).

Once the magistrate decided to take on a case himself, he might request more documentation or information before ordering a formal court session. In land-transaction disputes, he might order the plain-

---

*In our period, the unsalaried quasi-official known as the xiangbao in Baodi was usually called the *xiangyue* or *diyue* in Baxian and the *zongli* in Danshui-Xinzhu (Dai Yanhui 1979: 9–20; Allee 1987: 415–17). He was also occasionally referred to in the Dan-Xin records as the *zongbao* (e.g., 23408, 1880.12. [d-7]), suggesting that something of the same process was taking place there as occurred in Baodi, where the xiangbao had emerged out of the once separate posts of xiangyue and dibao (Dan-Xin 22407, 1870.12.21 [l-44]); P. Huang 1985: 224). I use the same term for all three counties, which not only makes things simpler but is also in line with the language of the Qing code (Statute 334-8).

tiff to submit his deed for examination. In boundary disputes, he might order the runners or the xiangbao to measure the land (*kan-zhang*); sometimes, he would request a drawing of the respective plots. If an injury was involved, he would verify that the requisite "injury slip" (*shangdan*) was affixed to the plaint. This form, prepared by the Office of Punishment (Xing fang) after an examination of the victim, would note the exact location of the wounds, the condition of the skin if broken, the color of the swelling, and the like.* On other matters, he might simply order the runners, sometimes along with the xiangbao, to investigate the assertions of the plaint (and counterplaint) and report back (*cha fu*). Seldom did a magistrate side with the petitioner on the basis of the plaint alone. In the entire three-county group, there was just one such instance.†

Often the magistrate simply registered his preliminary reactions to the information as presented to him. He might indicate some skepticism by questioning "whether the assertions made in the plaint are true" (*shifou shushi*). He might express stronger doubt, saying something like "these are exaggerations intended to alarm" (*weiyan songting*), or "there's obviously more than meets the eye here" (*qi zhong xian you bieqing* or *xian you yinni bieqing*), or "there are gaps in the story" (*qingjie zhili*), or "the facts might be disputed here" (*qi zhong kong you jiuge*). If he suspected fraud, he might note that the plaint seemed to him deceitful or crafty (*diao*) and warn that "if this turns out to be false, the matter will be handled severely" (*ru xu ding xing zhongban*).

These preliminary comments became part of the public record; and both plaintiff and defendant usually learned of their content by

---

*In general, light injuries had little effect on a magistrate's ruling. The root cause of the fight would be quickly identified for what it was—a land dispute, a debt, or whatever—and the basic issue addressed. But some reference to the injury, such as "the slight wounds suffered have now healed" (*suo shou weishang quanyu*), was usually required before a case could be officially closed. More serious injuries of course constituted assault and battery, a matter for criminal proceedings.

†This was the case we encountered earlier, the rare instance of an agricultural worker (Jin Wende) suing his employer (Yang Fuqui). The magistrate found no legal grounds for sustaining Jin's suit but did contrive to give him a partial victory through his comments: "This impoverished individual from afar has labored for three years and has had a hard life. It seems to me not right to abruptly expel him. I am ordering the runners on duty to carry this instruction to Yang Fugui and to tell him that if Jin Wende has not behaved in a manner unbefitting his station, he should be kept, to avoid litigation." The three runners reported back the next day that they had verified that Jin was a good worker and that Yang had agreed to keep Jin. No mention was made of paying Jin what he sought nor of the fact that he had been beaten (Baodi 188, 1832.7.9 [d-2]).

one means or another before they came to court. They might learn of the magistrate's thinking at the yamen, for example, from the clerks and runners or from the bulletin board where these comments were posted (Ch'ü T'ung-tsu 1962: 47, 98; Shiga 1984: 154). Or they might learn what the magistrate had to say from their court summons (*chuanpiao*), which typically contained not only a summary of the charges but also whatever substantive comments the magistrate had made. Runners might display these documents as proof of their authority or convey the contents when serving the concerned parties.

It would thus be a mistake to think of the magistrate's words as intended only for his staff. Indeed, he sometimes specifically addressed his remarks to the plaintiff, perhaps asking the person to clear up some point in doubt or putting some question to him, where he would use the direct superior-to-inferior "you" (*er*). Instructions to the clerks, by contrast, were always couched in a detached, impersonal form, most frequently involving the simple word *chi* ("order" or "instruct"), as in "order the runners to summon for a court inquiry" (*chi chai chuanxun*).

The issuing of the summons marked the end of the initial stage. The simplest instruction was the notation on the plaint form, "Permission granted [*zhun*]. Summon for court inquiry [*chuanxun;* or *huanxun* in eighteenth-century Baxian]." Magistrates were very careful in the wording of these orders. If there was a counterplaint setting forth a different version of events, they might use the term *zhixun*, that is, order both parties to appear together before the bench (*chuan'an*) for cross-examination.* If in addition to the plaintiff and the defendant they were calling in witnesses, community or kin leaders, or xiangbao to assist the court, they would use the term *jixun* ("gather together for [court] inquiry").

If the case involved possibly "weighty," criminal offenses, the magistrate's language sometimes underwent a subtle shift. Chuanxun was the most neutral term. *Xun* could be applied to anything ranging from a simple inquiry with no threat of punishment to an investgiation that might end in a severe sentence. Because it was open-ended, the word had far less ominous overtones that its alternative, *jiu*. The order *chuanjiu* ("summon for investigation") immediately conveyed a sense of gravity and the implication that the

---

*As Alison Conner (1979) has observed, bringing two different parties with different versions of events into confrontation before the magistrate was a frequently employed method of judicial investigation during the Qing.

investigation might very well lead to some punitive action. The distinction between xun and jiu was by no means hard and fast, however. Indeed, the two were sometimes used together, as in *chuanxun jiu* or *chuan'an xun jiu* ("bring to the bench for inquiry and investigation"), in which case both meanings would be conveyed. A magistrate might use both words on purpose, especially with cases that fell in the gray area between the punishable and the nonpunishable. Throughout this study, I render xun in most instances as "inquiry," and use "investigation" for jiu and for those instances where xun was used in a context that suggested possible punishment.

Adding some kind of qualifier to the court summons was another well-used device that magistrates employed in these borderline cases. *Yan* was the most common, as in *yanchuan* ("summon sternly"), suggesting something more serious than a simple civil matter. (Yan was also a favorite reinforcing device in the purely criminal realm, applied often, for example, in connection with orders to arrest and to punish, as in "arrest vigorously," *yanju*, and "punish severely," *yancheng*.)*

The Middle Stage

The middle stage of a lawsuit, even more than the first stage, saw a considerable range of possible actions on the part of the magistrate, the runners and the xiangbao, and the litigants. Often, the defendant filed a counterplaint setting forth his side of the story. As noted earlier, magistrates would then typically call both parties to court to confront each other before the bench. One wordy magistrate noted: "Who's right and who's wrong, let's wait until everyone is gathered at court, and [I will] determine by cross-examination" (Baodi 106, 1882.2.18 [l-22]).

If the magistrate wanted more information, he might in his comments either instruct the runners and xiangbao to investigate and report back or, on occasion, ask the litigants themselves to supply additional material. In one case, for example, the magistrate, noting

---

*Subtleties of language were also applied to the various role-players in settlements. Community or kin leaders, the xiangbao, and runners were almost always said to "settle [the matter] reasonably" (*lichu*) or to "mediate" (*tiaochu*) it, as opposed to the implicitly more important action of the magistrate—to "determine the facts" (*duo* or *heduo*). The weightiest term of all, "adjudge" (*duan*) or permutations of it (e.g., "analyze and adjudge," *pouduan*, or "investigate and adjudge," *xunduan, chaduan, jiuduan*), was generally reserved for the magistrate alone.

the discrepancies between the two stories, ordered each petitioner to file a clarifying statement to answer his queries, provide documentation, and name witnesses. That led to further submissions (Baodi 166, 1837.7.30 [m-4]).

Sometimes one or both parties might decide on their own initiative to present additional information or to prevail on some third party to file a statement or petition on their behalf. The litigants might also file additional plaints if the situation changed, as when, for example, one party engaged in aggressive action against the other after the initial plaint and counterplaint (e.g., breaking into the other's house to argue, forcibly removing property, beating the other up). Or, one or the other might file further plaints to embellish his story or just to let off more steam. It was conventional for litigants to begin any follow-up plaint by referring precisely to the magistrate's instructions and comments on their earlier one(s).*

The magistrate generally read and commented on each additional submission from a litigant. When impressed with new evidence, he might amend his earlier instructions. He might order, for example, that a matter he had delegated to his runners be brought back to court, or that more witnesses be summoned, or that his runners investigate the matter further. If unimpressed, he might respond with a mildly irritated "[I have] already instructed that the parties be summoned" (yi pishi chuanxun) or "Wait for the court inquiry" (hou tangxun), or a stronger "Don't annoy the court" (wu du) or "Don't annoy the court with exaggerations" (wu yong song du).

The patience of litigants could wear as thin as the magistrate's, especially patrons of the heavily burdened late-nineteenth-century Danshui-Xinzhu court, whose runners often took an inordinate amount of time (by Qing standards) to carry out a magistrate's instruction. Litigants there often filed prompting petitions (cuicheng) in the hope of stirring the court to action. Sometimes a magistrate responded with an obliging "Order the runners to hurry with the summons" (cuichai chuanxun) or "Order the runners to hurry with the investigation and report back (or settle the matter reasonably)" (cuichai cha fu, or cuichai cha li). Other times a magistrate felt un-

---

*Cases with a large number of plaints and counterplaints and multiple court sessions generally had as their principals wealthy and powerful individuals or lineages. Danshui-Xinzhu stands out in this respect, especially from Baodi, where the overwhelming majority of the litigants were simple peasants. Differences in the experience of the three courts are discussed in the next chapter.

necessarily pestered and let a petitioner know it, with a blunt instruction like "Wait for the court inquiry; don't annoy the court"
(*houxun, wu du*).

In some cases magistrates showed their displeasure with the work
of their runners. A failure to resolve a particular matter might bring
only an implicit criticism on the runners' report, in the form of an
order to "go back once more and try to find a way to settle the matter" (*zai qianwang shefa chuli*). But the magisrate might also openly
reprimand or even punish a runner for failing to carry out his instructions, though this was comparatively rare (e.g., Baodi 190, 1860.7.7
[d-36]; Dan-Xin 22430, 1886.11.10 [1-67]). In exceptional circumstances, he might replace the runners initially assigned to the case,
instructing the yamen officials to "change the runners, and order as
before to . . ." (*gaichai, rengchi* . . . ; Baodi 105, 1881.9.3 [1-21]; Dan-
Xin 22526, 1888.5.15 [1-106]).

Though the principals in a case were obligated to obey a summons and come to court, witnesses or third parties sometimes would
plead to be excused. One summoned witness, for example, put his
version of the facts into a written petition and asked to be excused
from appearing in court. The magistrate was satisfied with the account and granted permission (Baodi 105, 1902.3.7 [1-23]). The term
for such a "release" was *zhaishi*, and our case records contain a number of such petitions, including some that were denied. The magistrate would sometimes, though not always, explain this action, indicating, for example, that the person was needed for the face-to-face
cross-examination.

About two-thirds of the three-county files end in this middle
stage. Some of these cases were resolved by the litigants themselves
or, more often, by community or kin mediators, galvanized into intensified efforts by the lawsuit. The others simply disappear from the
records, and we can only make some educated guesses about what
might have happened. Let us look first at the relatively few cases
where litigants reached a settlement on their own.

The mere act of going to court raised the stakes in a dispute. One
party might decide to give in: the defendant to pay up or the plaintiff
to withdraw his complaint. Or both parties might become more conciliatory and work out an understanding themselves. Nine of the
Baodi and three of the Dan-Xin cases were resolved in this manner
(e.g., Baodi, 187, 1850.5.17 [d-46]; Dan-Xin 22709, 1887.3 [1-115];

Baodi 169, 1866.2 [m-25]; Baodi 168, 1867.9 [m-26]). The plaintiff in such circumstances was expected to submit a petition to the court explaining why he wished to close the case, and the magistrate would routinely grant permission, unless he had reason to believe that some criminal offense was being concealed (e.g., Baodi 169, 1866.2 [m-25]). But few plaintiffs, once satisfied, in fact took the trouble to advise the court and get the case closed. It is reasonable to assume that this accounts for a fair number of the "incomplete" cases in the records.

More commonly, the filing of a plaint intensified the efforts of community or kin mediators to work for an out-of-court resolution of the dispute. A court summons only increased the pressures, especially when accompanied by some strong comment from the magistrate. A plaintiff or defendant would for good reason take the magistrate's remarks as a preliminary indication of how a court judgment would go. One or the other might therefore become more conciliatory, thus preparing the way for an informal settlement. Mediators succeeded in settling 114 of our three-county suits.

Again, upon a satisfactory resolution of the matter, the court was supposed to be notified and asked to close the case. Often it was not the plaintiff, but the group of mediators—community or kin leaders, the local xiangbao, or one or more local notables—who took on this task. These spokemen usually mentioned somewhere in their petitions that the two parties had observed the appropriate ritual of apologizing to each other (bici jianmian fuli, or peili)), or that the offender had apologized or otherwise made amends, and that both parties wished to end the suit (juyuan xisong). In the event injury was involved, some reference also would be made to the fact that the wounds had healed (shang yi quanyu).

There were circumstances in which the magistrate might refuse to end a suit. Where a civil dispute involved serious injury, for example, he might insist on a formal court session. Thus, in response to a petition to close a case from the mediators of a rent dispute, the Baodi magistrate observed that "this involved assault and battery, with verified serious injury. . . . The matter may not be settled [this way] to close the case" (Baodi 100, 1839.5.18 [l-12]). But the magistrate usually welcomed the news of a settlement, endorsing the petition with the words "Permission granted to close the case" (zhun xiao'an). If he had issued a summons, he might add, "The summons is canceled" (xiaopiao) or "The court inquiry/investigation is waived" (mianxun/jiu). Often, he would preface these orders with the phrase,

"The court will be lenient" (*gu congkuan*), as a reminder to one and all of the majesty of his position. Sometimes, he would attach a warning to the effect that "if this person should cause trouble again, the matter will be dealt with severely" (*ruo zai zishi, ding xing zhongjiu*), or "if this person should engage in such unseemly behavior again, he will definitely be arrested and punished" (*ruo zai wang wei, ding xing ju cheng*).

As a final and routine step, the plaintiff or both parties filed "a pledge of willingness to end the lawsuit" (*ju ganjie*) with the court.* If the matter had been mediated, the pledge would mention that "kin and friends/neighbors have mediated" (*jing qinyou/lin shuohe*) or give the names of the mediators. Then it would summarize the settlement, which might involve no more than an apology from one or both parties, but might also involve complex arrangements for resolving the dispute. The petitioner would then conclude by noting that he had no disagreement with the terms (*bing wu yishuo*), that he wished to end the suit (*qinggan xisong*), and that he was therefore entreating the magistrate to waive the court inquiry (*ken en mianxun*). Often the mediators would also file a pledge verifying the terms of the agreement, thereby adding the moral weight of the community or kin group to it. The case would then be officially closed.

But here too litigants sometimes settled their differences without troubling to get their cases formally off the books. With no petition to that effect in the official record, we cannot tell how many of the 264 "unresolved" cases were truly so. My own view is that cases settled informally, whether by the litigants or by mediation, probably account for a substantial proportion of the 154 cases that end with the issuance of the court summons (109 in Baxian, 6 in Baodi, and 39 in Dan-Xin). Once the parties reached a settlement, after all, they lost most of their incentive to go through all the trouble of dealing with the court. But they did not have the option of formally declining to accept a summons from the runners or of asking them to convey back to the court that the dispute had been settled. The job of the runners, as agents of the yamen, was only to serve the summons; they were not expected to report on informal community or kin settlements. That was up to either the xiangbao or the litigants to do. If the xiangbao was lax, and the litigants savvy enough to know that

---

* Matthew's Chinese-English dictionary renders *ganjie* not quite accurately as "bond." The *gan* is as in *qinggan*, or willingly, the *jie* as in *jie'an*, or close the case. Hence my translation of pledge of willingness to end the suit.

the courts were not particularly vigilant about seeing a civil dispute to its conclusion, a case would simply be left hanging at this point. The court itself would do nothing more.

We can also impute at least some unresolved cases to lapses on the part of the courts' runners. The records show a number of instances of runner delays or outright negligence, documented by the magistrate's expressions of irritation. Those problems could have been just the result of inefficiencies in the system or case overload, or both. But it is almost certain that at least some runners were bribed by litigants to refrain from serving a summons. By not reporting on the outcome of a summons, a runner could effectively sabotage the investigative intentions of the court (more below).

A handful of the incomplete records go one step beyond the issuing of a summons, with the runners reporting that they were simply unable to serve the party. The reports cited various reasons—one or both principals were in hiding, had run away, were ill or otherwise immobilized, and so on—and account for 22 of the Baxian, 12 of the Baodi, and 4 of the Dan-Xin cases.

Finally, in 29 cases, there is no way to tell what the outcome might have been. With only fragments of sheets or obviously missing documents from the evidence of later ones, these files are incomplete in the full sense of the term.

The Final Stage: The Court Session

Once an out-of-court settlement proved impossible, the parties to the suit came before the magistrate in a formal session. He usually made a decision on the spot, and that decision, we now know, was very likely to be in favor of one or the other party (close to three-quarters of the 221 adjudicated cases). Occasionally, he might try, for the sake of future family or community relations, to salvage something for the loser, for example, ordering a rich person who won his case to make a token charitable concession to his poorer kin or neighbor (e.g., Baxian 6:1:720, 1769.11 [l-4]; 6:2:1416, 1797.6 [l-16]; 6:4:2552, 1852.11.19 [d-20]). But the surprise is how seldom magistrates ever seem to have made an attempt to work out even such merely symbolic compromises—in just 6 percent of the 170 one-winner cases.

Several considerations might enter into the far less common instance of a finding for neither side (33 cases). Sometimes the court's investigation turned up facts that removed misunderstandings, and with them, the cause of complaint. For example, in several Baxian and Baodi cases, the court's evidence was enough to persuade a party to a betrothal contract that the defendant had not acted in bad faith as he had thought (e.g., Baxian 6:1:1760, 1784.3.19 [m-9]; Baodi 168, 1871.8 [m-27]). Sometimes the court found the claims of both parties legitimate and ruled accordingly. In disputes over family property among legal heirs, for instance, magistrates simply ruled for equal division (e.g., Dan-Xin 22601, 1845.6.19 [i-1]). And sometimes the court found both parties at fault or both claims without merit. All told, such rulings governed in 22 of these cases.

Only very rarely (just 11 instances) did magistrates act as arbitrators. One common occasion for such an action was land boundary disputes that resulted from shifts in old boundaries after flooding (e.g., Dan-Xin 22506, 1878.2 [l-86]; Baxian 6:1:733, 1773.3 [l-7]).

There were of course cases that were not settled even with a formal court session. The magistrate might find, for example, that he did not have sufficient evidence for a judgment and order further investigation or another court session. A definitive ruling might come only at a subsequent session. A few case files ended with the order for further investigation. In those instances (5 in Baxian and 1 in Baodi), the dispute may have been resolved by informal mediation or left hanging through inaction on the part of the litigants or the court. However, the vast majority of cases that reached a formal court session ended in some kind of magisterial judgment, if not in the first session, then in a subsequent one.

Even with a definitive judgment, at least the party at fault, and often both parties, were required to file a pledge of willingness to end the suit. The loser's would include some language about accepting the verdict, as in this pledge in a land dispute: "[The court has ruled that] I am hereafter not permitted to roll my cart over [my neighbor's] crops. This [document] certifies that I willingly file this pledge [to end the lawsuit]" (Baodi 104, 1869.8.10 [l-4]). In credit disputes, the pledge would usually spell out how much was to be paid when (Baodi 191, 1871.1 [d-10]; Baodi 193, 1876.11 [d-11]).

Justice in the Intermediate Realm

Of particular interest is the largest group of cases that ended in the middle stage of the process, those where the formal and informal justice systems interacted to settle disputes. What follows is a closer look at the various ways in which the two systems influenced each other. The emphasis will be on illustrating with case examples how third-realm justice operated.

The Court as Catalyst Prompting a Settlement

The act of filing a plaint inevitably brought the formal system into any process of informal negotiations toward a settlement. From then on, both parties had to consider the legality of their positions and how the magistrate was likely to act if matters reached a formal court session. They also had to weigh potential gains against actual costs. There were, first of all, the statutory costs of filing counter-plaints and petitions, of charges for witnesses if any, and of the fees for a formal court session. I will take up these fees in detail in Chapter Seven. For now, let me just provide an inkling of what could amount to a considerable outlay by citing Dai Yanhui's figures for late Qing Taiwan: 0.4–0.5 diao of *cash* for a petition form, 0.4–0.5 silver yuan for the fee for filing the form, 0.4–0.7 yuan for the scribe's fee, 0.3–1.0 yuan for the summons fee, and 3.0 or 4.0 yuan up to over 10.0 yuan (sometimes as much as 100 or more yuan) for court fees (Dai Yanhui 1979: 706–8).* On top of this, there was the cost of entertaining or paying off the runners, clerks, and xiangbao, and if one had to wait at the county seat for the court session, of living expenses.

The threat of a court session alone could induce the disputants to settle their quarrel on their own, as occurred in nine of the Baodi and three of the Dan-Xin cases. In early 1850, for example, Wang Dianfa had purchased on credit 11 pieces of sheepskin, worth 4.4 diao, from Yue Xiang. He had repaid two diao of the debt, but when Yue asked him to pay the rest, and got only excuses in return, he seized some of Wang's clothing, a sickle, and a pipe. In anger, Wang brought suit on the seventeenth day of the fifth month. Three days later, the magistrate issued a summons for Yue to come to court. Their initial anger gone by then and faced with the prospect of a court appearance, the two men quickly settled. On the twenty-second, Wang petitioned to close the case, stating that he had paid Yue the balance, and that Yue had returned his property (Baodi 187, 1850.5.17 [d-46]).

---

*The *cash*-to-yuan exchange rate rose and fell quite sharply during the late Qing. According to Usui 1981: 77–79, there were between 800 and 2,000 *cash* to the yuan from the 1810's to the 1860's. For the subsequent period, 1870 through the 1900's, Bernhardt 1972: 248 cites a low of 855 and a high of 1,252.

More commonly, a lawsuit intensified community or kin efforts to mediate a settlement. Liu Zhenkui filed suit against his father-in-law, giving the following particulars. His wife often returned to her natal home for long visits, but he and his brother had recently divided up their household, and there was no one else to take care of his aged parents. For that reason, he did not want his wife to continue to return home. But his wife's father, Zhang Qi, insisted, and the two had come to blows, resulting in his own injury. Because of the claim of injury, Liu was immediately examined by the Office of Punishment, which noted that he had "a wound to the left side of his skull, about six-tenths [*fen*] of an inch long and two-tenths of an inch wide. No other injury." The magistrate accepted the case and issued a summons for a court inquiry. Within eight days, three mediating neighbors, Li Guoying, Chen Maolin, and Wang Junheng, had smoothed things over. They reported that they had brought the father-in-law and son-in-law together, that both regretted what had happened and now wished to end the dispute, and that they (the mediators) were therefore petitioning for the summons to be canceled. The magistrate observed: "Since you people have mediated and settled the matter, permission is granted to cancel the summons and close the case. Order both parties to file pledges of willingness to end the lawsuit" (Baodi 170, 1814.6.9 [m-16]).

Mediation sometimes did not succeed until the very late stages of a lawsuit. On the ninth day of the ninth month, 1771, Li Kunzhang filed a suit with the Baxian court, claiming that he had sold his land conditionally to Zeng Rongguang for 200 diao, but that Zeng refused to let him redeem it, beat him, and injured him. The magistrate accepted the case, noting "permission granted" (*zhun*). Zeng filed a counterplaint claiming that after the conditional sale Li had borrowed seven diao from him but had not repaid it, had tried to keep him from planting the winter crop on the land, and had beaten and injured him. The magistrate issued a summons on the next day for both parties and several witnesses to come to court for cross-examination. Two runners went out on the eleventh day and brought back the litigants, but could not get the witnesses to come. Both parties were examined for their injuries, which turned out to be much less serious than they had claimed. On the twentieth, the magistrate instructed that the witnesses be summoned. The next day, Li filed another plaint, this one charging that Zeng had sent some relatives to his house, and that they had forcibly cut down and removed a tree.

He urged that the guilty parties be arrested. The magistrate noted on this second plaint: "Wait quietly for cross-examination; do not meddle further." At this point, on the twenty-sixth day, five people representing themselves as the *xiangyue* petitioned to close the case. They had gathered both parties together and clarified what happened: the plaintiff Li had pledged the land to Zeng for 200 diao but later wanted Zeng to raise that price (*jia dangjia*) (presumably because the price of land had risen in the meantime). Zeng had refused. The mediators resolved the dispute by getting both parties to agree to a new conditional-sale price of 207 diao (thereby adding what Li had later borrowed from Zeng to the original price). They destroyed the old sales document and made up a new one. Both parties agreed to abide by these terms and to file a pledge of willingness to end the dispute (Baxian 6:1:728, 1771.9.9 [1-35]).

We catch a glimpse here of the powerful incentives at work on both litigants to reach a mediated settlement. There were the mounting costs of staying in town to await the court session. There were also the impending witness fees, once the court issued the summons. And, of course, there were the court fees to come. Add to that the consideration that the magistrate had indicated some displeasure at the exaggerations both parties had made about the injuries they received, and it is easy to understand why they would willingly accept a mediated settlement even after coming this far in the litigation.

The Role of Court Opinion

If magistrates chose to express their preliminary opinions on plaints, counterplaints, and petitions, their influence on community or kin mediation was that much greater. Any indication of displeasure, suspicion, or predisposition alerted the litigants to the likely outcome of a court session and therefore affected their posture in the mediation process. The Baodi magistrate, for example, made no attempt to disguise his feelings in the case of Mrs. Feng, née Tu, a widow whose husband and son had both died and who was left with just her child-bride daughter-in-law. Mrs. Feng claimed she was being taken advantage of by the defendant, a fellow villager named Li Wanlai, who had tried to marry off the daughter-in-law to a Tang in another village for his own gain. On her plaint, the magistrate observed: "Li Wanlai is not even a relative. How dare he try to marry off your son's bride to a Tang? If what you say is true, then he has indeed broken the law. Wait for the order to summon [you both] quickly to court." This reaction by the magistrate was enough to prompt Li to make concessions and accept mediation: he agreed to pay Mrs. Feng 36 diao as a betrothal price for her deceased son's child-bride (Baodi 171, 1896.5 [m-22]).

Alternatively, the magistrate's opinion might prompt a plaintiff with less than full justification on his side to make concessions, which would then lead to a mediated settlement. Zhang Guoqi filed a plaint against Zhang Liu and his son Zhang Han, alleging that they kidnapped his wife some seven months earlier. The magistrate commented: "You have only just brought suit, more than half a year after it happened. There's clearly more to the story. Wait for the summons and the court investigation and determination." For Zhang Guoqi, that was indication enough that his fabricated story was not likely to go unchallenged. Just 10 days later, he filed a petition to end the suit, this time telling the truth. He explained that he was so poor that he had been forced to go away to work and could not take care of his family. He had therefore married his wife to Zhang Han and had also entrusted his children to him and his father, Zhang Liu. When he returned, however, he learned that they were not treating his wife and children well. He got into a fight over it with Zhang Han, and Zhang Han told him to take his family back. With no better chance of supporting them than before, he had trumped up charges against the Zhangs. Relatives and friends had now mediated, he stated, and Zhang Liu and Zhang Han had agreed to continue to house his family and would return his children when they were grown. He was therefore petitioning to end the suit. The magistrate commented: "You were wrong to bring suit as you did, but in consideration of the fact that you have submitted this petition yourself, the court will be lenient and will not investigate further and hold you accountable" (Baodi 164, 1850.9.25 [m-19]).

When a magistrate reacted against both plaintiff and defendant, both would feel the pressure to settle. Han Yanshou sued Jing De and Han Xi, claiming they had borrowed 40 diao from him, set up gambling in Jing De's house, and refused to repay the money. The defendants countered that Han Yanshou had a long criminal record and owed them money. The magistrate commented that he thought the plaintiff and defendants were clearly fellow gamblers arguing over winnings and losses and ordered them brought to court for investigation. That was enough to motivate both parties to settle. Just one day after the summons was issued, a mediator, Rui Wenqing, petitioned to end the case. The two parties, he said, were relatives who had been involved in some financial dealings. Neither was involved in gambling. They had now straightened out their accounts and settled things. The Plaintiff Han Yanshou regretted his actions and had apologized, bringing the two sides back to their earlier good relations. On this representation, the magistrate agreed to cancel the summons, but not without reiterating his conviction that the dispute actually involved gambling debts. He warned both the litigants and the mediator against future offenses (Baodi 193, 1898.2.18 [d-31]).

In another pattern, the court's judgment of what the facts were could influence a settlement. Xu Wanfa lodged a complaint against his neighbor Yang Zongkui when the two got into a brawl over a fence that Xu had built at the boundary between their houses. Yang maintained that the fence encroached on his property. Since Xu rented his place, the case also involved his landlord; and since a neighbor saw the brawl, he was involved as a witness. Yang submitted a counterplaint, with drawings, and charged that the witness had helped to instigate the suit. Xu then submitted a follow-up plaint, also with a drawing, and charged that several other people were helping Yang with his suit. The magistrate ordered that everyone be brought to court. The other parties named in the plaints filed a petition to be excused from the court summons, but the magistrate denied their request. The runners managed to bring in most of them, but the court inquiry produced no definitive results. The magistrate then ordered his runners and one of the witnesses to go out and measure both plots according to their original deeds. Those measurements apparently backed up Xu's claims. Yang submitted yet one more statement to argue his case, but the magistrate took the position that the facts had now been established. When he summoned both parties to court for a repeat session (fuxun), it was clear how he would rule in the case. At this point, Yang gave in. The mediators marked out both plots and got the disputants to agree to abide by the settlement. Yang and Xu then both petitioned to end the suit, and the magistrate agreed to let the matter rest without a second court session (Baodi 100, 1845.10.7 [l-14]).

The Xiangbao

The two-way interaction between formal and informal justice is perhaps best seen through the person of the xiangbao. As I reported in my 1985 book, nineteenth-century Baodi records on the appointment and removal of these officeholders show that though some were men of real wealth and towering presences in the community, the majority were owner-peasants of relatively modest means who were placed in their positions by the truly powerful as a buffer between themselves and the state. Many clearly thought of the post as a thankless burden to be avoided. The Baodi documents contain many examples of nominated xiangbao who ran away to avoid having to serve—and in one case, of someone blackmailing another with the threat of nominating him. (But there are also a few examples of men who grasped at the chance to enrich themselves through tax embezzlement; P. Huang 1985: 225–31.)

As someone who was confirmed by the county yamen but nominated by community leaders, the xiangbao was intended to be at once an agent of the court and a representative of the local community. It was up to him, along with the runners, to convey to the litigants and their communities the opinions, summonses, and warrants of the court. In very minor disputes, as noted earlier, he might even be asked to settle matters in the magistrate's stead. At the same time, he was responsible for conveying community or kin opinion and mediatory efforts back to the court (which distinguished him from the official runners).

On occasion, he might instigate or become involved in the mediating process. The simple act of the xiangbao being asked to look into the matter was enough to start the process in the case of Zhang Yusheng's suit against his neighbor Bian Tinglu. Zhang had received a four-mu plot as security for a loan and had planted it in wheat. But his neighbor Bian claimed that half a mu was inside the boundaries of the Cais' gravesite, and in his capacity of caretaker of that site, he had proceeded to harvest it with three members of the Cai lineage. Zhang stated that he had then contacted Yuan Qi and other village leaders (*shoushi*) to help resolve the dispute, but that they had declined to intervene. The magistrate indicated his skepticism right from the start: "If you are merely cultivating land used as security for a loan, as you claim, why would Bian and the others take your harvest for no reason, and why would village leaders Yuan Qi and the others refuse to intervene? There must be more here than meets the eye. It is hereby ordered that the *xiangbao* investigate the matter with the village leaders Yuan Qi and the others and report back." Whatever the actual truth of the matter, this instruction set in motion a mediation process that ended with the xiangbao, Liu Mingwang, along with the village leaders Yuan Qi, Wang Lin, and Li Yi, petitioning the court nine days later to close the case. On investigation, they reported, they found that the boundary between the two properties was unclear. They had suggested that Zhang rent the one-half mu in dispute from the Cai family for 1,500 *wen*. Zhang and Bian had both accepted the arrangement and were willing to end the lawsuit. The magistrate noted: "Since this has been settled reasonably, permission is granted to close the case" (Baodi 101, 1851.8.8 [l-15]).

Sometimes the xiangbao mediated cases entirely on their own, as occurred in nearly a fifth of the mediated cases (7 of 36) in Baodi. In one of these, Ma Zhong brought suit against Zhang Enpu, from whom he had borrowed 1,830 wen. Mao claimed that he had retired the loan in two payments, one to Zhang and one to his son, that Zhang had nevertheless continued to press him for payment, and that in the course of a fight over this, he had been injured. The Office of Punishment examined Ma and noted that he had been "scratched by nails in two spots on the left side of the forehead, punched and scratched under his left eye, where the flesh swelled some with a greenish tint, and his skin above the lip had been scratched open in one spot. Otherwise, no injury." The magistrate commented in response to the plaint that he found "gaps in the story" and ordered the xiangbao to investigate. Next came a plaint a week later from Ma's nephew Ma Fugang, claiming that Ma's injuries had gotten worse, and that he was running a fever and had no appetite. This time the magistrate noted: "I have ordered the *xiangbao* to investigate and report. Do not make false statements and offend the court."

We can surmise that a comment like this from the magistrate would have enhanced the power of the xiangbao, as it plainly did here. It took Gao Shenglin just nine days to report back that he had looked into and settled the matter. The plaintiff, Ma, as it turned out, had not in fact cleared his debt in full, so he (Gao) had arranged for him to do so. Given that Ma's wounds had healed, and that both parties agreed to the settlement, they now wanted to end the lawsuit, if the court so pleased. The magistrate noted: "The court will be lenient and allow the case to be closed" (Baodi 192, 1886.4.2 [d-29]).*

I found one instance of court runners collaborating with a

---

* From the Danshui-Xinzhu records, it appears that xiangbao (known generally as *dongshi*) did not play a particularly prominent role in this process there: only one turns up as instrumental among 25 documented mediated resolutions (Dan-Xin 23203, 1877.10.28 [l-125]). The reasons for this difference are unclear. As for Baxian, it is impossible to say either way. The records generally refer to the mediators broadly as *yuelin*, a term that embraces both the xiangbao (*xiangyue*) and "relatives and neighbors" (*qilin* or *zulin*).

xiangbao to settle a dispute (Baodi 107, 1882.2.18 [l-18]). But this would have been a rare occurrence. Runners did not have either the status in the local community or the official authority to act as mediators.

Sources of Abuse in the Third Realm

The semiformal nature of third-realm justice was the source both of its strength and of its weakness. When the system worked as it should, the concerns of both formal law and informal justice were well served. But the fact that third-realm justice worked in largely ad hoc ways, without clearly spelled-out guidelines and procedures, left considerable scope for abuse.

Xiangbao Power and Abuse

As the critical intermediary between the court and society, the xiangbao could abuse the justice system in both directions. As the eyes and ears of the court, he could be pivotal in the stance it took and thus had the power to greatly influence the outcome of any litigant's case. At the same time, by foot-dragging, dereliction of duty, or an outright misrepresentation of facts, he could also thwart even the best-intentioned efforts of the court to get at the truth and uphold the law. (But the court also had ways to keep such abuses in check. The court's own runners were an important source of information. A xiangbao could not easily falsify the facts without their collusion, and vice versa. The practice of routinely assigning more than one runner to carry out a court order, whether for investigation or to serve a summons, also provided some protection from abuse.)

In the Baodi loan dispute between Ma Zhong and Zhang Enpu presented above, the xiangbao's influence derived not only from his role as mediator but even more from how he represented the facts. His siding with the defendant Zhang Enpu in his claim that Ma still owed him money, whether true or not, could only have been decisive in persuading Ma to settle out of court. Had Ma persisted in his litigation, he would have faced a magistrate strongly predisposed against him on the basis of the xiangbao's report.

In eighteenth-century Baxian, to give another example, one frequent source of dispute was the claim of a family's moral right to its ancestral gravesite on land it no longer owned. Some exploited the claim for material advantage, even long after the sale. Thus, in 1797,

Yang Wenju camped out on the ancestral gravesite of land that his grandfather had sold three decades earlier and cut the bamboo on it for his own use. On receiving the owner Xu Yuyin's plaint, the magistrate ordered the local xiangbao to investigate and report back. Neighbors attempted to mediate the dispute, but Yang refused to cooperate. In the meantime, the xiangbao reported back that the facts were indeed as Xu represented them. The magistrate then ordered that Yang be summoned to court. At this point, Yang gave in, and the community mediators petitioned the court to close the case (Baxian 6:2:1418, 1797.3 [l-44]).

The power of the xiangbao was the greatest when a magistrate decided to delegate a case to him. We saw earlier in the chapter that not one of the cases left to xiangbao and/or runners appears to have been resolved. Here we can only speculate on what actually occurred. Perhaps the xiangbao simply lacked the clout to bring a dispute to a clear-cut resolution, especially where the litigants were wealthy and powerful lineages, as was often the case in Danshui-Xinzhu. Almost certainly some, given this considerable latitude, were bribed into inaction.

The most elusive and yet probably the most important and frequently exercised power wielded by xiangbao was in their ability to stall the judicial process by simply failing to perform their assigned duties. Two cases give us a glimpse of this foot-dragging technique. Instructed to summon the defendant in a marriage dispute in Baodi, the local xiangbao reported that the defendant had gone somewhere and could not be found. Evidently irritated, the magistrate noted that he would send a runner to summon the man and reprimanded the xiangbao pointedly: "Do not try to cover things up again by claiming that the defendant has gone away." But the magistrate's irritation apparently made no difference, for the records of the case end there (Baodi 168, 1868.10 [m-30]). In the other instance, also from Baodi, a widow brought suit against an alleged debtor. The magistrate ordered the xiangbao to bring both parties in for cross-examination. But the xiangbao reported that the widow actually lived in another county, and that her relatives and friends verified that her claims were groundless. This conscientious magistrate noted his skepticism of the xiangbao's report and instructed that a record be entered of his behavior. Once again, however, no further action was apparently taken, the magistrate's good intentions notwithstanding (Baodi 190, 1860.7.7 [d-36]).

Runner Power and Abuse

In contrast to the semiofficial xiangbao, who were situated entirely in the third realm, the yamen runners belonged more to the first realm of formal justice, or at least to the borderline between the two. As hirelings of the yamen, they could not formally represent a community or kin group before the court; they could not, for example, petition that a case be closed because it had been successfully resolved by mediation. On the other hand, they were only partly salaried. To judge by a report from the Xinzhu magistrate to his superiors in 1888, he paid his runners a mere 0.08 yuan a day, or about 29 yuan a year, called a "subsistence stipend" (gongshi), compared with 1,000 yuan for his judicial secretary (xingming muyou) and 800 for his tax secretary (qiangu muyou), called an "honorarium" (shuxiu; Dan-Xin 11407: pp. 1–3).* Most runners probably sought supplementary income from gifts and squeeze. Unlike the magistrate and his personal staff, moreover, they were generally permanent residents of the county, subject to the importunings of local circles of influence.

Where the local xiangbao office was for whatever reasons defunct, runners became the magistrate's sole source of information on a case. Take the tangled tale of Mrs. Wu and Mrs. Gao, for example. The only point on which they agreed was that Mrs. Wu had some years earlier taken the daughter of Mrs. Guo as a child-bride for her son. Mrs. Wu came to court claiming that Mrs. Guo had kidnapped her now grown-up daughter and abetted in her adultery. On receipt of the plaint, the magistrate noted that the charges, if true, were serious ones and ordered the runners to investigate and bring Mrs. Guo to court. Mrs. Guo, in the meantime, had filed a counterplaint explaining the background to the dispute. By her account, when the girl grew up, she and young Wu had not gotten along, and Mrs. Wu had therefore pressed her to redeem her daughter. She had done so, for 40 yuan, and subsequently married the girl to Yang Rui. Mrs. Wu was simply hoping to extort more money from her by fabricating these charges. The runners, after investigation, reported that the facts were indeed

---

*Dai Yanhui, citing an unnamed 1888 Xinzhu source, gives the same figures I give for the magistrate's two principal assistants but the unrealistically low figure of 6.3 yuan (a year) for the runners (Dai 1979: 698, 703–11). I suspect that Dai relied on this same document but overlooked the subsistence stipend figures for the runners and relied instead on the standard statutory figure of six taels a year for the position. In the article on which this chapter is based (P. Huang 1993b: 283), I relied on Dai.

as the defendant Mrs. Guo stated in her counterplaint. There is no report from the xiangbao or any mention of him in the case file. Given the runners' report, Mrs. Wu had little choice but to give in. Mediators then settled the case on that basis and petitioned to have the case closed. The magistrate required both parties to file pledges of willingness to settle and close the case (Dan-Xin 21207, 1890.11.28 [m-7]). Here the runners' assessment of what actually transpired was clearly decisive in shaping the outcome.

Obviously, in such instances, runners could work the system to their own advantage. One case, in particular, smacks strongly of bribery. In Xinzhu on the fifteenth day of the fifth month in 1888, Xiao Chunkui filed a plaint charging that his neighbor Lin Jiao had enlarged his land at Xiao's expense by taking advantage of a recent flood to fill in an old ditch on his own land and dig a new one on Xiao's. The magistrate first ordered Xiao to submit his land deed for examination and then, upon a prompting petition from Xiao on the twenty-fourth, ordered runners sent out to investigate. A week later, the runners, Wang Chun and Li Fang, reported they could find no evidence that the ditch on Xiao's land was newly dug. In the seventh month, Xiao filed another petition, charging that Lin Jiao had bribed the runners and asking that new ones be sent. Though the magistrate's initial reaction was that "there is no need to change the runners," he nevertheless ordered further investigation. It was four months before the runner Wang Chun (Li Fang having died in the meantime) got back to him, saying that he now saw some signs suggesting that the ditch may have been recently dug. Two weeks later, Xiao filed a statement claiming he had been vindicated and charging again that Wang Chun had been bribed by Lin Jiao. At this, the magistrate agreed to assign two new runners to the case. Another four and a half months passed. Now the magistrate was advised that since the area where the old ditch supposedly lay had already been planted, there was no way the two new men could tell whether there had ever been a ditch there. Still determined to uncover the truth, the magistrate then instructed the runners to question local residents. On the ninth day of the fifth month, almost a full year after the original plaint, the runners returned with an ambiguous report, saying that it was possible the ditch had been moved. The magistrate, evidently out of steam, noted that he would wait for the plaintiff's prompting petition before taking further action. At this point, the record ends. Presumably, Xiao finally gave up (Dan-Xin 22526, 1888.5.15 [l-106]). The defendant Lin Jiao, by the looks of it, had managed to thwart Xiao's efforts, as well as the magistrate's, by bribing both sets of runners.

In another case of possible bribery, on the eighteenth day of the second month, 1882, Feng Zhihe filed a plaint that his cousin Feng Fude had repeatedly encroached on his eight mu of land. The magistrate instructed: "Order the runners to investigate and settle things reasonably." The defendant, Feng Fude, turned out to be a wealthy and powerful man who had been titled for meritorious military service (with the equivalent of an official rank of the sixth grade [*liupin*]). He responded by asserting that Zhihe had dug a ditch between their two fields that was causing problems of access for others. On the twenty-first, he filed charges of his own, claiming that Zhihe had broken into his house, damaged its contents, and terrorized everyone. The magistrate responded by having both men summoned for an investigation. On the twenty-seventh, the plaintiff's father, Feng Fusheng, reported that his son had been injured by Fude and was suffering from dizziness as a result. He further charged that Fude had a criminal record for sodomizing a young child. This brought no more than the magistrate's comment that he had already ordered an investigation. On the twenty-ninth, the runners, with the local xiangbao, reported that, "in accordance with the household division documents of the two parties, [they had] clearly delineated the two plots," and that "both sides now wish to end the suit." The magistrate readily obliged: "Cancel the summons." The records end there (Baodi 107, 1882.2.18 [l-18]). Though we cannot tell for certain what the truth was in this case, it seems quite possible that the defendant, Feng Fude, had managed to avoid going to court by bribing the runners and the local xiangbao into reporting an amicable settlement.

Like the xiangbao, the runners could also shape the outcome of a lawsuit just by foot-dragging and failing to bring the summoned parties to court. In one case, after the runner reported that the defendant could not be found, the plaintiff charged that the runner had been bribed by the defendant acting in collusion with a "litigation monger." In another case, the irate magistrate had an obviously dilatory runner punished with 100 blows of the heavy stick. But neither case went any further (Dan-Xin 22420, 1882.3.3 [l-57]; 22430, 1886.11.10 [l-67]). Both runners, it would seem, had successfully sabotaged the process.

We can only speculate that a substantial proportion of the very large number of incomplete case records might have involved runner abuse. This would include those instances in which the records end with runners reporting that one or the other party could not be found, as well as those that end simply with the issuance of a court summons. Between them, those two categories account for 131 of the 152 incomplete records in Baxian, 18 of the 26 in Baodi, and 43 of the 86 in Danshui-Xinzhu.

Formal, Informal, and Third-Realm Justice

Justice in the third realm, then, needs to be distinguished clearly from more strictly informal justice. In the latter, there was no expression of opinion from a magistrate. Community and kin mediators operated on their own, albeit mindful of the law, to try to maintain peaceable relations through compromise.

Household division, as I argued in the last chapter, offers perhaps the best example of informal justice. Over time, customary practices evolved that were remarkably effective for dealing with the stressful situation of parceling out family property among brothers. First, community and kin leaders joined with the heirs in protracted discussions to divide up family property into equal shares. Assignment of the shares was often decided by the drawing of lots. The process was then formalized by written documents witnessed by the participating mediators.

Qing law took the stance that it was immoral for close relatives to engage in litigation; the community or kin group was expected to settle their disputes. As the magistrate put it, in rejecting the suit of a younger brother against his elder brother, who controlled the family's property and refused to divide up, "Blood relations should not crawl prostrated around a court" (Dan-Xin 22524, 1888.2.23 [1-104]). Similarly, in a loan dispute between affinal kin, the magistrate commented: "You two are close relatives but have come to court over a minor matter of debt. That violates the proper affectionate relationship among marital kin" (Dan-Xin 23312, 1887.1 [d-35]).

This is not to say that informal justice operated entirely separately and independently of formal law. In the case of household division, the customary practice of equal division among sons was given formal legal sanction during the Tang. Thereafter, the congruence between social custom and legal stipulation made for a nearly univeral observance of the principle and minimized disputes and litigation. Where principle and practice diverged, as they increasingly did with the spread of conditional sales of land, ambiguities in the law encouraged the growth of legal challenges for disputes, as we saw in Chapter Two (see also P. Huang 1990: 106–8).

Third-realm justice must also be distinguished from the more strictly formal justice of court adjudication. In civil no less than in criminal cases, magisterial adjudication was governed above all by codified law. But just as the informal system was influenced by the formal system, so informal justice could play some part in the formal system. If the great majority of rulings were grounded in law, there was still a handful of cases in which the magistrate chose to follow the tack of compromise, simply upholding, for example, a settlement reached through mediation (Baodi 171, 1885.5.18 [m-21]) or ruling that the matter should be turned over to community or kin for mediation (Dan-Xin 22513, 1884.3 [l-93]).

It was only in the third realm that formal and informal justice operated on relatively equal terms. The magistrate's opinion, to be sure, carried all the weight of the official legal system. But that opinion was expressed within an ideology that deferred to informal justice, so long as that justice worked within the boundaries set by the law. Thus, magistrates routinely accepted peacemaking compromise settlements worked out by community and kin mediators in preference to continuing on to court adjudication. Even when legal violations were involved, mediators could gain court acceptance of their informal settlement by papering them over. We have seen, for example, how a dispute that probably involved illegal gambling was settled informally with the court's approval by being represented as a clearing up of accounts in legitimate transactions.

The framework within which formal and informal justice interacted was partly institutionalized and partly ad hoc. Mediators (as well as litigants) could almost always address the magistrate through petitions, and the magistrate's comments, in turn, were almost always conveyed back to them. Those practices ensured a routinized interaction between the two. At the same time, however, the communications were extremely abbreviated. Petitioners were limited to a single sheet of 300-odd characters per plaint, and magistrates usually ventured at most a few sentences. Much reliance, moreover, was placed on the semiformal official xiangbao and the runners as intermediaries, which allowed considerable scope for corruption and abuse.

At its worst, then, the semiformal process saw formal law under-

mined by runner and xiangbao abuse or false community representation, and informal justice misshaped by arbitrary court opinion. At
its best, however, third-realm justice successfully resolved disputes
by attending to the twin considerations of peacemaking and law,
through the joint working of the two. The system was one that embodied both the positive and the negative aspects of Qing justice.

CHAPTER SIX

Two Patterns in the Qing Civil Justice System

Y DATA SHOW TWO sharply different patterns of opera-tion in the courts' disposition of civil cases. In one, illus-trated by Baodi and Baxian counties, the system functioned relatively simply and efficiently. The majority of the litigants were small peasants engaged in ordinary disputes over land transactions, debt obligations, marriage contracts, and inheritance. The standard process—of plaints and counterplaints from the litigants followed by a formal court session with all parties present—worked well enough. Most cases were resolved within a few weeks, sometimes even days, by a single court session and a single judgment from the magistrate. Some cases went on for months. Only a few dragged on for years.

In the other pattern, illustrated by more complex and differenti-ated Danshui-Xinzhu, many of the cases that came to court were prolonged by clever litigants who took advantage of the loopholes in the system. Quite a number of these litigants were wealthy and pow-erful individuals or institutional entities, like lineages and landlord groups, who were ready to concoct any story to get their way. Mul-tiple court sessions were common, judgments were frequently con-tested, and lawsuits often ran on for years, sometimes even decades. Very few cases were resolved within weeks, let alone days.

Official Qing sources generally blamed these problems on the unprincipled actions of what the code called "litigation mongers" (*songgun*) and "litigation instigators" (*songshi*).* But the evidence gathered here suggests that the problems need to be seen in a larger

---

* A literal rendering of songgun as "litigation stick" does not work in English. Among other possible alternatives, I chose "monger" as best capturing the code's per-ception of this kind of abuse as habitual. Likewise, it would be a mistake, I think, to

context. The Qing legal system evolved from, and was designed for, a relatively simple peasant society, in which litigants were supposed to be terrified by the imposing and punitive posture of the court into voluntary acceptance of court rulings. It was not equipped to deal with the products of a commercialized and increasingly differentiated society: well-to-do and sophisticated individuals and entities, who were not nearly so easily intimidated as simple peasants. Structural change in the composition of litigants, more than the evil actions of litigation mongers and instigators, or simple population growth, was what accounted for the increased burdens on the courts and the growing proportions of unresolved cases.

The Qing code itself, complex and multilayered document that it was, in fact came close to acknowledging the real situation. Where official sources universally condemned litigation specialists of whatever stripe, it drew a distinction between malevolent litigation abusers and benign litigation advisers. Our case records will help us flesh out those categories. They will show also what the code never did acknowledge: the emergence of a type of legal adviser who approximated the modern-day lawyer, serving the interests of his clients within the boundaries set by law. The conceptual and discursive structure of Qing legal culture in fact precluded any acknowledgment of the existence of such figures. Their emergence is another indication of the divergence of legal practice from official representations.

Let us begin, as before, with an overview of the quantitative evidence. Table 14 shows the incidence of multiple court sessions in the three counties. The Baodi court clearly had little difficulty clearing cases that came before it, dispatching all but 6.7 percent of them in a single session, and needing only one additional session for the three exceptions. The Baxian court was also relatively efficient: 13.3 percent of its 98 cases went over into additional sessions. Most (11) required only a second session, and the other two only a third. The Danshui-Xinzhu figures stand in sharp contrast to those for the other counties and not just in the proportion of cases that had to be carried over (29 of 78, or 37.2 percent). More than half of these required three or more sessions, and about a third of those required at least seven. One, which we will come to in due course, went to fully 12 sessions.

Table 15 provides a first glimpse at the reasons for these differences. In Baodi, litigants almost always accepted a court judgment as

---

translate songshi literally; the code in no way meant the "shi" in the conventional meaning of master/teacher.

TABLE 14

Incidence of Multiple Court Sessions in Baodi, Baxian, and Dan-Xin

(N=adjudicated cases)

Sessions	Baodi (N=45)	Baxian (N=98)	Dan-Xin (N=78)	Total (N=221)
2	3	11	13	27
3	0	2	3	5
4–6	0	0	8	8
7–9	0	0	4	4
12	0	0	1	1
TOTAL	3	13	29	45

TABLE 15

Reasons for the Multiple Court Sessions

Reason	Baodi (N=3)	Baxian (N=13)	Dan-Xin (N=29)	Total (N=45)
Two issues	1	0	3	4
Additional information required	2	3	3	8
Noncompliance	0	8	9	17
Litigation abuse	0	2	9	11
Litigation instigator	0	0	2	
Litigation monger	0	0	1	
Multiple false accusations	0	2	6	
Litigation adviser/agent	0	0	1	1
Multiparty litigant	0	0	4	4

final. There was not one instance among the 45 cases of a plaintiff or defendant returning to court to complain that the other had not complied with the magistrate's judgment or trying to get a rehearing by filing additional charges, making gimmicky arguments, or presenting contrived facts.

In Baxian, there were eight instances of noncompliance that brought one or the other party back to court to appeal for enforcement. And there were two instances of blatant and repeated attempts to manipulate the system on the part of an abusive litigant. On the whole, however, the Baxian court worked almost as well as the Baodi one: in most cases a single court judgment was all that was needed.

It is in the figures on the Danshui-Xinzhu court that the stresses on the system become truly conspicuous. Noncompliance and litigation abuse between them were responsible for the bulk of the prolonged cases. Most of the others were the work of multiparty corporate litigants. In all four of the cases shown in Table 15, such groups entangled the court in elaborately convoluted representations that required numerous court sessions to sort through and adjudge, and then to enforce.

The Baodi-Baxian Pattern

Let us now try to breathe some life into these figures with a few illustrative cases, beginning with the place where the system worked quite smoothly, Baodi county.

The Baodi Court

All the Baodi caes that went to a second session did so for one of two reasons. The first was when the case involved more than one issue, and the court chose to deal with them in separate sessions. To elaborate on an example cited earlier, Tian Fulu had piled dirt in front of his house, which spilled over into the road and caused traffic to go around through Tian Younian's field. Younian complained, and the two got into a fight. Fulu's son Yongheng slashed Younian on the left side of his forehead with a knife. At this, Younian filed suit against both father and son and then had his wound examined and recorded. A summons was issued the next day, ordering all the parties to court the following month. At this session, the magistrate dealt only with the injury issue, ordering that Tian Yongheng be held in the yamen jail for wounding Younian. The original source of the dispute was put over for two months, to allow for the busy planting period. At that session, the magistrate ordered Tian Yongheng to pledge that he would remove the dirt from the road. He was then released to a guarantor who petitioned on his behalf (Baodi 105, 1884.2.20 [1-8]).

In the other type of case, also relatively simple, a second session was made necessary because the court found that additional information was required. In 1865, for example, Zhang Qingtai charged that Geng Dewang had forcibly taken his wife while he was away. Geng claimed that Zhang had sold his wife to him for 90 diao, that the transaction had been witnessed by a go-between, and that he had written proof of this. The problem, as it turned out, was that Zhang had received only 60 diao and wanted the rest of his money. At the first court session, just 14 days after the plaint, the magistrate decided he needed to hear from the go-between before making a ruling. Some two weeks later, the go-between, Li Tao, was brought to court along with the principals. This time, the magistrate verified matters to his satisfaction and ruled that Zhang's was a false charge, but that he should be paid 10 more diao to complete the sale and settle the dispute (Baodi 169, 1865.5.9 [m-12]).

Both these reasons for delay can be said to be "ordinary," in the sense that they were part of what the Qing legal system considered routine operations. Such problems were expected to occur in every county court, as indeed they did in both Baxian and Danshui-Xinzhu. As Table 15 shows, both courts deferred their rulings in three cases pending more information, and there were three instances in Danshui-Xinzhu of an additional session to resolve a second issue. In sum, the Baodi court moved rapidly toward definitive resolutions of the relatively simple cases that came before it from relatively simple litigants.

The Baxian Court

In the Baxian court of the 1760's to the 1850's, we see the beginnings of the kinds of pressures on the system that were to later plague the Dan-Xin court. In particular, a growing show of recalcitrance on the part of losing parties pushed courts into having to take further action. One of the eight losers who made so bold was the impoverished peasant Li Da who had had to sell his land. After a time, during which the land changed hands two more times, Li began to live there again, building a shack for himself and his mother, and even going so far as to cut down 48 cypress trees, as well as some bamboo. The current owner, Tan Guangyang, brought suit on the thirteenth day of the first month, 1797, and the magistrate issued a warrant to bring Li to court. Li managed to hide for a while but was finally brought to the yamen for a court session toward the end of the third month. At that session, the magistrate had Li punished with 25 blows of the heavy stick and ordered him to file a pledge to dismantle the shack and move off the land within eight days. Li Da did the one but not the other, perhaps because he had nowhere else to go and perhaps also because he supposed there would be no follow-up on the court's order. At any rate, on the eighth day and again on the nineteenth day of the fourth month, Tan petitioned the court to enforce its judgment. In response, the magistrate had Li brought in and held in custody until his mother moved off the land. He was released only after she had moved and only on the pledge that he would cause no more trouble (Baxian 6:2:1415, 1797.1.13 [l-15]).

Four of the other noncompliance cases concerned debt obligations. For example, the merchant Liao Dengkui hired a boat owner named Zhang Liangcai to transport his herbs and rice to Hubei, but Zhang sold off the rice himself and pocketed the proceeds, along with 88 silver taels he had taken out in Liao's name from the merchant's shop.* Confronted with what he had done, Zhang acknowledged in writing that he owed Liao 88 silver taels, plus the 8,200 wen he got for the rice. But when he did not pay off the debt, Liao brought suit. At the court session the following week, the magistrate ordered Zhang to pay up as documented. Liao waited for about a month, then filed a new plaint charging that Zhang had still not paid him. At this second session convened later that month, the magistrate ordered that Zhang be held in custody and ruled at first that he pay within three days, but then bent to Zhang's plea that he could not pay without an extension in time, pending receipt of the proceeds from his next trip. Zhang was finally released when a guarantor paid 20 taels on his behalf and pledged with him to make good on the balance within 10 months (Baxian 6:2:2410, 1815.3.9 [d-11]).

Debt obligations were often difficult to enforce because of the debtor's inability to pay. Compromises were often necessary, as this magistrate understood. In another case, involving a failed and bankrupt shop, the court required the defendant to pay off only 20 percent of the outstanding loan. The plaintiff filed petitions to argue for more, even charging that the defendant had bribed the yamen's clerk to avoid meeting his obligations in the first place. That necessitated a repeat court session, at which the original judgment was upheld (Baxian 6:4:2566, 1852.10 [d-26]).

The two instances of litigation abuse that crop up here are still of a rather simple sort. In one, the widow Zhong, née Zhang, filed suit against Jiang Rongfu, who had bought the land containing the Zhongs' ancestral gravesite. Mrs. Zhong had buried her firstborn there many years earlier and was charging that Jiang had plowed up the grave and planted the site. On investigation, the magistrate determined that the widow herself had let the grave deteriorate, that Jiang had not in fact touched or desecrated it, and that she had fabricated the charges with the intention of extorting money from Jiang. The widow's son, Zhong Wenfang (in whose name she had brought

* The value of the silver tael against the silver yuan varied from place to place and over time. Under the standardization of 1910, the silver yuan was set at a fixed measure in weight of 0.72 tael (*Cihai* 1979, 3: 3923). On the value of the silver yuan against copper *cash*, see Appendix B.

suit), was ordered to acknowledge that the charge was false and to pledge not to cause any further trouble.

The case would have been little different from any of a large number of false-accusation cases if it had rested there. But the widow's son Wenfang then brazenly submitted another plaint, this time charging that Jiang would not allow him to repair the grave. The magistrate had to convene a second court session. At that session, satisfied that Zhong's charges were again false, he had Zhong punished by 25 blows with the heavy stick and locked up. Zhong was released only after filing a new formal pledge that he would cause no further trouble (Baxian 6:3:2638, 1822.8.5 [1-24]).

The Danshui-Xinzhu Pattern

That the Dan-Xin court's experience was altogether different from the others is immediately clear from just a cursory glance at the case records. Where the Baodi-Baxian files typically contain only one brief plaint and at most a counterplaint, many of the Dan-Xin files bulge to overflowing with plaints and counterplaints and petitions, often lengthy ones. There is a striking difference also in their calligraphy and prose, indicating the participation of well-educated men, including degree-holders (albeit almost always just holders of the lowest "government student," or *shengyuan*, degree) in the litigation process. One can only now and then detect the hand of a literatus (apart from the magistrates) in the Baodi-Baxian documents; many were written in the calligraphy and prose of the semiliterate. The two groups of documents, in fact, reflect substantial differences in the educational level of local society and the degree of complexity of local government.

Social Composition of Litigants

Table 16 shows the social composition of 500 of the 628 plaintiffs in the three courts. The differences between Baodi and Danshui-Xinzhu are especially striking. In Baodi, fully 70.1 percent of the identifiable plaintiffs were peasant cultivators, and only 8.5 percent in one of the higher status or income groups (landlords, degree-holders, merchants, big lenders). Close to the reverse was true in Danshui-Xinzhu, with only 16.5 percent of the plaintiffs peasant cultivators and fully 50.5 percent people of some means or status. What is more, Baodi did not have any corporate plaintiffs at all, compared

TABLE 16
Social Background of Plaintiffs

Background	Baodi	Baxian	Dan-Xin	Total
Wage worker	11	8	1	20
Peasant cultivator[a]	82	78	29	189
Undifferentiated town resident	2	54	26	82
Landlord	0	10	41	51
Degree-holder	2	9	14	25
Merchant	4	21	8	33
Big lender[b]	3	8	16	27
Big landlord[c]	1	3	18	22
Corporate entity[d]	0	3	10	13
Other[e]	12	13	13	38
TOTAL	117	207	176	500

NOTE: The social background could not be determined in 128 of the 628 cases. The Baxian records were particularly bad in this respect, accounting for 101 of the unknowns (out of 308 cases), compared with just 1 (of 118) for Baodi and 26 (of 202) for Dan-Xin.
[a] Includes both owners and tenants, usually not differentiated in the records.
[b] With loans of more than 100 chuan, diao, or yuan.
[c] With 100 shi or more in rent, or five or more tenant households.
[d] Encompasses groups, villages, lineages, guilds, and commercial and business corporations.
[e] For instance, soldiers, boat-people, bannermen, and yamen functionaries.

with Dan-Xin's 5.7 percent. Finally, while town residents (other than those enumerated above) accounted for just 1.7 percent of all plaintiffs in Baodi, they totaled 14.8 percent in Danshui-Xinzhu.

Baxian, as one might expect, fell somewhere in between, with 37.7 percent of the identifiable plaintiffs peasant cultivators and 24.6 percent in the more well-to-do/higher-status category. Baxian differed significantly from both in one respect, however. Because the county encompassed the "regional metropolis" of Chongqing in this period, the proportions of town residents and merchants were high relative even to Danshui-Xinzhu (26.1 percent vs. 14.8 percent, and 10.2 vs. 4.5).* But Baxian's countryside does not appear to have been as stratified as Danshui-Xinzhu, with landlords accounting for just 6.2 percent of the plaintiffs, compared with Dan-Xin's 33.5 percent.† Nor did it have the highly developed lineage organization that the migrants from Southeast China took with them to Taiwan; corporate

*The county's population more than quadrupled with the growth of Chongqing, climbing from a still modest 218,079 in 1796 to 990,500 in 1910. *Baxian zhi xuanzhu*, 1989: 144–45; Skinner 1977: 290; Reed 1993: 49.
†Danshui-Xinzhu had richer soil and was more recently settled (and therefore more sparsely populated) than the other two counties. The one made the land more attractive to absentee landlords; the other meant that holdings had been subjected to fewer generations of partitioning.

entities figured hardly at all there. Litigation in Baxian, as we have seen, was still fairly simple as late as the 1850's.

For our purposes, the really telling contrast is between Baodi and Danshui-Xinzhu: it was the difference between a simple peasant society and a relatively differentiated and stratified society. In one, litigants behaved much as the system expected them to: court judgments were generally accepted as final without further complications. In the other, more well-to-do and higher-status litigants made for a comparatively sophisticated legal culture, where noncompliance, litigation abuse, and legal maneuvers were common.

Perhaps the most telling symptom of the difference between the two is the wholesale reliance of Dan-Xin litigants on the prompting petition (*cuicheng*). Where the Baodi court, uncluttered with new lawsuits and unresolved old ones, was able to act promptly on cases, its Dan-Xin counterpart, for all that it served a relatively sparse population, was so overburdened that it almost never acted without repeated promptings from the litigants.

Noncompliance

As we saw in Table 15, noncompliance was one of the Danshui-Xinzhu court's major headaches, occurring in nine of 78 cases. Baodi was at the other extreme, with no instances in 45 cases. Baxian departed more in complexity than in numerical incidence: seven of Dan-Xin's cases required at least three sessions to resolve (two three sessions, two five, two seven, and one an astounding 12), compared with just two of eight in Baxian (and none more than that).

Interestingly enough, the legal battle that entangled the Dan-Xin court in 12 sessions, the largest number in our files, was waged not by a specialist, as one might expect, but by a litigant acting on his own, the elderly (seventy-three sui) defendant, Liu Qinwu, brought to court by his kinsman Liu Guichun. Guichun's grandfather had allowed his impoverished nephew, Qinwu's father, to cultivate a piece of land to which he held topsoil title rent-free. The subsoil was owned by another party, to whom the impoverished nephew paid rent. The arrangement continued for some 20 years. Then, in 1875, after the deaths of both parties to the original arrangement, Guichun demanded that Qinwu pay him topsoil rent, which he did to the tune of 620 shi of rice over a period of six years.* Now, in 1880, Guichun,

---

* If we assume one shi of rent per mu, the land in dispute would have totaled 103+ mu, making Liu Guichun quite a well-to-do landlord and Qinwu quite a "rich" tenant peasant.

his family's fortunes in decline, wanted to sell the land and, unable to get Qinwu to give up his rental, had filed a plaint against the old man. Qinwu promptly filed a counterplaint, claiming that his father had been given the right to cultivate the topsoil in compensation for a 900-yuan loan he had made to Guichun's grandfather to redeem some lineage land he had illegally sold.

At the first court session, on the twenty-ninth day of the eleventh month, 1880, both sides stuck to their stories, and the magistrate was required to summon other members of the lineage as witnesses in an effort to clarify the facts. By the second session, on the fifth day of the twelfth month, the magistrate had doped out that Qinwu's claim was a pure fabrication and ruled accordingly: Guichun's grandfather had indeed owned the topsoil free and clear, and so Guichun should have the right to dispose of it as he saw fit. On the other hand, since Qinwu's father had paid subsoil rent on the land for 20-plus years, an obligation that properly fell to the owner of the topsoil, Qinwu should be reimbursed for those payments. The court calculated the fair sum of those payments to be 400 yuan and ordered Guichun to give Qinwu 450 yuan before repossessing the land.

The seventy-three-year-old Qinwu, however, insisted on being paid twice that amount, 900 yuan. On the next day, the magistrate repeated his original ruling. Nevertheless, Qinwu pleaded brazenly that he "dared not accept the judgment" as ordered by the magistrate, because his family would be left with no land to cultivate.

Since Qing law required that litigants voluntarily accept the court's judgment, the case could not be officially closed so long as Qinwu held his ground. On the twenty-first, the magistrate considered the case yet again: this time he pointed out that he had already granted Qinwu 150 yuan more than the 300 the lineage kin had originally set in their attempt at a mediated settlement. But Qinwu still refused to accept the judgment. Thoroughly exasperated, the magistrate complained that Qinwu was "taking advantage of his old age to refuse to comply" and ordered him held in the county jail pending another court session.

At that session, held three months later, on the twenty-eighth day of the third month, 1881, the magistrate decided to allow the obstinate old man another 50 yuan, raising the amount Guichun was to pay to 500 yuan. But this was still not enough for Qinwu. He opted to stay in jail rather than accept the settlement. There he sat until the thirteenth of the fifth month, when the bailiff reported that he had taken ill. Alarmed, the magistrate instructed immediately: "Have the doctor Pan Shouyin go immediately to examine Liu Qinwu and take care to give him medicine as needed. Make sure he recovers." The magistrate, no doubt, was afraid of the consequences of having an old man die in his jail over a civil dispute.

To make a long story short, the defendant Qinwu was able through sheer obstinacy to get the magistrate in the next few court sessions to raise Guichun's obligation little by little to 650 yuan. Only then, at a court session on the thirteenth day of the eighth month, did he accept the court's terms. The final details of the settlement, including the disposition of the current year's crop and the differences over the exact boundaries of the land, required four more court sessions to work out. The case was not closed until the middle of the twelfth month, 15 months after it first came to court, when all parties concerned filed the appropriate pledges of acceptance of the court's judgment and willingness to end their dispute (Dan-Xin 22418, 1880.8.23 [1-55]).

This case illustrates well the scope that was open to a persistent and savvy litigant, especially an elderly one, to force a magistrate's hand. The legal requirement that a court judgment be voluntarily accepted by the litigants gave Qinwu the opening he needed to prevent a definitive resolution until he got what he wanted. Once he showed that he was willing to go the distance by remaining in jail, which he did for almost a full year, the court had few recourses left. No magistrate could impose harsh physical punishment on a man his age over a civil matter, and none, surely, would have been willing to risk having such a litigant die in his jail. The considerable stakes involved—of fields whose topsoil rent totaled over a six-year period no less than 620 shi—no doubt contributed to the old man's resolve. He was, in the end, able to parlay the originally proposed settlements—300 yuan suggested by community mediators and 450 yuan by the magistrate's first ruling—all the way up to the final figure of 650 yuan.

In another of the Dan-Xin noncompliance cases, three parties had formed a partnership with a stake of 5,000 yuan to buy land. Since Zeng Yiji had put up the most money, he was in charge of keeping the record books and collecting rent on the land. Later, Yiji, who was apparently rather a simpleton, turned over the record books and the Zeng family's rights to the rents to the corporate entity of his affinal kin, the "Zheng Jili," in return for a loan of 2,000 yuan. That was in 1857. Thereafter, the Zheng lineage took all rents from the Zengs' land. The third party to the venture, the Xus, went along because they regularly received more than their share of the rents from the Zheng Jili.

The case first came to the attention of the court in 1869, when Zeng Yiji's grandson Zeng Chaozong brought suit to recover the record books and the Zengs' right to the rent on the land they owned. The magistrate ruled that he could do so but only on condition that he repay his grandfather's debt to the Zheng Jili. Though Zeng Chaozong insisted that he owed only 1,500 yuan, and that what the Zheng Jili had collected in rents over the past 17 years more than covered that amount, the court was unmoved. Zeng had no choice at the court session but to agree to the terms of the judgment, promising to pay within half a month. But after paying only 500 yuan, he began to collect rents from the tenants, and once he got the rents, he refused to make any additional payments.

The case came back to court in 1875 on the complaint of the Zheng Jili. The Danshui subprefect ordered that the tenants should make their payments to the lineage until such time as Chaozong cleared his outstanding debt. Here there was special urgency and incentive for the court to make a clear-cut ruling on the payment of rents, for the Zheng Jili refused to pay tax on them on the grounds that the money was going to Zeng Chaozong, and he denied his tax liability on the grounds that title to the land had not yet been formally returned to him.

Finally, Zeng Fengchun, Chaozong's degree-holding uncle, submitted a statement to say that other members of the Zeng lineage had collected 1,000 yuan to pay off the balance required by the court within two months. With that payment, on the sixteenth day of the seventh month, 1875, all outstanding issues appeared to be settled: the Zheng Jili received the 1,500 yuan due it, and the account books, land deeds, and rent-collection rights were all returned to the Zengs.

But now a dispute erupted among the Zengs over which branch of the family had the right to the books. On the twenty-fifth of the third month, 1876, Chaozong's first cousin (*tangdi*) Zeng Jinrong submitted a petition to claim the books. Since his branch of the family alone had come up with the money to pay off the Zheng Jili, he asserted, it should be the one to collect the rents. Zeng's plaint was countered by the other five branches, which charged him with attempting to monopolize the rents.

Then the next year, 1877, the Zengs' corporate entity, the Zeng

Guoxing, filed a new charge, claiming that the Zheng Jili owed it 20,000 yuan for all the rents collected over the course of 17 years. It charged also that the Zheng Jili and the Xus, the third party in the original venture, had ganged up to withhold tax payments on the rents received from the land. At this point, the court ordered that a complete accounting of all records be made to settle things once and for all.

On the twenty-second day of the fifth month, 1878, the magistrate issued a summary judgment based on a thorough check of all the available records. He noted the foolishness of Zeng Yiji in entering into the original arrangement, pledging land worth 5,000 yuan as security for a mere 2,000-yuan loan, and his even more foolish course of giving up 17 years of rents instead of paying off the loan. He also noted the greed of the Zheng Jili in taking advantage of the simpleminded Zeng Yiji. But however much he deplored the lineage's actions, he did not let this cloud his judgment of the legalities of the case. The Zheng Jili may have been immoral and greedy in its actions toward its affinal kin, but it was acting within its legal rights and was entitled to charge interest on its legitimate loan against the rents collected over the course of 17 years. In a detailed accounting, the court tallied up the rents collected on the land, which just about offset the interest on the original loan, plus two later loans totaling about 1,300 yuan. On balance, the magistrate found, the Zengs still owed the Zheng Jili 326 yuan. As for the Xus, who had collected 2,475 yuan more than their due in rents, albeit with the willing consent of the Zheng Jili, they must pay one-quarter of that sum, part of which would be applied to the amount the Zengs still owed the Zheng Jili, and the remainder to the "losses" the Zheng lineage had sustained.

But now it was the Xus who were unhappy. Their spokesman, Xu Guozhen, in collusion with Zeng Jinrong, got two tenants to back up their charges that the Zheng Jili had collected rents from them that ought to have been credited to the Xus' court-ordered payment. In this, the final twist to the case, the magistrate, in a seventh session, on the twenty-first of the eleventh month, 1878, rejected the Xus' plaint as groundless and ordered them to pay up immediately. Matters were finally closed with all the parties filing their pledge to accept the court's ruling (Dan-Xin 22410, 1875.3.14 [l-47]).

This example, more than the preceding one involving the stubborn elderly "rich" peasant, illustrates the great complexity of

Danshui-Xinzhu society. All the principals to the suit were corporate entities. And all engaged in different kinds of maneuvers to bend and twist the law to their own benefit. Between them, they managed to keep the dispute going in court for a full decade.

The record for persistence, though, goes to the three parties to a court battle over rents and taxes, in a case that took more than twice as long to settle. A tenant group, numbering more than 80 house-holds, complained that their landlord, a lineage with the corporate name "Wu Shunji," was extracting extra rent by using nonstandard large measures. To get the court on their side, they asserted that the lineage was concealing land newly brought under cultivation from the tax registers, a charge that brought the county yamen into the fray. The lineage defended its rents, contending that if the court did not uphold the rates, it would not be able to pay its taxes. The yamen was less concerned with the rent dispute than with registering all of the Wu land and bringing it onto the tax rolls. The result of the complex maneuverings of the three parties was a lawsuit that dragged on from 1852 until 1878, with a total of more than 60 plaints, counter-plaints, petitions, and reports, and a total of six court sessions. The entire file runs on for fully 223 pages.

The court ruled, in 1860 and 1861, that there was substance to the charges and claims of both the Wu Shunji and its tenants. The lineage had been paying only nominal taxes of 25 shi. The court took the opportunity to register fully 500 jia of land, on which the Wus were henceforth to pay 500 shi a year in tax. As for the tenants, they were all to pay the Wu Shunji a rent of six shi a jia. The records then show multiple attempts by the court to enforce its rulings on both taxes and rents. The last documents indicate that the Wu Shunji was still resisting the tax assessment as late as 1876, 1877, and 1878 (Dan-Xin 22202, 1852.2.8 [1-9]).

Litigation Abuse

Even more than noncompliance, the Danshui-Xinzhu court was burdened by litigation abuse. Litigants who knew the loopholes of the system manipulated it to their own ends. They entangled the court in a mass of plaints, counterplaints, and petitions. Some of them resorted to a host of false charges and fabrications of fact, each eating up court time as the magistrate investigated.

Melissa Macauley (1994: 89–92) has shown how Qing provincial officials, prodded by the Jiaqing Emperor in 1807 to report on the problem of unresolved litigation, were nearly unanimous in placing the blame on evil songshi and songgun. In their usage, these were fuzzy and catch-all terms. But the Qing code, multilayered document that it was, in fact used these terms in quite specific meanings mainly in the statute and substatutes devoted to "Instigating Litigation" (*jiaosuo cisong*; Statute 340 and Substatutes 340-1–340-12), and secondarily in the statute and substatutes on "False Accusations" (*wukong*; Statute 336 and Substatutes 336-1–336-27). It identified in addition a third category of litigation abuse.

The *"litigation instigator" (songshi)*. According to the code, this kind of abuser composed false plaints for others or else represented them in false accusations (Statute 340). Such people also sometimes initiated false charges themselves. Regardless, the code stipulated, they were liable for the same punishments as a false accuser (Substatute 340-9): by two grades of added severity above what they falsely accused another of in the case of relatively light crimes (that were punishable by lashes with the light bamboo), and three grades of added severity in the case of more serious crimes (Statute 336). Local authorities were directed to be vigilant against such people; allowing them to abuse the system through negligence would be punishable, and complicity in their activities would be treated as a serious criminal offense (Substatute 340-4).

By way of illustration, we begin with a boundary dispute among three groups of producers. The plaintiff was a tea-producing group, all surnamed Liu, with the corporate name of "Jin Liuhe." Its land adjoined the Sizhuang people's cattle-farm on the west, and the Luos' crop farm on the south. Troubles began with disputes over damage done by Sizhuang cattle to the Lius' tea plants and came to a head when a joint Sizhuang-Luo force of "hundreds of armed men" raided the Lius' land, destroying numbers of houses and tea plants. The boundaries of the Lius' tea farm, as it happened, were well documented and clear and distinct. It was the land deed of the Sizhuang cattle farm that was fuzzy, giving it an excuse to encroach on the tea producers. The Luos had simply seized the opportunity to gang up with the Sizhuang and move onto Liu land in the south.

During the lawsuit, the Luos were represented by their own Luo Ayuan, but the Sizhuang hired a government student (shengyuan) named Liao Qionglin to act for them. Liao was clearly the mastermind behind the subsequent maneuverings of the co-defendants. First he filed a counterplaint, contending that the Lius (or more accurately, the Jin Liuhe) had set fire to their own houses in order to fabricate charges. But the court cut through that nonsense at its very first session, on the twenty-ninth day of the eighth month, 1885, just five days after the Lius filed their initial plaint. Whatever the facts with respect to the boundaries, the magistrate ruled, the defendants were wrong to raid the plaintiff's farm and destroy plants and burn houses. Liao, the court already suspected, was responsible for insti-gating the trouble (*congzhong suonong*), and it ordered him held un-til the facts could be clarified.

Liao then filed several additional counterplaints, charging that the Lius had encroached on the Sizhuang farm's land. The Lius, for their part, filed repeated prompting petitions for court action (includ-ing a plaint to the prefectural court, which instructed the county court to expedite its handling of the case). The original magistrate, in the meantime, moved on to another post, and his replacement was reluctant to act without sizing up the situation for himself. In his first comment on the case, late in the eleventh month, he noted that "each side has insisted on its version of things. No judgment can be rendered until the real facts have been established."

In the meantime, the Sizhuang and the Luos took further aggres-sive actions. On the fourth day of the first month, 1886, the Lius reported that the defendants had raided their tea farm again, damag-ing more plants and houses. This time, they had captured one of the raiders, Peng Xu Huoyan, whom they hauled into court for the sec-ond formal session 10 days later. Peng testified that he was a hired worker who owed Liao Qionglin's wife money, and that it was Liao who had sent him on the raid. But the magistrate was not fully con-vinced that Peng was telling the whole truth. And Liao claimed in a petition on the twenty-second day that Peng had actually been hired by the Lius to frame his two parties.

Now the magistrate decided to go to the disputed site to check things out for himself. This field trip brought him to comment that the boundaries were in fact well defined, that he could not under-stand why the defendants were "causing so much trouble," and that he suspected there might be "someone who was behind the whole thing." At this, Liao submitted yet another statement, charging once again that the Lius had planted tea on the Sizhuang cattle farm's land. This time, the magistrate did not mince any words. "I have al-ready investigated the site myself and know the truth," he noted on the petition; the land deed that Liao had submitted was thus clearly phony. At the third court session, on the ninth day of the fourth month, the magistrate issued his summary opinion: the boundaries delineated in the Lius' documents were perfectly clear. He went on to censure both the defendants and their representative. The Lius' neighbors had encroached on their land and acted in a most "barbaric" manner; and the man the Sizhuang farm had hired to take charge of the suit *(baosong)* had acted in a disgraceful manner, violating the rules of proper behavior for the literati *(bushou wobei)*. The magistrate, it is clear, considered Liao Qionglin a litigation instigator.

The final disposition of the case was made at still another court session (the fourth) six months later. But somehow by then, Liao, who almost certainly would have drawn some punishment, was dead. The magistrate commented simply that "the instigating government student . . . Liao Qionglin died, and therefore the court will not deliberate further over the matter." He accepted petitions from outside mediators and the litigating parties to close the case with a settlement involving clear delineation of the boundaries, appropriate compensation to the Lius, and pledges from the defendants (Dan-Xin 22514, 1885.8.24 [l-94]).

Not all "litigation instigators" were hired guns. Zhang Yuanhai, for example, managed very well on his own to engage his two neighbors, Zhang Shunyi and Wu Bang, into a protracted court battle. Yuanhai had served as the middleman for a rental contract between Shunyi and his kinsman, Zhang Qian, and knew that they had not drawn up a formal written document. He saw in this an opportunity to extort money from Shunyi. He began his machinations by urging Qian to take advantage of the situation and not pay rent to Shunyi. Then, when Shunyi sued Qian for rent payments, on the thirteenth day of the twelfth month, 1890, Yuanhai told Qian to collude with a certain Wang Yifang in a counterplaint asserting that the land did not belong to Shunyi at all but was actually owned by Wang. Yuanhai himself filed a plaint charging Shunyi and his other neighbor, Wu Bang, with building a dam that caused water to flow into and damage his fields.

When the case came to court six months later, the magistrate, confronted with the maze of charges and claims, took no action and simply ordered that the disputed sites be measured out and their ownership verified. Even as that process was in train, Yuanhai filed another plaint, charging that Wu Bang had encroached on his land, taken his farm implements, and prevented him from cultivating his land.

That charge was disposed of in a second court session, almost a full year later (in the fourth month of 1892). The magistrate, with the reports on the land measurements now in hand, ruled that Zhang Yuanhai's accusations against his neighbor, Wu Bang, were false, and ordered Yuanhai to pledge his acceptance of the court's judgment. But that still left Yuanhai's accusations against Zhang Shunyi on the docket. This issue was not resolved until almost another full year later (twentieth day, second month, 1893). By that time, Shunyi had died, and his widow was the one taking up the cause. Once again, the magistrate found against Zhang Yuanhai, holding that his charge was pure folly, for he could easily have redirected the flow of the water that ostensibly damaged his land.

In quick order the court then disposed of the tenant Qian's claim that Zhang Shunyi's land actually belonged to Wang Yifang, though that required two more court sessions. On the twenty-third, the magistrate ruled that Wang's was a false claim, and that the land was to be turned back over to Shunyi's widow. The dispute between the tenant Qian and the widow was settled in the fifth and final session the following day. Qian was ordered to pay the rents he owed, and the widow Zhang was given leave to find herself a new tenant (Dan-Xin 22223, 1890.12.13 [l-30]).

Zhang Yuanhai, it is clear from the records, was responsible for all the crisscrossing false claims and charges. Apart from causing no end of trouble for his two neighbors, Zhang Shunyi and Wu Bang, he created a mess that required the court five sessions and three years to unravel. Nevertheless, he managed to get off scot-free. His success in getting the tenant Zhang Qian and Wang Yifang to act in their own names effectively shielded him from direct responsibility for their false claim. As for his own false charges against his neighbors, they were civil offenses and not of an order to justify punishment in the court's eyes.

The Qing court's approach of dealing with one issue at a time, while effective and perhaps even necessary, helped keep Zhang Yuanhai from having to answer for all of his separate actions at one time. In none of the judgments did the magistrate specifically rebuke Zhang for instigating all the false charges. And so this crafty individual got away with a flagrant manipulation of the system without ever being identified as a "litigation instigator."

Zhang's case reveals the scope for this sort of legal abuse. The civil system had no real deterrent, since men of his savvy knew punishment was seldom administered in civil cases. In Zhang's case, the strategy was to snarl up the court in a mass of fabrications with multiple plaintiffs. Though he failed in the end to get what he wanted, he managed through his convoluted maneuverings to prevent the court from focusing in on all his schemes at one time. The fact that he could get away with what he did could only encourage a culture of litigation abuse in Danshui-Xinzhu.

The "litigation monger" (songgun). "Habitual" *(jiguan)* was the way the Qing code characterized this type of abuser. The "litigation monger" was someone "who acted in collusion with the yamen clerks to manipulate and cheat the simpleminded rural people, and intimidate and extort [from them]" (Substatute 340-6). Or he might be a yamen clerk himself—the scribe *(daishu)* who exploited his position as the transcriber of plaints and petitions to advise or encourage litigants to fabricate facts and make false charges (Substatutes 340-10, 340-12). When caught and proved guilty, these culprits were to be severely punished, by banishment to distant borders (Substatute 340-6).

Examples of such official corruption are understandably hard to come by. The Dan-Xin civil records contain just one detailed case, but it is a telling one. In 1870, twenty-six-year-old Du Qingji, an educated but not yet degree-holding "junior student" *(tongsheng)*, filed charges against his maternal uncle Zheng Shu. According to his plaint, his grandfather had entrusted the family's properties to Zheng when he died, and Zheng had betrayed that trust by selling nine pieces of property totaling more than 3,000 yuan's worth for his personal enrichment. Du listed all nine properties, along with the ostensible middleman in the transactions.

The astute magistrate, however, observed immediately that, by Du's own account, he would have been more than twenty years old at the time his grandfather died, in 1867. It made no sense that the grandfather would have entrusted the family's properties to a maternal relative when his own grandson was full-grown. Moreover, the magistrate found, Du had been held in the county jail by a predecessor of his.

Du claimed that his incarceration had been the result of a false charge by his uncle Zheng acting in cahoots with his step-grandmother. The magistrate commented in response that if Du had been imprisoned, it must have been because he was misbehaving. Even so, he directed his runners to look into the matter.

The uncle, Zheng Shu, now gave his version of things in two counterplaints. First of all, he denied that he had been put in charge of the family property. He pointed out that three of the grandfather's four sons were alive and well at the time he died, so the old man had no reason to entrust the family properties to an outsider. Second, he pointed out that Du owed him money, and he had the account records to prove it; Du was filing false charges to avoid having to pay off his debt. Finally, he showed that six of the nine transactions Du had listed had been made by others, not him. As for the remaining three, all had been witnessed by prominent men, not by the person Du had named. For the time being, the case rested there. Only 10 years later, when Du sued his uncle again, do we learn that this first lawsuit was settled by informal mediation.

In this 1880 suit, heard by a new magistrate, Du had the wit to represent himself as thirty-two sui (four years younger than he claimed before) to support his assertion that he had been a minor at the time his grandfather died. He repeated the same charge: that his maternal uncle Zheng Shu had abused his grandfather's trust and enriched himself. He also submitted what he claimed to be the will of his grandfather, which spoke of properties totaling "several tens of thousands of yuan," along with a now-pared-down list of four properties that Zheng had "forcibly occupied" or "stole and bought." This magistrate was no more easily fooled than the other. If Zheng indeed had charge of the family's properties and had done the things Du complained of, why had none of the sons brought suit? "The charge is clearly false; the plaint is rejected," he wrote.

But Du persisted with still another plaint, repeating the same charges. Once again, Zheng Shu was forced to respond. He had bought the land in question from Du's grandfather after it had been inundated, he said. Later he had leased it out to tenants, who had reclaimed it. Du, seeing that the value of the land had gone up, was simply trying to extort money from him. Zheng had the original sales document to prove that the transaction had taken place. This would probably have sufficed, but what clinched the matter were two mediation documents from the first lawsuit, which Zheng presented to the court. In one, drawn up in 1870, the very year of the original filing, Du admitted that he owed Zheng 81 yuan and had fabricated charges against him to avoid repaying the loan. It bound him to repay

30 yuan immediately and another 20 yuan later. Zheng in turn would forgive the remaining 31 yuan, out of consideration for Du's poverty, and accept Du's apology and pledge not to cause any more trouble. The document was witnessed by several mediators and signed by Du.

In the other document, dated three months later, in 1871, Du acknowledged that the land he had fussed about had in fact been sold outright to Zheng. The Du family had recently suffered multiple deaths and was completely impoverished. Du wished to renovate the ancestral grave in the hope of changing the family's fortunes. Zheng, out of kindness, gave Du four yuan to help him. Du acknowledged the gift and promised not to cause any further trouble over the land. This document too was witnessed and signed.

Even when confronted with this evidence at the court session on the eighteenth day of the second month, 1880, Du tried to wiggle out by claiming that he had been tortured into acceding to these agreements. The magistrate was not convinced. In his summary judgment, he recounted the facts about the land in question and again voiced his skepticism by wondering why, if the transaction was illegitimate, none of the other branches of the family had objected. Then, pronouncing Du "a habitual troublemaker who had repeatedly passed himself off as a yamen clerk or runner to try to extort money from people," he ordered that he be made to wear the cangue and placed on public exhibit as a warning to others. Three weeks later, on Du's plea of sickness and repentance, and his aunt's petition for mercy, the magistrate allowed his release.

Apparently, Du saw this as only a minor setback, for a year and a half later, in the eighth month of 1881, he submitted yet another plaint to yet another new magistrate to charge Zheng yet again. This time, after repeating the same tale about his grandfather's decision, he claimed that one piece of the land Zheng had supposedly bought was the family's sacrificial land, that it had not been sold at all, only pledged as security for a loan, and that Zheng had refused to let him redeem it; instead, Zheng had contrived a deed of sale and placed the land on the tax registers. But he, Du, moral and filial man that he was, could not bear to see his family's ancestral sacrifices terminated; he begged the court to restore it to its rightful owner.

The magistrate commented immediately that his predecessor had already punished this man, who should know enough by now to mend his ways. How could he offend the court thus again? But Du persisted with another plaint. This time the magistrate commented:

it was a well-established fact that the contested land had been sold irrevocably. He concluded with a threat: "Is this man bent on getting himself punished for false accusations in accordance with the law?"

Two years later, in 1883, when a new magistrate arrived on the scene, Du filed yet two more petitions. He concocted a similar claim and asserted that the arrival of the new magistrate now gave him the opportunity to right a long-standing injustice. Reluctantly, the magistrate heard the case on the sixteenth day of the second month, 1884. At this session, the magistrate found out that Du had been working for some time as an assistant scribe (*bangshu*) in the yamen and was a habitual "litigation monger." He also examined an account book of Du's, about which we have only this brief but most intriguing reference from the magistrate's judgment: "On examination, half of Du Qingji's account book records charges imposed by yamen runners on cases they oversaw. There can be no doubt that Du is a litigation monger. It is hereby ordered that [the account book] be burned, so that it cannot implicate others." Though we can only speculate, this strongly hints at other abuses by Du and the complicity of the yamen's runners.

As for the disposition of Du, the magistrate, after recounting his predecessor's judgment of four years earlier, observed first that Du had filed multiple false accusations, and that if he was not punished severely, the problem of litigation-mongering would get out of hand. But after this initial and very correct observation, he went on to an unexpected conclusion: in light of the fact that Du was repentant, the court would allow him a chance to redeem himself. If in the future he was found hanging around the yamen offices and making trouble, the court would hold the chief scribe (*zongshu*) responsible and punish him along with Du. Thus the case ended.

Du, after wasting the court's time (and causing Zheng no end of trouble) on all these phony plaints, went essentially unpunished. We can only wonder whether the magistrate felt constrained in his actions by the suspicion that Du's offenses were only the tip of an iceberg that involved many other "litigation mongers" in the yamen (Dan-Xin 22406, 1870.9.29 [l-43]).

The "false accuser" (wugao zhe).   With this label, the Qing code was referring mainly to a nonhabitual offender who acted with or without the assistance of a hired "litigation instigator." Such a person, as we have seen, was to be punished with added severity over and above that called for by the crime he fabricated. Those who hired an agent to act on their behalf (*guren wugao zhe*) were to be punished as if they themselves had falsely accused another (Substatute 340-5).

False accusations were quite common in all three counties and ran at close to the same proportion in each, accounting for eight of the 45 adjudicated cases in Baodi, 15 of the 98 in Baxian, and 13 of the 78 in Danshui-Xinzhu. Where Danshui-Xinzhu differed from the other two counties was in the crassness of the false accusers: nine of the 13 leveled multiple false charges that resulted in more than one court session, compared with none in Baodi and just two in Baxian. It is, of course, in the protracted cases involving multiple false accusations that we get the clearest picture of the really abusive false accuser.

In 1881, for example, Xu Guo fabricated a land deed and charged that Xu Qishi had encroached on his land. What gave him the opening for his fraudulent claim was the pervasive use of "white deeds" (*baiqi*) in Xinzhu as a way to escape official taxes on land transactions. These documents, which were not registered with the authorities and not legally valid, were easy to contrive.

At the first court session, four months after he filed his plaint, the magistrate took the standard posture toward these unofficial deeds. Since Xu Guo's deed had not been registered and no taxes had been paid, he had no legal right to the land. Accordingly, it was to be made public property in support of the local academy. At this, Xu Guo promptly petitioned for a second hearing, pleading that he had been unaware of the fact that the deed he submitted was a white one rather than a proper red one (*hongqi*). He had pledged out his land to another, he said, and had had to borrow the deed to show to the court. Only then did he learn that it was a white one. He offered to pay the tax on the land. He then repeated his original charge that Xu Qishi was encroaching on his land.

The magistrate responded by setting a second court session three months later. Here, still innocent of Xu Guo's fabrication, he ruled that, "in light of the fact that he [Xu Guo] was repentant," he would allow him to pay half the value of his "land" to make up for the unpaid taxes. This Xu Guo gladly did, for the sum was modest because he had contrived a mere 19-yuan purchase price on his fake deed. Upon receipt of his payment, the court issued and authenticated a red deed, without taking the trouble to locate the border of Xu Guo's "property."

Xu Guo was now armed with an official deed over his fictitious piece of land. That allowed him to file further fraudulent claims. First, he and his nephew charged that a man named Fang Huan was encroaching on their land. Fang Huan, it turned out, had conditionally purchased the land of the original defendant, Xu Qishi. Xu Guo was thus still after the same site. When the court took up this plaint a year later (midway through 1883), the magistrate was still not wise to Xu Guo's scam and ruled carelessly that the two pieces of land had distinct boundaries, which should be observed. Neither party was to encroach on the other's property.

Encouraged, uncle and nephew then filed further complaints against Xu Qishi and Fang Huan for encroaching on their land. The result was still another court session 10 months later. Only at this, the fourth hearing, did the magistrate investigate the matter and put the pieces together. After recounting exactly what Xu Guo had done, he upheld Xu Qishi's rights over his land and had Guo's red deed canceled on the spot. Xu Guo and his nephew got by with a mere warning that if they filed false accusations again, they would be punished severely (Dan-Xin 22419, 1881.12.3 [1-56]).

This case illustrates further the wide scope for abuse in the civil system. Although magistrates had the discretion to impose light punishment for false accusations in civil cases, few actually did so. That left an opening for Xu Guo's type of abuse. He went off free as a lark, after entangling the court with his series of false charges and claims for two and a half years.

Elderly false accusers, protected by the code's stipulation that their sentences might be commuted from physical punishments to monetary fines (Substatute 1-8), could be particularly brazen. In one case, the seventy-one-year-old (*sui*) Wu Shimei took a scattershot approach in an attempt to recover two pieces of land that his widowed sister-in-law had recently sold to a man named Zeng Liansheng. One of these she had a clear right to, since Wu's deceased brother had inherited it. But the brother had held title to the other in name only. A friend of his, who had worried that people might think ill of him for selling the plot to a nephew (his sister's son), had persuaded the dead man to front as the buyer.

The complication of title gave Wu Shimei the opening he needed to claim that the land in question was really family property that he had shared with his brother. First, he filed a plaint on the third day of the ninth month, 1890, pressing that claim and charging that the tenant on the land, Hu Xin, had not paid rent for three years. Next, in an attempt to explain away his inability to produce the documents for the land, he filed a declaration that they were in the hands of his widowed sister-in-law, who was managing the family's property. Then he filed another plaint, charging that his sister-in-law had sold the family property illegally to Zeng Liansheng. And finally, in a fourth submission, he asked the court to examine the division document between himself and his brother. At the same time, he induced some of his people to go to the land in question, start an argument with the tenant, and forcibly remove four oxen.

The court was indeed befuddled by Wu's multiple fabrications and actions. At the first court session, the magistrate ruled only that the oxen be returned. Emboldened, Wu's people made further trouble for the tenant, and Zeng, the new owner, filed a formal complaint with the court. The magistrate ordered that runners be sent to protect the tenant's cultivation rights. But Wu countersued, accusing Zeng of making a fraudulent charge. He even had the gall to file a prompting petition for an early court judgment.

All parties were finally brought in for a third and final court session. There, on the twenty-second day of the fifth month, 1891, all the relevant documents were examined, and the magistrate, after detailing the facts of the case based on this evidence, ruled that Zeng's purchase was legitimate, and that the widow must pay the real owner of the one piece of land its purchase price. As for Wu, he was reprimanded for his "rascally litigiousness" (*diaosong*) and "indiscriminate attacks" on people (*wangjie*). "He should be punished," the magistrate observed, "but considering his advanced age, the court will be lenient and merely reprimand him."

This old man had the temerity to challenge the court with yet another petition. This time, the magistrate rebuked him in a harsher tone: "He takes advantage of his advanced age to engage in rascally behavior and protracted litigation. He is hoping still to overturn the court's judgment. It is really preposterous!" He rejected the petition out of hand. But he again stopped short of punishing Wu (Dan-Xin 22222, 1890.9.3 [1-29]).

Together, these case histories tell about a culture of litigation abuse that was not present in Baodi or Baxian. The Qing legal system counted on inducing submission and compliance from simple litigants by the force of the court's intimidating presence. That was one reason for donning the penal posture. That approach, though reasonably successful for peasant litigants like those in Baodi and

Baxian, did not work at all well with the more worldly litigants of late-nineteenth-century Danshui-Xinzhu. Clever litigants knew the openings left by the civil system: repeated false claims and accusations could go unpunished, because punishment was seldom used in civil cases; contrived facts could enmesh the court in a mass of detail; refusal to accept a magistrate's judgment could keep a court from closing a case; and so on. Such actions entangled the Danshui-Xinzhu court with more and more unfinished business, so much so that it became more and more resistant to handling civil cases and acted only on multiple plaints and repeated prompting petitions.

Benign Litigation Advisers

Eager as the Qing officials were to lay the mounting burdens on the Danshui-Xinzhu court to knaves and scoundrels, the rise of litigation abuse was in fact symptomatic of a deeper problem: the widening gap between a system designed for a simple peasant society and the reality of an increasingly complex and sophisticated society. The latter gave rise not only to widespread litigation abuse but also to the increasing use of benign litigation advisers who operated within the boundaries of the law.

The Qing code, a more complex document than simple official pronouncements, provides us with good clues to this benign group, just as it does to the abusive one. It identifies two kinds of advisers that could be tolerated, if not fully endorsed. There were, first of all, the private scribes who helped others to write up their plaints and petitions truthfully, without adding or subtracting facts. These men were distinguished from the yamen scribes, whose job it was to write down litigants' complaints accurately. There were also the specialists who helped redress grievous wrongs by advising the ignorant of their legitimate rights. Both groups were excluded from the designations of litigation instigator/monger (Statute 340; Substatute 340-12).

The Danshui-Xinzhu records document in addition a third type of specialist, not acknowledged in the code: a modern lawyer-like professional hired by clients to press their legitimate interests. The emergence of this last type of legal specialist perhaps says the most about the limits of the old system.

Private scribes. Earlier on we saw peasant litigants coming to the yamen scribes to take down their stories and prepare the proper documents. But this was more the exception than the rule in Danshui-Xinzhu. More than 80 percent of all plaints (and counterplaints and

petitions) in the late Qing case records, as Yasuhiko Karasawa (1993)
has demonstrated, were brought to the yamen in written form. The
largest number, 59 percent of the 2,982 civil and criminal plaints he
counted, were identified on the lead to the plaint form as "self-
drafted" (*zigao*), and another 9 percent were identified as "self-drafted,
[yamen scribe] edited" (*zigao shanbian*)—as opposed to simply *shanbian* ("[yamen scribe] edited"). Some 14 percent were submitted on
nonofficial forms.*

Since the vast majority of peasants were barely literate, if at all, it
is obvious that many of these litigants had turned to others for assistance. But none dared own up to that because private scribes, like litigation counselors, were at best semilegitimate in the eyes of the law.
Although the code excluded both groups from the punishable categories of "litigation instigator" and "litigation monger," it stopped short
of condoning their activities (Statute 340). By the letter of the law, if
a plaintiff was unable to compose his own plaint, he was to relate his
story to a yamen scribe, who would write it down exactly as he told
it (Substatute 340-12). By implication, then, no plaintiff could turn
to a private party to compose his plaint. For this reason, not one of
these plaints even hints that a third party had a hand in it.

All the same, we might speculate a little on the types of people
who drafted these documents. In the countryside, it seems to me,
truly professional scribes who depended entirely on such services for
a living must have been quite rare. Though litigation was by no
means uncommon, there was probably not enough demand among
the villagers in a smallish area to support a full-time plaint-writer or
legal adviser. More than likely, the "self-drafted" form of a village
plaintiff was the work of one of the various amateurs and semipro-
fessionals who helped compose family division documents, loan
agreements, land transaction documents, letters, and other written
material: village or market-town teachers, aspiring or lower degree
holders, literate village leaders, xiangbao, or even itinerant fortune-
tellers or geomancers. Some of these might make this an important
sideline, working out of a stall advertising their services in a busy
section of town or setting up shop on market day in a market town.

In large towns and cities like county seats, on the other hand, professional plaint-writers may have been quite common. Though there
is little way to tell what they might have charged for such services,

---

* The Baodi and Baxian plaints do not have such leads or indicate in any other way
how the forms were prepared.

we do have Gangyi's late-nineteenth-century account telling of how, as a magistrate, he had visited a "litigation instigator" (songshi) in disguise in order to expose him. In that account, Gangyi speaks of paying a fee of two yuan for the service of writing up a plaint (Gangyi 1889: 15). Such a sum would have been prohibitive for most peasants, doubling or tripling the cost of filing a lawsuit. Or, put another way, it represented the expense of feeding an adult male peasant for 25 days.* Such a charge was of course perfectly manageable for the wealthier and more powerful litigants who appeared so frequently in the Danshui-Xinzhu records.

Litigation advisers and agents. The services provided by a private scribe could range from the simple act of writing down what he was told in a language and form deemed appropriate for a legal plaint to the provision of complex legal advice and services. Here we enter into the realm of professionals who resemble modern-day lawyers. But the state never accorded this group even the semilegitimacy conferred on the private scribes, whose existence was formally acknowledged in the code. Although the code conceded that there were people who provided benevolent legal advice to others, it defined them in the narrowest of terms. A benevolent adviser was someone who helped redress a grievous wrong (shenyuan), like being falsely accused of murder or robbery (Statute 340); "minor" matters, like not being repaid a debt owed or having one's property rights violated, would simply not quite fit under the word yuan. The possibilities, as well as the limitations, of the code's conception are well illustrated in the following passage from Wang Youfu, a legal secretary of the early nineteenth century:

Good people minding their own business who are taken advantage of by the abusively powerful or are incriminated by their enemies and bandits . . . might only be able to pound their own chests and swallow their grievance. . . . If they turn to a common scribe . . . they might be treated perfunctorily, [and their plaint] might only annoy the reader and not deliver the needed message. In such a situation, if an intelligent and able person composes for them a plaint that effectively exposes the evil plot and dramatically focuses attention on it, and instructs them on how to answer questions at court . . . , so that the injustice can be righted and the evildoer punished for false accusations, [such] a person not only does no harm but actually serves the good of society. (*Muling shu* 1848, 18: 21b)

* This figure is based on an 1888 budget report from a magistrate to his superiors, showing an expenditure of 0.08 yuan a day for the board of a runner (Dan-Xin 11407, 1888.1). Litigation expenses are discussed in detail in the next chapter.

Wang went on to urge that the term songshi be reserved for such benevolent advisers; the term songgun would be used only for people deserving of the pejorative label. "Those who manipulated the ignorant rural people . . . to enrich themselves were just 'litigation sticks.' How could they be termed 'master' [or teacher]?" "In my view," he concluded, "the litigation sticks should certainly be punished, but the litigation masters ought not to be prohibited."

Wang's view, however, did not quite amount to a call for the modern-lawyer type of legal adviser. He remained within the framework of the Qing code's conception of the benevolent litigation master: one who would right the grievous wrongs committed within the existing system. The conceptual structure of the legal system itself was in fact not questioned. The magistrate's relationship to his subjects was like that of parents to children; it made no sense to think of lawyers representing the children before their parents. Lawsuits over "minor matters" were by definition undesirable; it made no sense to think of lawyers representing their clients' legitimate interests. To entertain such notions would have gone against the fundamental concepts of the legal system.

In the dominant official discourse of the Qing, it is clear, the *song* of the compound songshi, which meant litigation and was by definition undesirable, came to overshadow the more benign *shi*, meaning teacher or master, so that in the end, the term songshi in general official usage carried only a pejorative meaning: he was a "master at evil litigation." Even as sophisticated a legal specialist as Wang Huizu (1730–1807) subscribed entirely to such a view. He wrote, for example, "Those who instigate litigation are the *songshi*; those who hurt the people are the local bullies [*tugun*]. If we do not get rid of these two kinds of people, there is no possibility for giving good governance to the people" (*Muling shu*, 1848, 18: 21a). Even the very narrowly conceived benign litigation adviser of the code could not but recede into the background of official consciousness.

Given the posture of the Qing official world, it is no surprise that examples of a modern-lawyer type of litigation adviser/agent are hard to find. The following case from Danshui-Xinzhu provides a rare illustration. In 1884, Xie Mayuan brought suit against the Lins and the Pengs over some land that he had left "wild" after he tried to reclaim it and failed. The defendants had subsequently opened it up and cultivated it. The dispute had come to court before, in the Tongzhi years (1862–74), and the magistrate had ruled then that the land should be evenly divided between the Xies and those who reclaimed it. But the judgment had not been enforced. Now Xie was trying to assert full title to the land; the Lins and Pengs were as adamant that the land belonged to them.

The magistrate stuck to the earlier ruling of his predecessor, at the court session on the twenty-fourth day of the fifth month. But neither side, it was clear, was willing to abide by it. At this point, the plaintiff Xie Mayuan brought in Xie Wenhui, a government student and putative kinsman, to press the case for him. Wenhui filed a second plaint, charging that the Pengs had forcibly occupied the Xies' uncultivated land. And he filed repeated prompting petitions to urge a new court session. Thanks to his efforts, two more court sessions were held, in the eighth and eleventh months of the following year, 1885. Again the magistrate upheld the first court's ruling. Again it turned out to be unenforceable.

Wenhui then filed no fewer than seven petitions, which brought yet another court session, in the sixth month of 1887. This session produced a new ruling: local mediators were to set a fair price on the land, and either the Lins and the Pengs would buy Mayuan out or he would pay them an appropriate amount for the labor they had expended in opening the land up to cultivation.

To obtain payment from the reluctant Lins and Pengs, the plaintiff's energetic agent, Xie Wenhui, continued to press the court hard. He filed two statements charging that the mediators were dragging their feet, which was detaining him from taking the local-level imperial examination (*xiangshi*), as he had planned; he filed petitions at the prefectural court (which urged prompt action from the county); he petitioned for another court session; and he filed four additional plaints to charge that the runner had improperly released the Pengs from their summons to court.

At this point, a new magistrate arrived on the scene, who noted on Xie Wenhui's latest petition his displeasure with Xie's actions: "This case has dragged on for years and, in spite of the repeated judgments of the previous magistrates, the case has still not been closed. It is all because of this one government student who is bent on pressing his one-sided view." At the court session (it was by now the twelfth month of 1889), the magistrate reiterated his displeasure with Wenhui, dubbed his efforts "persistent litigiousness" (*jiansong buxiu*), stopping just short of calling him a litigation instigator or litigation monger, and ordered that the matter be settled by local mediators.

We next find Xie Wenhui filing five more petitions, now in request of court sessions to force each of the Pengs to pay up. At this point, on the twenty-fifth day of the twelfth month, 1890, one Lin and one Peng did pay up, 70 yuan and 50 yuan, respectively. Wenhui then filed seven more petitions to force court sessions and payments from the last two Pengs. One paid 140 yuan in 1891, and the other, Peng Laobang, finally paid 100 yuan in 1893. Those amounts apparently amounted to about 20–30 percent of the current worth of the reclaimed land. With those payments, Xie Wenhui finally let up, and the case file, fat with 40-odd plaints, counterplaints and petitions, ends (Dan-Xin 22513, 1884.3.3 [l-93]).

Xie Wenhui, it is important to note, acted throughout within the law; at no time did he fabricate facts or level false charges. In our terms, he was "only doing his job" for his "client" Xie Mayuan, as a persistent lawyer might. But it is clear that the magistrates concerned did not, could not, think of him in such a way. The pat categories available from standard Qing legal discourse were either the malevolent litigation instigator/monger or the very narrowly conceived benevolent litigation adviser. Xie did not fit either. The magistrates, for lack of any other category to put him into, were inclined as time passed to the less charitable view. After all, Xie was responsible for entangling the court in a 10-year lawsuit over a "minor matter" that ideally should not have come to court at all. Though the magistrates never quite brought themselves to call him a "litigation instigator" flat out, they clearly thought of him in those terms when they pronounced him a "litigious" (*jiansong*) troublemaker.

The appearance in Danshui-Xinzhu of "lawyers" like Xie Wenhui speaks volumes about the growing divergence between the Qing legal system and the realities of an increasingly complex and differentiated society. Litigants like Xie Mayuan were both sophisticated enough and wealthy enough to seek professional legal advice. Indeed, given a court that was so overburdened that it resisted as much as possible involvement in civil lawsuits, the services of a professional were essential to getting action from the court. But those professionals, in turn, compounded the burdens on the court.

Synchronic Patterns and Diachronic Changes

Many of the differences between Danshui-Xinzhu and Baodi-Baxian can of course be attributed to local characteristics. In Danshui-Xinzhu, corporate lineages were much more highly developed. So were corporate business entities. The greater fertility of the land, coupled with relatively recent settlement and sparse population, made for a higher incidence of big landlords and of complex land relations. Here the practice of dual landownership was well entrenched, with a clear distinction between subsoil and topsoil rights; there was no comparable practice in Baodi and Baxian. The land, moreover, was fertile enough to sustain two levels of land rents, the *dazu* "big rent" on the subsoil and the *xiaozu* "small rent" on the topsoil, a practice that set it apart also from those areas where dual ownership was pervasive, notably parts of the Yangzi delta. Topsoil owners there almost always cultivated the land themselves. Only rarely did one rent out to a tenant for a "small rent," as in Danshui-Xinzhu (P. Huang 1990: 107–8, 157–58).

Relatively recent settlement also made for distinctive problems. There were more cases involving newly reclaimed land. Tenants who opened up uncultivated land, we have seen, felt entitled to compensation for their labor, or even to proprietary rights over the land. That became one frequent source of dispute between landlord and tenant. At the same time, the state had a special concern with bringing new land onto its tax registers. Such cases were rare in well-settled Baodi and Baxian but quite common in Danshui-Xinzhu.

Differences like these should be seen as synchronic variances. Projected to wider areas, we might think of Danshui-Xinzhu in terms of the most fertile agricultural areas in China, for example, Fujian-Guangdong, and of Baodi in terms of dry-farmed areas like the North China plain. Baxian, perhaps, was more representative of the wet-rice areas of the upper, middle, and lower Yangzi regions—more fertile than the North China plain but less fertile than the southeast and the south.

But we can also see some of the differences between the three areas as diachronic. A case could be made that late-nineteenth-century Danshui-Xinzhu represented a more "advanced" version of its contemporary Baodi. The Ming and Qing saw the long-term growth of commercial exchange in many areas of China, a development that extended to even the dry-farmed North China plain with the expansion of the cotton economy (for a detailed account, see P. Huang 1985).

With commercialization, we might suggest, some places on the North China plain became more and more like nineteenth-century Danshui-Xinzhu economically and socially. Even places like Baodi were to see accelerated commercialization in the twentieth century, when the county would become one of the major centers of production of "improved native cloth" (*gailiang tubu*; P. Huang 1990: 128). In time Baodi would come to have the same kind of diversified and urbanized economy, and complex and differentiated society, as Danshui-Xinzhu. It too would come to have multiparty corporate and business entities similar to those in Danshui-Xinzhu.

In the case of Baxian, my sample stops with the 1850's, on the eve of the coming of new changes to the county. But the influence of modern Chongqing city would in time bring the Baxian countryside too to something like the differentiation of Danshui-Xinzhu. A longitudinal study across the late nineteenth century and into the twentieth might reveal some patterns of change similar to those suggested by the contrasts between Baodi and Danshui-Xinzhu.

To sum up, the civil legal system of the Qing was intended for and dealt much better with the relatively simple peasant society of nineteenth-century Baodi than it did with the more complex society of late-nineteenth-century Danshui-Xinzhu. In Baodi, the court was well up to the task imposed by its caseload, dispensing justice simply and efficiently. In Danshui-Xinzhu, the court had come to be entangled in crisscrossing difficulties of noncompliance, fraudulent claims, and legal machinations. Unresolved cases accumulated because of difficulties of enforcement or protracted maneuverings by the litigants. The Danshui-Xinzhu court, in fact, was coming to resemble very much the overburdened situation described in eighteenth-century official complaints about Fujian (Macauley 1994: 86–89).

In part, no doubt, the mounting pressures on the Danshui-Xinzhu court stemmed simply from the increased frequency of land and debt transactions that came with commercialization and population increase. More buying and selling of land and lending and borrowing of money, and more complex forms of those transactions, brought more disputes, and then lawsuits. But the explanation for the difference in the two courts' pattern of operations needs to be sought mainly in their disparate social contexts. Wealthy and powerful individuals and corporate entities were rare in rural Baodi but common in Danshui-Xinzhu. Such litigants tended to be more knowledgeable, less compliant, more persistent, and more manipulative of the legal system than simple peasants. They were the ones who could spare the time, trouble, and expense to hire legal advisers/agents and engage in a protracted lawsuit. Their emergence was finally responsible for the increasing proportion of unresolved cases and the mounting burdens on the Danshui-Xinzhu court.

CHAPTER SEVEN

Extent, Cost, and Strategies of Litigation

I F I T I S T R U E T H A T large numbers of small peasants went to court over civil matters, as the preceding chapters have indicated, something is plainly wrong with the conventional picture of extortionate legal expenses imposed by rapacious yamen clerks and runners. If court expenses were indeed so prohibitive, most people should have shunned the courts; it makes no sense to think that small peasants went to court over relatively small stakes at exorbitant cost.

Old sources like magistrate and legal secretary handbooks support both views. Thus, Fuma Susumu's excellent recent article (1993) draws on those sources to argue for, on the one hand, the high incidence of litigation and, on the other, the abusiveness of clerks and runners. Fuma does not take up the inconsistency of the one phenomenon with the other.

This chapter attempts to get at what actually was by disentangling the empirical evidence on actual practice from the more purely moral and ideological representations. I begin by examining the available evidence on the extent and the costs of civil litigation to attempt to arrive at an approximate sense of what those actually were. On that basis, I attempt to make some suggestions also about the probable actual practices of local government, as opposed to their representation in official discourse. Finally, I analyze litigant strategies and choices against this background.

The apparently contradictory actions and choices of litigants become readily understandable when seen in the context of a paradoxical system that was at once intimidating and accessible, moralistic yet practical. When we distinguish clearly between the representational and the actual dimensions of civil litigation and local government, we can arrive at a more plausible picture of how things worked. We can also explain how and why the image of pervasive yamen abuse took hold. Most important, we can see that the widely held presumption that greedy, corrupt clerks and runners kept all but litigation abusers out of the court system simply cannot have been true. The fact is that many common people went to court for the legitimate purposes of settling disputes and protecting their rights.

The Extent of Civil Litigation

What follows is a tentative discussion on the extent of civil litigation based on a preliminary search through the available evidence. It draws on three types of information: references in magistrates' accounts to their experiences; magistrates' monthly reports to their superiors; and annual county court registers. Each source yields a somewhat different set of numbers.

Let us first dispense with the kind of information that has helped to distort the picture. A notable example is the passage from Lan Dingyuan about his tenure as the magistrate of Chaoyang county in Fujian in 1728, as quoted by Melissa Macauley (1994: 88): "In one day, [I] received 1,000 to 2,000 plaints. On the day(s) with the least activity, [I] received 1,200 to 1,300 plaints." Taken on its face, this passage suggests that Lan dealt with an astronomical and ultimately implausible number of cases. With an average of, say, 1,500 cases a day for a year of, say, 300 days, he would have handled 450,000 cases, or more than one lawsuit per person in the county. But as Lan indicates in the preceding clause, he was in fact referring to "the one day in three when [the yamen was] open for receiving plaints" (*Luzhou gong'an*, 1765: 10). He was talking about the 72 or so days of the year (three of every 10 days in the eighth through the third months) when the court accepted lawsuits involving "minor matters." That reduces the number down to less than one-fourth of what might otherwise be presumed.

More important, Lan's "petitions and plaints" (*cizhuang*) should not be taken as a reference only to new lawsuits. As Wang Huizu wrote in his autobiography about his experience in Ningyuan county in Hunan in 1787, he received 200+ petitions and plaints each day the yamen was open for receiving plaints about "minor matters"

(Wang Huizu 1796: 2: 9), but as he noted elsewhere, "new plaints that should by law be accepted totaled no more than 10. The rest were all just counterplaints [*suci*] and prompting petitions [*cuici*]" (cited in Fuma 1993: 476, n. 11). A ratio of one new lawsuit to 20+ petitions and plaints received would reduce Lan's numbers to a still clearly hyperbolic 5,400 cases a year. That number is way out of the range indicated by other sources.

More credible are certain anecdotal references cited by Fuma Susumu. There is the magistrate Zhang Woguan of Guiji county in Zhejiang near the end of the Kangxi reign (1662–1722), who speaks of "one hundred and several tens" of petitions and plaints a day, of which those containing "true facts" (*zhenqing*) totaled no more than "one or two out of 10." Then there is Wang Huizu's number of 200+ petitions and plaints a day in 1787, by then on a two-in-10-day sched-ule (the third and the eighth days, as opposed to the earlier third, sixth, and ninth days) for receiving "minor" cases, of which only about 10 were new lawsuits. And finally, there is the figure for Xiang-xiang county in Hunan some time in the Qianlong reign (1735–95), which speaks of 300 to 400 petitions and plaints on such days. If we take Wang's figure of 10 new lawsuits a day for a total of 48 days (six days a month for eight months), we would get a figure of 480 cases a year. That is less than ¹/₁₀ of the figure implied by Lan Dingyuan, or about one case for every 250 persons, or every 50 households.* If we count in terms of the numbers of litigants, including both plaintiffs and defendants, we would be talking about twice these numbers (Fuma 1993).

Three anecdotal accounts from the nineteenth century suggest similar, if somewhat lower, numbers. Liang Zhangju, writing rhetori-cally in 1837 as if to question Wang's numbers (of 200+ petitions and plaints a day), remarked: "Even though there are lots of litigation documents [*songdie*], can the number in one day exceed 100 sheets? Of the 100 sheets, can those cases that require attention exceed 10? It is not difficult to record 10 cases a day. On the next day, another 100 sheets are received. But more than half are counterplaints. The plaints that need to be recorded are reduced again from 10 to five" (Liang Zhangju 1837, 5: 4 [245]). Ruan Benyan of Funing county in Jiangsu, in 1887, speaks of receiving "on the third and eighth days for receiving plaints, about 60 to 70 sheets each day," or about a half of Zhang Woguan's figures (and a third of Wang Huizu's; Ruan Benyan

---

* The Ningyuan county population was 23,366 households in 1816.

1887, 3: 8). A last source, Qian Xiangbao, a magistrate who served in Henan during the Guangxu reign (1875–1908), boasts of how, after he punished the "litigation mongers" (*songgun*) severely, the number of plaints declined from "a hundred and thirty or forty" to "just forty or fifty."* At the end of the year, after he had been on the post for six months, he wrote, he had closed a total of 130 civil (*zili*) cases, of which half were leftovers from the previous administration (Qian Xiangbao 1920, 1: 18; see also 4: 14). If we take the number 130 as ⅝ of the year's total (since the yamen received such plaints five of the six months in the second half of the year, but only three of the six months in the first half), that would mean about 200 cases a year.[†]

Together, these anecdotal references suggest a ballpark range of perhaps 200 to 500 new civil cases a year, with the petitions and plaints coming in at perhaps 10 times that rate. How does this jibe with the second major source of information, the magistrates' monthly reports to their superiors? Here we turn to Governor Fan Zengxiang's comments on plaints and reports he received (for scattered months and years) during his tenure in Shaanxi province from 1901 to 1908 (Fan Zengxiang 1910, vols. 1–3), specifically the 33 "monthly reports on self-managed cases" (*zili cisong yuebao*) that had been adjudicated (as opposed to the cases "reported upward" [*shangkong*], not to be confused with appeals, also described as *shangkong*). As shown in Table 17, in the great majority of instances, the county magistrate closed an average of five "minor" (i.e., "self-managed") cases a month, or roughly 60 cases a year (though magistrates accepted civil plaints only on certain days, they worked on those cases all during the year).

Governor Fan suspected that the magistrates included "in their monthly reports only three or four out of 10 of their cases" (Fan Zengxiang 1910, 13: 32a). As the reader will recall, this is just about the same proportion adjudicated in the three counties (35 percent). According to Fan, because "the common judicial secretary and clerk did not hope for praise or reward, but only the absence of reprisal," they

---

* The majority of those, he went on to note, had mainly to do with the conditional and outright sale of land and houses because many of the buyers did not pay the necessary taxes and obtain the official deeds. When the sellers learned about it, they would try to extort money or resell the land, hence the frequent disputes.

† Mu Han (1845, 1: 32) speaks hypothetically of a magistrate closing "three or four [civil] cases each day, amounting to 80 or 90 a month." If we assume that cases formally closed amounted to about 55 percent of all cases received (the proportion in our three counties), he was proposing an inflow of more than 150 cases a month, or 1,200 cases a year—too high to be taken seriously.

TABLE 17

"Minor" Cases Adjudicated per Month by County Courts,
Shaanxi, 1901–1908

County	Cases (N=173)	Source (juan, page)
Baoji	4	14: 9b
Changan	5	18: 15b
Changwu	9	18: 24b
Chaoyi	4, 4, 4, 7	10: 29b, 13: 20a, 14: 12b, 15: 10a
Chengcheng	3	14: 14a
Chenggu	16, 4	13: 27b, 16: 38b
Dali	3	17: 39b
Dingyuan	4	19: 14a
Fuping	4, 4	18: 5a, 28b
Heyang	5	13: 21a
Huayin	3	13: 42b
Lintong	6, 4, 8, 7	10: 28a, 13: 31b, 15: 9b, 10a
Lonan	4	13: 16a
Pucheng	6, 4	10: 25b, 19: 43b
Sanyuan	6	11: 21a
Shanyang	3, 3	11: 27b, 12: 23a
Shiquan	6, 4	16: 39a, 18: 22b
Xianning	4	15: 36b
Xianyang	5, 5	18: 10a, 15b
Yichuan	11	18: 32b
Yijun	4	18: 24a
AVERAGE	5	

SOURCE: Fan Zengxiang 1910, vols. 1–3. Fan's comments on the lawsuits reported to him as provincial governor from 1901 to 1908 are not dated.

often "listed just two or three cases to meet the reporting obligation" and generally chose the unimportant and simple ones that could be summarized easily. If we take the number of civil cases reported in the registers as representing about 35 percent of all cases actually dealt with by the county court, then most counties in Shaanxi at this time actually handled an average of perhaps 15 cases a month, or 180 cases a year. It is a figure that is quite close to the extent indicated by the qualitative evidence in magistrates' writings.

As my final source on the scale of county civil litigation during the Qing, I used the 24 annual case registers (*cisong anjian bu*) of Baodi for 1833–35 and 1861–81, which contain one-sentence listings of all cases, civil, criminal, and administrative, handled by the court during the year. Table 18 shows the total of cases received each year, broken down into four categories: "civil" (as defined in this book), physical fights or assaults (*dou'ou*), administrative (involving mainly the appointment and duties of xiangbao and paitou), and major crimes.

TABLE 18

Baodi County Cases, 1833–1835, 1861–1881

Year	Civil[a] (N=209)	Fights and assaults (N=274)	Administrative (N=78)	Criminal[b] (N=367)	Total (N=928)
1833	16	22	10	42	90
1834	11	20	14	20	65
1835	14	14	4	30	62
1861	2	15	4	13	34
1862	1	10	1	13	25
1863	6	10	3	15	34
1864	10	3	0	6	19
1865	8	7	0	14	29
1866	2	1	4	6	13
1867	8	7	4	11	30
1868	13	4	9	11	37
1869	12	16	3	8	39
1870	10	14	0	7	31
1871	7	17	4	7	35
1872	8	9	1	6	24
1873	6	8	3	12	29
1874	7	10	2	12	31
1875	4	18	1	16	39
1876	6	9	1	22	38
1877	8	22	3	23	56
1878	8	14	1	17	40
1879	19	8	0	23	50
1880	11	10	5	19	45
1881	12	6	1	14	33
AVERAGE	8.7	11.4	3.3	15.3	38.7

SOURCE: Baodi 329: *Cisong anjian bu*, 1833–35, 1861–81.

[a]Includes 5 cases pertaining to matters other than land, debt, marriage, and inheritance (including old-age support): 1 for 1833, 1 for 1871, 2 for 1872, and 1 for 1873. 31 of the 209 cases involved a physical assault or fight (*ou* and *dou'ou*) in addition to the explicitly identified civil issue.

[b]Includes minor offenses such as theft.

The number of civil cases is plainly much lower than the figure given in the other two types of sources, lower even than what Governor Fan Zengxiang termed the "just two or three cases listed to meet reporting obligations." The average for the 24 years works out to just under nine cases a year. Even if we add half of the "physical fight and assault" cases, on the assumption that they were at bottom concerned with civil disputes, the total, at just under 15, is still lower than the product of the kind of perfunctory and formulaic reporting Fan spoke of. The problem is: how are we to understand these numbers, and the gap between them and the ones suggested by our other two sources?

On the one hand, the Baodi numbers can be seen as "hard" in the sense that they are seemingly the actual cases recorded for a given year. They come from the archives of the county yamen. They should, on the face of things, contain a comprehensive listing of all cases handled by the court. On the other hand, since these registers were official documents that were sent upward, they were probably subject to the kind of logic Governor Fan noted. It seems likely that only cases that were closed were entered into these registers, and even then perhaps just a fraction of those. Unfortunately, there does not appear to be a register of the sort I found for Shunyi county for 1927, which (as we saw in Chapter Two) listed cases on receipt and then tracked them with markings when they were closed. If we take Fan at his word, then the actual civil cases handled by the Baodi court may have been closer to three to four times the number reported, or 50 or so cases a year.

That figure is still of course much lower than the numbers suggested by the other sources. One possible explanation is the distinctive characteristics of the county, at once centrally located and yet little commercialized. It was close enough to the capital to have been well controlled, in contrast to, say, the peripheral county of Ningyuan, near the southern border of Hunan, where Wang Huizu served in 1787.* Yet it was a county of the lean soil typical of the North China plain and not nearly so prosperous and differentiated a society as Danshui-Xinzhu, where one might expect more commercial transactions and hence of disputes related to those transactions.†

For now, I would propose that we think of 50 to 500 a year as the plausible range for the county courts' annual civil caseload during the second half of the Qing. Many counties, perhaps, hovered around 100 to 200 cases a year. For an average, we might think of something on the order of 150 cases per county per year.

That number makes sense if compared with the available data for the Republican period. As shown in Table 19, 236 county courts reported an average of 249 new civil cases in the year 1936. That figure is supported by the data for five counties given in the "new gazet-

---

* Wang wrote, for example, about a gang of 60 to 70 bandits who had operated in the county for more than 16 years (Wang Huizu 1796, 2: 5a,b).

† We should be careful not to see a simple one-to-one relationship between degree of commercialization and incidence of litigation. As I showed in the previous chapter, as a court became more burdened by the sophisticated maneuverings of well-to-do litigants, it also became less accessible to the peasants. Thus, the court of a simpler and less-commercialized county like Baodi was more accessible to peasants than the court of Danshui-Xinzhu.

TABLE 19

Civil Cases for "China" (236 Counties) and Five Selected Counties,
1918–1944

County	Year	Number of cases[a]	Annual average
236 counties	1936	58,844[b]	249
5 counties	1918–44	2,700	270
Songjiang (Jiangsu)	1918	187	
Songjiang	1924	130	
Shunyi (Hebei)	1927	101[c]	
Linhai (Zhejiang)	1928	821	
Linhai	1929	853	
Shunyi	1930	126[c]	
Suixian (Hubei)	1935	163[d]	
Suixian	1936	101	
Ningdu (Jiangxi)	1940	146	
Ningdu	1944	72	

SOURCES: 236 counties: *Sifa tongji, 1936*, 2: 1–8. Songjiang: *Songjiang xianzhi*, 1991: 258. Shunyi: *Minshi anjian yuebao biao*, 1927, *Minshi susong anjian nianbao biao*, 1930. Linhai: *Linhai xianzhi*, 1989: 234. Suixian: *Suizhou zhi*, 1988: 431. Ningdu: *Ningdu xianzhi*, 1986: 367.

[a] Sources give the data by three different, but roughly comparable, categories. All figures are for cases heard (*shouli*) except as noted.

[b] The official judicial statistics volume for 1936 lists totals for 236 reporting counties in 19 provinces. I have excluded cases reported by local courts in the 19 provincial capitals and the cities of Shanghai and Beiping and all first-instance cases reported by three superior courts.

[c] Cases newly received (*xinshou*).

[d] Cases concluded (*shenjie*).

teers" published in recent years, which show an average of 270. Considering the somewhat greater accessibility of Republican courts as a result of the formal recognition of civil lawsuits and the standardization of court fees, the increase, of about two-thirds by 1936, makes sense. As we saw in Tables 7 and 8 (Chap. 2), the proportion of civil cases increased from a third of all cases to about a half between the Qing and 1936.

To give a comparative sense to this estimated scale of Qing litigation, Table 20 converts the numbers to a rate of civil lawsuits per 100,000 population and compares the Qing with Republican and postrevolutionary China, as well as contemporary America. These very rough indicators suggest that the incidence of civil litigation in China may have gone up by a half or more in the Republican period, and then further doubled by the late 1980's. By 1989, the incidence was just over three times that of 1750–1900.

Not surprisingly, the number of suits remains very much lower than in the United States: just one lawsuit in China for every 39 here. Contemporary America is a society in which enormous numbers of

TABLE 20

Civil Lawsuits per 100,000 Population for Qing,
Republican, and Postrevolutionary China
and the Contemporary United States

Country	Date	Cases
China	1750–1900	50[a]
China	1936	83[b]
China	1989	163[c]
United States	1980	6,356[d]

[a]This is a very rough estimate, based on an average of 150 cases per county per year, and an average county population of 300,000.

[b]See Table 19, note b.

[c]The number of civil cases received (*shou'an*) was 1,815,385; the population was 1,111,910,000 (*Zhongguo falü nianjian 1990*: 993; *Zhongguo tongji nianjian 1990*: 89).

[d]An estimated 14,600,000 civil cases were filed nationwide (extrapolated from complete reports for 28 of the states); the population was 229,712,000 (*State Court Caseload Statistics: Annual Report 1980*, pp. 14, 55). The state of California's figure for the year was 6,725 (ibid., p. 58). The figures do not include the 73 civil cases per 100,000 population handled by federal courts that year (*Annual Report of the Director of the Administrative Office of the United States Courts, 1981*: 200). The four largest categories of civil lawsuits were small claims, domestic relations, torts, and estates.

civil lawsuits come from divorce, auto torts, and inheritance. Chinese society simply did not and does not have anywhere near comparable numbers of disputes over such matters. Contemporary America is also a culture in which a resort to law to settle disputes has become deeply ingrained. In contemporary China (as in the Qing), the great majority of civil disputes are resolved by extrajudicial mediation, not—as is almost always the case in our society—by the courts. A ballpark sense of the relative proportion is provided by data compiled in recent years. In 1989, the 1,000,000-odd Chinese mediation committees reportedly handled some 7,341,030 disputes, compared with 1,815,385 civil lawsuits handled by the courts (*Zhongguo falü nianjian 1990*: 993, 1011). That suggests that just one of four disputes undergoing mediation becomes a lawsuit. The stark contrast between Chinese and American rates of litigation, then, stems from both China's lower incidence of civil disputes (one dispute requiring mediation for every ten U.S. lawsuits) and the reliance on extrajudicial mediation.

Whatever the precise comparative dimensions, we must not underestimate the importance of formal law in Chinese society, today or in the Qing. The working figures for the Qing suggest a degree of litigiousness that brought around 150 cases annually to the county courts, or about one new lawsuit each year for every 2,000 people (assuming an average population of 300,000 per county). If we think in terms of litigants (i.e., both plaintiffs and defendants), rather than lawsuits, and of households (with an average of five members), rather than individuals, one in every 200 households would have had someone involved in a new lawsuit each year. Over a 20-year period (and barring repeats), or about the timespan of clear recall in the three villages studied by Japanese ethnographers, that would mean one in every 10 households had someone involved in litigation. The village data presented in Chapter Two suggest a roughly comparable incidence: an average of six lawsuits per village for the 20 years from the 1910's to the 1930's, or roughly one new litigant for every nine households.* Though low by contemporary American standards, that figure was high enough to put litigation in the memories of most peasants and the collective recall of almost all villages. There is no question that formal law played a major role in the lives of the majority of the population. Simple peasants may have feared the courts, but not enough to keep them from using the courts to settle their disputes and protect their rights.

The Cost of Civil Litigation

The extent of civil litigation is of course crucially linked to the expenses involved. I propose here to set aside for the moment the issues posed by the possibly hyperbolic anecdotal evidence about the rapacious behavior of clerks and runners, and examine instead the available evidence on what might be considered the "normal" charges for civil litigation.

The scale of the legal fees levied in the Republican period is suggestive of what obtained in the Qing. In Shunyi county in 1940, a plaintiff paid 0.60 yuan for the plaint form, 0.10 yuan to the scribe for every 100 words, and a 0.15-yuan summons fee for witnesses living within 10 li (1 li = 0.3 miles) of the court, 0.23 yuan for 10–15 li, 0.30 yuan for 15–20 li, and 0.38 yuan for 20–25 li (KC, 1: 116). The standard "adjudication fee" (*shenpan fei*) was 4.50 yuan for non-property-related cases. For property cases, there was a graduated scale, rising from 0.45 yuan when less than 10 yuan of property was at issue to, for instance, 4.5 for 75–100 yuan, 33 for 900–1,000 yuan,

---

* At the time of the Mantetsu surveys, the three villages had a total of 315 households (P. Huang 1985: 316, 317, 319).

TABLE 21

*Agricultural Laborer Wages, Land Prices, and Wheat Prices,
Shajing Village, 1936–1942*

Year	Year-laborer wages (yuan/year)[a]	Land prices (yuan/mu)[b]	Wheat prices (yuan/shi)
1936	30	45	6
1937			12
1938			22
1939	40	100	23.5
1940	90		42+
1941	130	150	
1942	170	200	50

SOURCES: Wages: KC, 2: 55, 88, 261, 267; cf. KC, 1: 45. Land prices: KC, 2: 265, 268; cf. KC, 1: 40, 91; 2: 171, 227. Wheat prices: KC, 2: 70, 238, 252, 354–55.
[a]Cash wages only (i.e., does not include the value of the worker's room and board).
[b]Middle-grade land.

and 105 for 8,000–10,000 yuan, with 4.5 yuan tacked on for every 1,000 yuan over that (KC, 1: 312–13). Though a litigant was required to pay the *shenpan fei* up front, the fee was refunded if the case was settled before it reached a formal court session (KC 1: 307; cf. P. Huang 1991: 8). The cost to a litigant, in other words, was about one yuan for filing a plaint and another 4.5 yuan to see a lawsuit involving up to 100 yuan through to a court judgment. For a major lawsuit involving property of about 1,000 yuan, he or she would pay 34 yuan.*

As a measure of the burden of a suit, consider the figures on agricultural wages, land prices, and wheat prices in this area on the eve of wartime inflation (Table 21). In 1936, a year-laborer could file a plaint for a cost of about 1/30 of his annual cash income. For a common dispute involving no more than 100 yuan, he could see it through to a court judgment for another 1/7. To be sure, a year-laborer could ill-afford a suit involving 1,000 yuan or so, but then he was unlikely to be engaged in a dispute over what amounted to more than 30 years' income. For a landowner, on the other hand, such a cost, though high, was not prohibitive. As we see in Table 21, one mu of middle-grade land in this area was worth, on average, 45 yuan (ranging from 30 to 60 yuan) at this time, and, as noted in Chapter Two, a peasant could borrow up to 50 percent of the land price if he offered the land

* For most peasants, lawyers' fees were not a consideration; hardly any ever employed lawyers, even at this late date.

as security in the arrangement called *zhidi jieqian,* and up to 70 percent if he offered it in conditional sale (dian). Putting up one or two mu of land would usually see him through.

Another way to think about the cost of litigation is in terms of its value in consumption grain, the principal expenditure in the livelihood of peasants. The average annual grain consumption of a male adult was about three shi.* By that measure (again in 1936), a filing on a small suit amounted to ⅙ of a shi of wheat. For a major suit, the cost would have equaled five shi of wheat, or 1.66 of an adult male peasant's annual grain consumption.

For the late Qing, Dai Yanhui cites figures for Xinzhu of 0.40 to 0.50 diao (or about the same fractions of a yuan) for a petition form, about the same for the filing fee, and 0.40–0.70 yuan for the scribe's fee (Dai 1979: 706–8). That would put the cost of filing a plaint at 1.20 to 1.70 silver yuan.† If the case went on to a court session, the plaintiff would have had to pay from three or four yuan to 10 yuan in court fees; for a major lawsuit, those fees could range up to 100 yuan or more (ibid.).

These figures are not too different from the litigation charges (*songfei*) reported by the Baxian county magistrate in 1906.‡ He notes, first of all, a fee of some 0.70 silver yuan (700 wen), for "issuing a receipt and sending to judgment" (*kaidan songshen*). In addition, if a summons was issued, the plaintiff had to pay about three yuan, and if a court session was held, another yuan. If the court had to send a clerk or runner to measure land, or to investigate, there would be a charge of 0.80 yuan for a distance within 40 li. For more than 40 li, there would be a surcharge of 0.20 yuan for every 10 li. If runners had to be sent (presumably for other purposes than serving a summons or measuring the land or investigating), there would be a further charge of five yuan.§ If a repeat court session was required, there would be

* Or some 40 catties a month, about the level of the rice allowance in Songjiang county in the 1950's (P. Huang 1990: 184).

† That sum is basically consistent with the data in the 1957 Xinzhu county gazetteer, which speaks of a registration (*guahao*) and recording (*dengji*) fee in the Qing of 1.40 yuan for filing a lawsuit, plus an initial registration fee of 0.08 yuan, or 80 wen (*Xinzhu xianzhi* 1957, 4: 307). On the fluctuating exchange rate between the copper *cash* and the silver yuan in the Yangzi delta area between 1879 and 1910, see Bernhardt 1992: 246–47 (Table B.2).

‡ This document is translated in full in Reed 1993. I am grateful to Bradly Reed for sharing the document with me and allowing me to use it in this study. For the sake of comparison, I have converted the magistrate's figures from wen to yuan.

§ According to the magistrate, both the plaintiff and the defendant had to pay the above fees.

an additional fee of 0.16 yuan. Thus, though it cost a litigant under one yuan to file a plaint, he had to pay at least another four yuan to see a common lawsuit through to adjudication. Major suits involved added charges.

This was at a time when a shi of rice sold for just under six yuan (Bernhardt 1992: Table B.2). In other words, a litigant paid the equivalent of about ⅙ of a shi of rice to file a plaint, and about ¾ of a shi of rice to see a common lawsuit through to a court judgment, the same rate we saw in the Shunyi of 1936. For a major lawsuit, the cost could run up to many times more, just as in Republican Shunyi.

Data are harder to come by for earlier periods of the Qing. Wang Huizu provides a ballpark figure for the mid-eighteenth century:

A peasant household that has 10 *mu* of land, with the husband doing the cultivation and the woman the weaving, can support several mouths. The cost of a single lawsuit amounts to 3,000 *wen*, and they would need to borrow money to meet the expense. Within two years they would have to sell their land. If they sell one *mu*, they will have one *mu* less of income. They will then be caught in a spiral of borrowing and selling. Within seven or eight years, they will lose their means of subsistence. The poverty comes in seven or eight years, but the initial cause is actually the plaint and its acceptance [by the court]. (*Muling shu*, 18: 9a)

We might speculate that Wang was probably talking here about a major and complete lawsuit, not just the filing of a plaint or a common lawsuit involving a sum of under 100 yuan. Assuming that is the case, Wang's figures are quite consistent with the late Qing and Republican data, working out to about one year's wage for an agricultural wage-laborer (i.e., 2,000–5,000 wen of copper *cash*; Li Wenzhi et al., 1983: App. Table 1, pp. 230–32).

These scattered and not completely satisfactory figures suggest that the cost of civil litigation in the Qing, though high from the point of view of the small peasant, was not entirely prohibitive. Barring irregular charges, it was relatively inexpensive for a litigant to file a plaint in order to gain leverage in a mediated settlement. Though Wang Huizu is surely correct about the long-term implications of an average middle peasant owning, say, 10 mu of land, entangling himself in a major court case, a more well-to-do middle or rich peasant would find the expense bearable. If the dispute involved a large enough stake, it probably seemed worthwhile to a peasant to go to court.

This is not to deny the "horror tales" of astronomical litigation expense, which have been abundantly cited in past scholarship and illustrated in some detail in Chapter Three by the case of Hou Zhenxiang (of Houjiaying village) who, out of fear of possible criminal prosecution for the suicide of his daughter-in-law, sold 20 of his 40 mu of land to raise 2,400 yuan to smooth things over. What should be pointed out, however, is that such exorbitant expenses probably involved serious criminal charges and the risk of severe punishment. In those instances, litigants were understandably more easily intimidated into paying large sums, hence the greater opportunity for extortionate charges by petty officials. Civil cases involving large sums may have also offered such opportunities. But it would be a mistake to equate the common civil lawsuit with such charges. The substantial numbers of peasants who went to court over rather modest amounts would obviously not have done so had the costs run all that high.

Our seemingly contradictory images of exorbitant cost and frequent peasant litigation, then, can be reconciled in part by distinguishing between the common civil lawsuits and lawsuits involving large amounts of property or major crimes. Within lawsuits, we need to further distinguish between the mere filing of a plaint and a full lawsuit that proceeded to a court judgment. Major lawsuits involved much greater expense, more frequent use of litigation advisers, and more opportunities for official abuse. Common civil lawsuits, and lawsuits that involved the mere filing of a plaint to leverage an opponent, on the other hand, remained relatively simple and inexpensive. They were what provided even small peasants with the needed access to the courts to settle their disputes.

"Yamen Worms"

Even for the lawsuits involving stakes large enough to make extortionate charges believable, we should not take Qing official discourse at its word. On close examination, it will be evident that the Qing state and its officials blamed rapacious runners and clerks for the failings of local government in much the same manner and for much the same reasons as they blamed litigation instigators/mongers for mounting caseloads.

The Qing code dubbed abusive yamen staff "yamen worms" (*yadu*). Though the term applied to both clerks and runners (Substatute 344-7), runners were singled out with a derivative term, *duyi.* According to Substatute 344-3, these "worm-runners," who "intimidated and extorted from the poor people," were to be punished by degrees based on the amount they extorted. The word worms, of course, graphically conveyed the meaning intended: these miscreants would eat up the yamen from the inside, as worms might a book or a wooden structure; they were the cause of decay in the yamen.

As with litigation abusers, we do not have far to look for the reasons for such a formulation. Given the ideal of benevolent/humane government by moral men, failings in local government could only be blamed on the moral failings of immoral men. In fact, we might see moral magistrates and "yamen worms" as two sides of the same coin of the concept of "humane governance" (renzhi). Moreover, since magistrates were by official ideology superior men selected for their moral qualifications, few among them would have placed the blame on themselves; that left mainly the unofficial staff under them to blame.

Blaming "yamen worms" for the decay of local government was entirely consistent with blaming litigation abusers for the strains on the courts. To the Qing official mind, there was no contradiction between the two pictures of rapacious yamen staff and mounting caseloads, because the Qing state never acknowledged in its official legal ideology what has been demonstrated in this book: that large numbers of decent people went to court over legitimate concerns. They were therefore not faced with the problem of explaining the inexplicable: how small peasants could have gone to court over civil matters in the face of exorbitant legal expenses imposed by evil clerks and runners. Instead, they came up with a formulation that erased the contradiction: it was evil litigation abusers acting in cahoots with immoral yamen clerks and runners that explained the county courts' increasing problems. Decent people avoided the courts, as the state's moral ideology would have them do.

The two notions of "litigation sticks" and "yamen worms" thus sprang from the same basic conceptual structure. In fact, the definition in the code of the litigation monger overlaps with the conception of the yamen worms: the litigation monger was one who either acted in collusion with clerks and runners or was himself on the yamen staff.

The roots for the category yamen worms can be found in the way in which the Qing state conceptualized yamen clerks and runners from the start. Ideally, by official representation, clerks and runners, rather like civil cases, did not exist; if they did, their numbers were to be kept as low as possible. As Ch'ü T'ung-tsu (1962) has shown, the Qing state early on set unrealistically low quotas for clerks in each county, "varying from a few to less than thirty" (p. 38). Runner quotas were similarly set low, at between 15 and 50 (p. 59). The Qing code even contained a statute (No. 50) setting out the punishment for any magistrate who exceeded these quotas: 100 blows with the heavy bamboo for one too many clerks or runners, to increase by one grade for every additional three men, up to the added punishment of three years of penal servitude.

The actual needs of county governments were of course very much greater, especially with the growth of population and the increasing complexity of local government during the Qing. Hong Liangji (1746–1809) estimated that yamen clerks actually numbered 1,000 or more in large counties, 700 to 800 in medium-sized counties, and 100 to 200 in small counties (Ch'ü T'ung-tsu 1962: 39). As for runners, early-nineteenth-century sources spoke similarly of numbers ranging from several hundred to more than a thousand in each county. Liu Heng, magistrate of Baxian from 1825 to 1827, wrote of having reduced in one year the number of runners in his county from 7,000 down to 200 or 300 (p. 59).

When it came to the pay that clerks and runners received, we find a similar disjunction between official representation and actual practice. The statutory pay for clerks was set very low in the early Qing (at six taels in 1652) and then eliminated altogether in the first year of the Kangxi reign (1662; Ch'ü T'ung-tsu 1962: 45). The statutory pay for runners was likewise set at the very low figure of "about six taels in most localities" (p. 64). The state in fact took the same posture toward the pay of clerks and runners as toward their numbers: ideally it did not exist; if it had to exist, then it would be kept as low as possible.

The actual needs and incomes of clerks and runners, once again, were very much higher, the more so with the prolonged inflation of the Qing. Bradly Reed (1993) has demonstrated with archival materials from Baxian that yamen clerks and runners relied greatly on fees collected on lawsuits for their income. There was little statutory funding for county yamens; their actual operating expenses were met mainly by litigation fees. Enough income was generated from the clerks' posts that an imperial edict of 1800 observed: "When the term of a clerk expires, money is paid by his successor for the post. This is called *ch'üeh-ti"* (*quedi*; quoted in Ch'ü T'ung-tsu 1962: 52). By the early twentieth century, head runners in Baxian were earning as much as 1,000 taels, though the six-tael salary was still on the books.

As Reed (1994) has suggested, clerks and runners were probably not nearly so abusive or rapacious as official representations have made them out to be. "Hard" evidence on this subject will of course be difficult to come by, and the issue may never be settled to the satisfaction of skeptics. Nevertheless, I would speculate that the operational realities of most county yamen staff did not correspond with either the state's unrealistic ideal or its hyperbolic counterideal. To date, Reed's evidence from Baxian is the most solid available. The 1888 report of the magistrate of Xinzhu I mentioned earlier lends considerable support to Reed's findings. It seems safe to me to take the expenses set out in that report—2.40 yuan a month in subsistence wages (*gongshi*), or 28.80 yuan a year for the runners, 120 yuan to 300 yuan a year for the major clerks (Dan-Xin 11407, pp. 1–3)—as ballpark figures for the actual "salaries" of yamen clerks and runners at the time. While much higher than the statutory figures, they cannot be called princely, let alone exorbitant.

No matter how reasonable, however, the actual numbers and pay of clerks and runners were always under the shadow of official condemnation. The Qing state took its normative ideals seriously enough to promulgate a specific statute to restrict their numbers to the officially set quotas, as has been seen. And a model official like Liu Heng took pride in recounting how he forbade his clerks from charging any fees for inquests and paid the expenses out of pocket himself (Ch'ü T'ung-tsu 1962: 46). By comparison with those ideals, the actual practices of the yamens, no matter how justifiable, were always seen as somehow a little shady and not quite acceptable to the law.

Since state constructions did not distinguish clearly between justifiable illegal practices and truly abusive behavior, it was easy for Qing officials to conflate the two. Seen as illegitimate to begin with, clerks and runners were easy targets for vilification. A few instances of outrageous abuse by some could easily lead to a picture of all yamen staff as rapacious.

For us to capture the operative realities of Qing local government accurately, we need to draw a line between nonabusive and abusive practices, a distinction that I suspect was also made by men who saw themselves as honest and upright. What we need is a third category in between the official ideal and the counterideal. In this connection, Ch'ü T'ung-tsu's term of "customary fees" (1962: 44–49), though not clearly distinguished by him from the statutory and the corrupt, is a useful category.

Though admittedly illegitimate by the letter of the law and the regulations of the state, legal fees like those I have detailed are best thought of as customary and appropriate. They seem to have been widely accepted by magistrates and their clerk/runners as well as the populace. If they contravened the representational ideals of the state, they were plainly not of a piece with the fees extorted by truly corrupt "yamen worms."

Most Qing local yamens, I would speculate, must have operated more in the intermediate area of what was customary than the abusive area of what was corrupt. We would otherwise be hard put to explain how and why small peasants went to court in such numbers over modest sums. It seems to me more plausible to suggest that official moralizing caused the conflating of the customary with the truly corrupt into the hyperbolic category of "yamen worms." The actual practice of most local governments was probably not nearly so rapacious.

All this is not to deny that there might have been a long-term tendency toward increased yamen corruption, much like the tendency toward increased litigation abuse outlined in the last chapter. As Qing society became more differentiated and complex, and sophisticated and powerful litigants more common, both legal and illegal uses of litigation advisers likely increased. That trend, along with the higher stakes involved in litigation, may well have engendered more corrupt and abusive practices within the yamen. We have seen the case of Du Qingji in Danshui-Xinzhu, which illustrates the phenomena of both the litigation monger and the worm runners, as defined by the Qing code. The point here is not to deny the existence of such abuse; it is only to suggest that it could not have been nearly so prevalent as has been widely assumed. Otherwise, the numbers and types of civil lawsuits documented in this book could not have existed.

Some Litigant Choices and Strategies

The reality of civil litigants likewise differed from both the idealized image and the vilified image projected by the state. Most were neither moral gentlemen who stayed above petty disputes and litigation nor evil people like litigation instigators/mongers. They were simple decent folk who went to court as a final resort to resolve disputes or protect their interests. Most, moreover, were active agents rather than the manipulated passive objects that the state's constructs of litigation instigator/monger made them out to be. They chose strategies and actions appropriate to the resources at their command and the interests they wished to advance. Direct evidence for such choices are difficult to come by because we do not have for common litigants anything like the kinds of information we find in magistrate and legal secretary handbooks spelling out different actions and the rationales for them. Nevertheless, we have enough evidence to draw some clear inferences about litigant choices.

The Decision to File a Plaint

Most people in the Qing undoubtedly did see the courts as forbidding. They were forbidding, first of all, because of their penal posture. The point was made in many ways. The code was unmistakably punishment-oriented, beginning as it did by defining varieties, gradations, and instruments of punishment. Law itself was equated above all with punishment, as in the nomenclature for the judicial agencies of the government, from the Xingfang (Office of Punishment) of the county yamen up to the Xingbu (Ministry of Punishment) of the central government. Magistrates supposedly dealt only or mainly with punishable matters (xingshi), and all court sessions were held with instruments and personnel for punishment at the ready. Even though punishment was seldom used in civil cases, the threat was always present. Moreover, horror tales of rapacious yamen clerks and runners and of astronomical expenses abounded, a part of the legal culture of the Qing. The court, therefore, could not but have seemed intimidating to most of the populace.

Yet the courts also appeared accessible to many prospective litigants. The fact that magistrates seldom if ever used punishment in civil cases must have been quite widely known, considering the incidence of litigation. The fact that they consistently adjudicated according to the law to uphold property and contractual rights must also have been widely known. Certainly these proclivities were well understood by relatively sophisticated litigants and legal advisers. Most important, despite the tales of horrendous legal expenses and the ever-present threat of yamen abuse, the customary legal fees were not beyond the reach of most common people.

TABLE 22

*Informally Settled, Adjudicated, and Incomplete Cases
in Baxian, Baodi, and Dan-Xin*

County	Informally settled	Adjudicated	Incomplete	Total
Baxian (N=308)				
Number	53	98	152	303
Percent	17.2%	31.8%	49.4%	98.4%
Baodi (N=118)				
Number	45	45	26	116
Percent	38.1%	38.1%	22.1%	98.3%
Dan-Xin (N=202)				
Number	28	78	86	190
Percent	13.9%	38.6%	42.6%	95.1%
Total (N=628)				
Number	126	221	264	611
Percent	20.1%	35.2%	42.0%	97.3%

SOURCE: Appendix A, Table A.3.

The decision to turn to the formal court system in a dispute was thus made within a structural context that might be characterized as access under fear. The courts frowned on civil litigation in theory, but dealt regularly and consistently with civil disputes in practice. The courts were penal and forbidding in posture, but accessible and reasonable in action. Litigants deciding to resort to the courts were those who had enough at stake to overcome their fears and reluctance.

We must also bear in mind that the simple filing of a plaint did not mean that a litigant intended to pursue matters all the way to a formal court session. As Table 22 shows, in the majority of instances in our three county courts, the records end before a formal court session either because litigants reported they had settled matters informally (20 percent) or because neither the litigants nor the court chose to pursue matters any further (42 percent, including a few instances of damaged or lost records). In only 35 percent of the cases did the litigants persist in bearing the expenses of court adjudication.

A substantial proportion of litigants, we can infer, used the filing of a plaint as a way to add pressure on an opponent in a dispute. Some number clearly took the action on the spur of the moment, after a heated argument or physical fight. Others probably meant it as a bluff, a way to intimidate an opponent into being more compliant as the dispute was being mediated. For some no doubt it was a calculated move designed to bring court opinion into the mediation process. In the dispute in Shajing village over easement rights, for example, we saw how once Zhao Wenyou filed suit in the county court, he effectively altered the terms of community mediation in his dispute with Li Guang'en: the position that the court was expected to take became a part of the baseline for working out a compromise settlement. In this case, Zhao got most of what he wanted by just filing a plaint.

Whatever the motivations and strategies, a decision to file a plaint needs to be distinguished from a decision to see a case all the way through. The one, as has been seen, cost only a fraction—less than one quarter—of the other. This relatively modest cost is undoubtedly one of the reasons, perhaps the most important reason, why many people were ready to turn to the courts.

The Choice of Representation

Once having decided to file a plaint, litigants faced certain other decisions. One was whether or not to employ the services of a private plaint-writer. As we saw in Chapter Six, by the letter of the law, private scribes were illegal; the state intended plaintiffs to tell the simple truth to the yamen's scribes, who were supposed to write down what they were told without embellishment or change. This may have been the rule in Baodi, but the resort to private scribes was extremely common in Danshui-Xinzhu, where more than 80 percent of the plaints submitted were brought intact to the yamen. Though none of the litigants acknowledged the use of a private scribe, most, especially illiterate peasants, must have done so.

For many of the more sophisticated and powerful litigants, another early decision was whether or not to employ the services of a litigation adviser or agent. We have seen how the use of such legal services was not uncommon in Danshui-Xinzhu. But again, given the official proscription of such "lawyers," no litigant admitted to this. Take our prime example, Xie Wenhui. Actually a hired agent of Xie Mayuan's in his attempt to assert ownership rights over land that had been reclaimed by his tenants, Wenhui passed himself off as a member of Mayuan's family.

Obviously, not all written representations appearing on plaints corresponded in all respects to the original oral narratives of the complainant in the manner intended by the state. In subtle and not so subtle ways, the plaintiff's complaint underwent changes during the process of transcription. The changes may have been merely in form:

adapting spoken to written vocabulary and normal conversation to the standard "legalese" of plaints, such as the formulaic openings and closings, the standardized ways for plaintiffs to refer to themselves and to the magistrate, and so on. Or they could be substantial: adapting and repackaging the facts and the truth to fit legal categories and concepts (or what private scribes and advisers or yamen clerks thought to be legal categories and concepts).

In this sense, then, the composing of a plaint may be seen as the first meeting of informal society with formal law. To the extent that the litigants were illiterate peasants, it might also be seen as the first meeting of the peasants' predominantly oral culture with the bureaucracy's written culture. A detailed analysis of this subject would require focused investigation, to include changes in language, in nuance, in stereotypical depiction, and in conceptual categories.*

One major and common type of adaptive representation by litigants, as has been seen, concerned women who returned to their natal homes to get away from unhappy and oppressive relationships with their husbands and/or marital families. If the wife had the full support of her natal family, there was little her husband and in-laws could do to force her to come back. Informal mediation could not coerce the woman to return against her will. As for the courts, there was nothing in the legal stipulations about marriage and divorce that forbade a woman from returning to her natal family. A lawsuit based on such a complaint was unlikely to be accepted by the court. Under those conditions, husbands and their families often represented the case under some other rubric to gain the attention and support of the court. One common resort was to charge that the woman had been "abducted" (*lue*) or "seduced" (*you, youguai*), which was punishable by Qing law (Statute 275). Thus, in the Baodi case in which the sixteen-year-old bride hid at her grandmother's house to escape harsh treatment from her husband and his parents (Chap. 4), the father-in-law charged that she had been "seduced" by a "bandit" into running away. Such a charge got him the attention of the court (and also enabled him to file a complaint on a day other than those stipulated for filing on minor matters). The plaintiff, Chen He, though reprimanded by the court for bringing false charges and required to file a pledge with his son not to mistreat the girl in the future, nevertheless got what he wanted: the court ordered the girl to return to her

---

*Karasawa 1994 begins to explore the multiple implications of the meeting of speech with writing.

marital home. Of the 33 marriage-related cases from Baodi, 13 involved wives who had been ostensibly "abducted," "seduced," or illegally remarried, or had run away. Of those, fully six actually involved disputes over wives who had returned to their natal homes (P. Huang 1991b: 39ff).

Once again, such adaptive representations by litigants tell about the paradoxical structure of the system within which they operated. Although the courts regularly handled civil cases, the state took the posture that they did not. That posture was what led some litigants to represent civil disputes as criminal ones to gain the attention of the court.

The Decision to Terminate a Lawsuit

Another crucial decision was when to terminate a lawsuit. Informal mediation, as has been seen, had as its main principle and method the use of peacemaking compromise. Court adjudication, by contrast, was predicated mainly on formal law as embodied in the code. For peasants whose main interest was to patch up relations that had been damaged in the heat of a dispute, informal mediation would have been the preferred method. For peasants who believed themselves clearly in the right legally or morally, however, informal mediation seldom provided the clear-cut vindication that might have been desired. The courts were much more likely to produce such an outcome. But that had to be weighed against the expense of litigation.

To judge by the evidence presented in Chapter Four, most litigants employed a strategy of graduated steps. It was easy and fairly cheap to file a plaint and get a preliminary response about the dispute from the magistrate. That step generally led to intensified community mediation. It also increased the role that court opinion played in the process of mediation. The next step(s) would have been a court summons (plus a court investigation or land measurement, if needed). The final step was a formal court session. The expenses rose rapidly with each step, as did the degree of court involvement in the resolution of the dispute.

From this point of view, the graduated process of litigation may be seen as a continuing series of choices by the peasant litigant about the degree to which he wished to depend on formal rather than informal justice. Informal mediation was the cheapest and would produce the most compromise-oriented type of resolution, and formal court session the most expensive and the most clear-cut. The litigants, clearly, were not limited to just one choice between the informal system and the formal system; a continuum of choices was open to them in the intermediate sphere between the two systems. The further into the judicial process the litigant went, the greater the weight of court opinion, and hence of the law, in the resolution of the dispute. The knowledgeable peasant litigant acted to achieve the desired mix of compromise and law while balancing prospective gains against costs.

One pattern was where a plaintiff accomplished his purpose just by filing a plaint, as in the easement dispute referred to above; a mediated settlement followed shortly after. Often, however, things had to go much further. In the dispute over land boundaries between Xu Wanfa and his neighbor Yang Zongkui in Baodi in 1845 (cited in Chap. 5), for example, Xu could have chosen to drop his plaint when Yang countered and submitted a drawing of his plot as evidence. Xu opted instead to pursue matters up to a formal court session. Even then, with the drawings of both plots and with witnesses before him, the magistrate found that he did not have sufficient evidence to make a clear-cut decision. He had to send runners to conduct an official measurement of the land. That measurement supported Xu's claims. Only when it was clear how the second session would go did Yang give in to a mediated settlement.

The plaintiff Xu, we might infer, was bent on a judicial judgment because he knew from the start that he was in the right, and he felt so strongly about what was at stake that he persisted in the lawsuit against mounting costs. He had to pay the fees for the summoning of witnesses and for the first court session, and then for the land measurement. Still he persisted. Yet he agreed to terminate the case before the second formal court session, perhaps because he had got what he wanted, or perhaps because by the mediated settlement he had to compromise less than what another court session would have cost him. Here once again we witness active litigant maneuverings in the spaces left by the paradoxical coupling of the formal and informal systems in Qing justice.

There were, finally, choices open to the losing party even after a court ruling had been rendered. To be sure, the person was under immense pressures to comply with the judgment of the magistrate and his imposing court. Nevertheless, the obstinate or sophisticated litigant still had substantial room for noncompliance. He could refuse to comply with the requirement of pledging to accept the court's ruling, in the manner of the stubborn old man Liu Qinwu, detailed in the last chapter. The legal "loophole" that Liu used was born of the official representation that magistrates did not adjudicate but merely facilitated the resolution of a case. In criminal cases, that ideal led to the requirement that a suspect confess before a case could be officially closed. In civil cases, it led to the parallel requirement that the litigants file pledges of voluntary acceptance of the settlement. By refusing to file such a pledge even after the magistrate threw him in jail, Liu was able to keep the court from officially closing the case. His was admittedly only the power of the desperate, but it was enough in this instance for him to bend the magistrate to his will.

A litigant could also resist a court decision by failing to carry out what he pledged to do. In the case of Zeng Chaozong, also cited in the preceding chapter, the court was unable to make him live up to his promise to pay off his debt. Here too we see a litigant who was no mere passive object.

To return to the question posed at the beginning of this chapter, our image of rapacious yamen clerks and runners, it turns out, is based on a counterideal formulated by the Qing state. The structure of official Qing legal discourse was such that moral ideals were generally paired with equally moralistic counterideals. The ideal that local government would be staffed solely by morally superior men led to its counter of a local government corrupted by immoral clerks and runners. In the same way, the ideal that good people would stay above litigation was accompanied by its counter, that evil instigators/mongers would manipulate ignorant people into frequent litigation.

The reality of civil litigation in the Qing was not the same as either the officially constructed ideal of no minor lawsuits or the officially constructed counterideal of litigation abuse. Rather, people went to court in considerable numbers and for the legitimate purposes of settling civil disputes and protecting their property or contractual rights. The same applied to Qing local government. It was not the same as either the official ideal of the benevolent rule of moral men or the official counterideal of "yamen worms." Rather, the majority of the local yamens probably acted according to customary standards that might have been illegitimate but were not nearly so corrupt as the official counterideal made them out to be. The legal and political systems did not, could not, acknowledge these realities in theory, lest the fundamental Confucian principle of benevolent rule by moral men itself be questioned.

Nevertheless, the system that was so highly moralistic in representation did adapt in action to practical imperatives. The result was a system born of the interactions between moral ideals and practical imperatives, and characterized by couplings of paradoxical dimensions. Litigants operated within that structure. They were indeed intimidated by the penal and forbidding representation of the system, but they also took advantage of its relative accessibility and went to court with considerable regularity. Some made adaptive accommodations to criminal representations in their civil suits. Many employed private scribes, and some even litigation advisers/agents, though none admitted to such use because of their proscription by law. Many took advantage of their simultaneous access to both informal mediation and formal adjudication, maneuvering within the spaces between them to their own interests. Few behaved in the manner of the officially constructed images of evil litigation instigators/mongers or passive objects manipulated by them. Many were active agents pursuing legitimate interests. Their choices and actions become more understandable when we separate out practice from representation and see the system in terms of the disjunctions between the two.

CHAPTER EIGHT

From the Perspective
of Magistrate Handbooks

H O W , W E M U S T F I N A L L Y A S K , did Qing magistrates see the legal system and their own roles in it? How did the paradoxical legal structure outlined in the preceding chapters shape their thinking and actions? To answer these questions, we can turn to the older, standard materials on the subject: the legal handbooks that were widely used in the Qing. Those materials reveal much about both the representational and the practical realities of the magistrate's office. For readers who are not fully convinced by the argument in the preceding pages, a close look at the handbooks will serve also as a check on the evidence provided by the case records and the code.

The Ideology of Benevolent Governance

The *Compendium on Magisterial Service* (*Muling shu*, 1848), perhaps the most comprehensive magistrate handbook of the Qing period, gathering together selections from dozens of writers from the early Qing down to the nineteenth century, begins with observations on "the source of [benevolent] governance" (*zhiyuan*). Local government, the editor Xu Dong wrote in his preface, was the key to good government, because "if the departments and counties are well governed, then all in the empire will be well governed." And the key to good local government lay in the magistrate's "personal self" (*shen*). Xu's allusion here, obvious to all schooled in the Confucian classics, was to the theme of the first chapter of *The Great Learning* (*Daxue*), to what might be considered the organizing self-image of the Confucian "scholar-official": the purpose of learning was to cultivate the self morally, in order to bring order to the family, thus to govern the state, and thus to bring peace to the empire; the ideal was benevolent government (renzhi), also expressed as the [humane] government of moral men (renzhi).

More specifically, a magistrate must love the people (*qinmin*)— again a term and concept straight from that chapter. As the prominent eighteenth-century official Chen Hongmou (1696–1771) put it, "Officials are established and appointed by the court for the sake of the people; to fulfill their duties, the officials must love the people" (*aimin; Muling shu,* 1: 13a). County magistrates were in fact often referred to in Qing official discourse as *qinmin zhi guan,* literally, "officials loving the people." That the word love here means parental love is immediately conveyed by the word "qin," as found in the compound terms father (*fuqin*), mother (*muqin*), and parents (*shuangqin*). But the word "qin" in this context also conveys the notion of "being close to," as in *qinjin.* The term qinmin, in other words, carried the twin idea that magistrates occupied the crucial position of being the closest among all officials to the people, and that was why it was so important that they be moral men who were benevolent and kindly toward their subjects.

Chen Hongmou went on to push the parental simile further (borrowing from another part of *The Great Learning*—chap. 10): "The people call the [local] official father-mother [*fumu*], and refer to themselves as the children-subjects [*zimin*]. What is meant is that [the magistrate] must be concerned about all that affects the happiness and suffering of the people, as he might his own family" (*Muling shu,* 1: 19a). Another contributor, Xie Jinluan, identified only as a holder of the *juren* degree and an expectant official of the Qianlong (1736–95) period, elaborated on the principle: "If [the magistrate] would just take the two words father-mother and lodge them firmly in himself, so that whatever he feels in his heart or thinks in his mind, or says with his mouth and does in his actions, are those of the father-mother, then in less than three years, the world would be an ideally governed one" (1: 51b–52a).

Proceeding from these principles, the *Compendium* and other handbooks concluded that the "hearing of plaints" (*tingsong*) was the most important of the magistrate's multiple responsibilities, since it brought him closer to the people than any other. As Wang Huizu put it, in his widely read *Views on Learning Governance* (*Xuezhi yishuo,*

1793: 12): "The key to governance is loving the people" and "loving the people has to do with the hearing of plaints." The obvious implication was that the handling of civil disputes, though ostensibly of only minor importance, was in fact the most important activity of a magistrate.

But Wang and most of the other handbook writers could not make such an observation because it would have run directly counter to another part of the official ideology, also traceable to *The Great Learning* (chap. 4): society was supposed to be so harmonious and moral that there ought to be few, and ideally no, civil lawsuits. To have declared that handling such disputes was the magistrate's most important responsibility would have legitimized their existence.

Instead, Confucian ideology dictated that officials maintain that no truly moral person would stoop to litigation. Huang Liuhong, for example, chose to comment on this observation of a late-seventeenth-century magistrate in his influential *Fuhui quanshu* (A complete book concerning happiness and benevolence, 1694):

There are three causes for litigation. One, there are obstinate individuals. . . . They like to be assertive and to win. On the slightest provocation, they think they show their ability by filing a lawsuit. They pride themselves on knowing their way around the yamen. It all stems from their perverse nature. Second, there are greedy types. They want to swindle people. . . . If they do not get their way, they will file complaints upon complaints. . . . Third, there are litigation sticks who instigate lawsuits. . . . They have the hearts of tigers and wolves. . . . They have no steady work, and concentrate on prompting common people to file lawsuits. (11: 15a-b)

Huang's comment:

The key to putting an end to litigation consists first in calming one's emotions [*pingqing*], and next in forbearance [*ren*]. . . . The other party is not necessarily entirely at fault, and I am not necessarily entirely in the right. Besides, [if] there is no deep enmity or accumulated animosity, what purpose does it serve to assert oneself and win? . . . If one calms one's emotions with such thoughts, then the anger will pass, and there can be no reason for litigation. As for forbearance, if the other person is being unreasonable, bystanders will have a just opinion about the matter, [so] what harm can there be to me? . . . With such thoughts, the impulse [to litigate] will disappear. There can be no reason for litigation. (11: 13b)

By this formulation, litigation resulted from contentious or immoral people; no morally superior person would deign to think of it. In fact, the very act of engaging in a lawsuit indicated some moral failure on one's part.

A century and a half later, Xu Tong chose a selection from the prominent Manchu official Yuqian (1793–1841) that made just this point:

Those who are good at educating their families emphasize humaneness, righteousness, propriety, wisdom, and sincerity. The person who likes to litigate is one who is mean-spirited, and is therefore not humane. He also lacks balance and reason, and is therefore not righteous. He is contentious out of anger, and is therefore not a person of propriety. He squanders his money and bankrupts himself, and is therefore not a person of wisdom. He engages in treachery, and is therefore not a person of sincerity. (*Muling shu*, 17: 46a-b)

These views were echoed to varying degrees in all of the magistrate handbooks of the Qing. It was simply part of the standard legal discourse in the late imperial era. The moralizing, we might say, was wielded as part of the "officialese" of the Qing ruling elite. It may be likened to references to Marxist-Leninist theory and Mao Zedong thought in revolutionary China before the 1980's reforms. Just as Marxist-Leninist ideologizing established one's credentials as a member of the ruling elite in Maoist China, so Confucian moralizing in the Qing identified one as a cultivated gentleman, a member of the gentry or would-be gentry status group.*

The Practical Reality

The magistrate handbooks do not stop with just the moralistic constructs outlined above. They go on to give concrete and specific instructions about the actual practice of magisterial service. There was, we might say, not only a moral culture surrounding the office of the magistrate but also a practical culture. Huang Liuhong, after the discussion on the need for calm quoted above, went on to observe: "However, calming one's emotions is the conduct of a moral gentleman [*junzi*], and making allowances for people also is not something that the common person can do." That being the case, the reality was that there was plenty of "trivial" litigation (Huang Liuhong 1694, 11: 14a).

Huang's view of that litigation and how it should be handled combined both moral and practical notions. First, he noted that it was

---

*The view of litigation as somehow immoral and contrary to Confucian values received institutionalized expression in the Qing courts' stipulation that gentry degree-holders not engage in litigation. The plaint forms used in eighteenth-century Baxian and nineteenth-century Baodi explicitly state that plaints from gentry members would not be accepted. They had to be represented by proxy.

precisely because most complaints arose from the anger of the moment that the court system provided for a cooling-off period. Limiting plaints on minor matters to certain days and months ensured that "by the time the plaints are accepted, the person is already calm, so that the mediators may resolve the dispute over a cup of wine or a pot of tea." Such an approach, according to him, reflected "the deep concern of the father-mother [official] for the people" (Huang Liuhong 1694, 11: 5b). Yet, as he went on to note, magistrates would still have to hear a certain number of plaints, for there were "people who file plaints because they feel they have no alternative [*bu deyi*]." And the magistrate, similarly, "accepts plaints because he has no alternative" [when the dispute cannot be mediated and the plaintiff had a legitimate complaint; ibid.]. Regardless of the representations about how there ought not to be any lawsuits over trivial matters, in other words, the practical reality was that they existed.

One of the contributors to the *Compendium*, Yuan Shouding, a jinshi of 1730, put this operative reality into quantitative terms: "Those who file plaints of course have good reasons for feeling they have no alternative but to do so, but still the lack of forbearance is a cause. With forbearance, of 10 possible complaints, seven or eight would be saved. That is why those who govern emphatically and repeatedly admonish the people to forbear anger and be conciliatory" (*Muling shu*, 18: 17b-18a). What Yuan leaves unstated, obviously, is that the court was still saddled with two or three plaints it could not ignore.

Wang Huizu, as we saw in the preceding chapter, noted from his own experience as magistrate in Ningyuan county, Hunan, in 1787 that on a typical (minor matter) day, "new plaints that should by law be accepted totaled no more than 10." Though his intention was to emphasize the low proportion of new lawsuits, even that number ensured that "trivial" cases made up a major portion of the magistrate's caseload.

Fang Dashi, a nineteenth-century official with extensive experience as a magistrate, put the matter succinctly and clearly in the handbook he composed, appropriately titled *Plain Words* (*Pingping yan*, 1878). Under the heading, "Do not neglect minor matters," he wrote:

Household, marriage, land, debt, and theft cases are minor matters from the perspective of the yamen. But from the perspective of the people, they concern immediate interests and are not at all trivial. Moreover, even if those are considered minor matters, within any one department or county, there will be few weighty cases and many minor ones. If [the magistrate] is conscientious only when it comes to major capital and robbery cases, how many of those can there be in one year? (Fang Dashi, 3: 32a)

But Fang did not go on to draw the obvious conclusion from his argument: if indeed the key to good governance was in being close and loving to the people, and if indeed the hearing of plaints brought the magistrate closer to the people than any other activity, and if indeed the majority of plaints heard by a magistrate concerned "minor" civil matters, then the handling of those cases, more than of major cases, was in fact the key to good local governance. The representation that lawsuits over trivial matters really should not exist at all kept most of the handbook writers from coming to this obvious conclusion. In fact, they generally did not pay all that much attention to the handling of "minor" matters.

The one exception was Wan Weihan, who worked for some 30 years as a legal secretary for magistrates in the middle of the eighteenth century. In his *Important Aspects of the Skills of Serving as a Private Secretary (Muxue juyao,* 1770), he closed the logical link that other writers had failed to close: "[The work of] commenting on and disposing of plaints [through formal court sessions], though it is [considered trivial and is] done on the magistrate's own authority, is actually the most important thing in terms of winning the hearts of the people" (*de minxin;* Wan Weihan 1770: 5b).

The Moralistic and Practical Culture of Magisterial Work

Together, the paradoxical combination of moralistic and practical views made up an outlook that might be termed the *practical moralism* of Qing magistrates. It was "moralism" because of the insistence on the primacy of high moral ideals, but it was also "practical" because of their very pragmatic approach to the real problems of governance. The two were kept together as a single package, despite the tensions between them.

One way the two were kept together was to keep from drawing the logical conclusions from either perspective, to the direct contradiction of the other. The authors of magistrate handbooks never took the position of philosophical pragmatism that everything was to be measured by its practical results. Nor did they take the position that moral principles must rule out practical departures from those principles. In the culture of the Confucian magistrate, moralistic outlooks and practical considerations were two coexisting realities. As

Confucians, Qing magistrates were moralists; as officials, they were also practical men of the world.

Informal Mediation

Wang Huizu's detailed instructions on magisterial service provides a good illustration of what this "practical moralism" meant in operation: "It was good," he thought,

for a magistrate to be diligent at hearing and adjudicating a case [*ting duan*]. But there are instances when he should not take to excess a black-and-white approach. The best way to restore harmonious relations is the mediation of relatives and friends. While adjudication is done by law [*fa*], mediation is done by human compassion [*qing*]. When it is a matter of law, then there has to be a clear-cut position for or against. If it is a matter of human compassion, then right and wrong can be compromised some. The one in the right [*lizhi zhe*] can accommodate the feelings of a relative or friend, while the one in the wrong [*yiqu zhe*] can avoid the law of the court. . . . That is why mediators were established in ancient times. (Wang Huizu 1793: 16)

This was the only real path to harmonious relations, as he saw it: "For a magistrate to arrogantly believe in his own judiciousness and refuse to allow the withdrawal and closing of a case [*xixiao*] is not really a good way to maintain peace among the people" because "if right and wrong are distinguished, then there is a winner and a loser, and one is punished. That leaves bad feelings from which disputes might arise in the future" (pp. 13, 16). Let us be clear on what Wang was saying here. He was not instructing magistrates to take on the task of mediation themselves, in the manner that past scholarship has argued. On the contrary. He was plainly speaking of an extra-judicial process carried on by kin and neighbors.

As the above passage shows, Wang strongly believed that magistrates ought to choose such a resolution over adjudication when they could. But if no out-of-court settlement could be worked out, and the case continued to a formal court session, then the magistrate must analyze things clearly (*mingbai pouxi*) so that right and wrong could be clearly adjudged (*shifei pan*) (Wang Huizu 1793: 13). To do that, Wang Huizu emphasized, every magistrate must first of all study the code. To be sure, he said, a magistrate could not hope to know the code as thoroughly as a legal secretary because he had to attend to so many other matters. But "if he does not understand well the statutes and substatutes on land-house, marriage, debt, theft, robbery, homicide, assault and battery, litigation, fraud, . . . then when he is faced with two litigating parties and cannot ask the advice of his legal secretary, he will be hesitant and unable to decide a case. The litigation instigators will take notice [of such weakness]. Whereas if he knows the code well, . . . then he can easily adjudicate on the spot, and instill fear and respect among the litigation instigators." For that reason, every magistrate, "whenever he has time after a day's work, should study carefully one or two statutes and substatutes. Within a few months, he will be familiar with the essentials. Those who do not so do are resting on their laziness and causing trouble for themselves" (Wang Huizu 1800: 6–7).

In other words, despite the ideal in the moral culture that the magistrate did not adjudicate, in the sense of deciding what the truth was and of judging right and wrong from the standpoint of the law, but merely facilitated the revelation of the truth by the perpetrator through confession, the practical culture of the office demanded that he study the code in order to adjudicate effectively. For, according to Wang Huizu, magistrates "who adjudged cases without confidence, and end a court session by ordering a repeat session, unavoidably caused the cluttering up of their work. The source of the problem is traceable to their lack of knowledge of the statutes and substatutes." These observations Wang appropriately titled: "[Magistrates] must study the statutes and substatutes" (Wang Huizu 1800: 6).

Although Qing magistrates generally did allow cases to be withdrawn and closed upon successful extrajudicial mediation (and the petition of the plaintiff), in the manner called for by Wang, other handbook writers strongly disagreed. Take, for example, this advice by the *Compendium* contributor Chen Qingmen, a jinshi of 1723:

In household, marriage, and land [cases], [the magistrate] should examine carefully the plaint for truth and falsehood, and not accept cases indiscriminately [*lan zhun*]. When he rejects a case, he should explain his reasons for rejecting the plaint. . . . Once he accepts a case, however, he should always conduct his own interrogation and not allow it to be settled by mediation. When interrogating, he must act quickly and not let things drag on and get delayed. Once he has completed his investigation, he must adjudicate to resolve the case [*duanjie*]. He must not be ambiguous and vague [*hanhu*]. (*Muling shu*, 18: 19b)

Liu Heng (1775–1841) echoed him a century later: "[The magistrate] should not accept plaints lightly. But if he does accept a plaint, then he should always bring it to trial [*shen*]. When he does that, he should always adjudicate [*duan*], and not allow a mediated settlement." The problem, as Liu saw it, was that if a magistrate accepted a petition to close a case because of a mediated settlement, then litigation mongers would know that they could file plaints without restraint on the assumption that, right up to a few moments before the court session, they could end the matter by "a single sheet of petition to allow a mediated settlement." In acceding to such requests, "the official has no way of knowing [whether he is being duped by] the evil tricks of a litigation monger, and the falsely accused has no way of ensuring that the truth be known and justice done" (*Muling shu*, 17: 37a–37b).

The obvious difference in emphasis between Wang Huizu and Liu Heng was noted by Fang Dashi, who quoted from each in turn and then commented himself: "From the point of view of preventing false accusations, Liu's is the correct position. From the point of view of maintaining harmonious relations among kin and neighbors, Wang's is the preferable position" (Fang Dashi 1878: 2: 31a-31b). In practice, as our case records show, Qing magistrates generally followed Wang's advice.

Regardless, one thing that Chen Qingmen, Liu Heng, Wang Huizu, and Fang Dashi were all agreed on was the need to adjudicate unequivocally by law when a suit was not resolved by informal mediation. None of them advocated that magistrates themselves take on a mediatory as opposed to an adjudicatory role. Their differences were over whether or not to allow the closing of a case by petition from informal mediators, not whether or not to adjudicate by law. The image their writings project of the magistrate presiding over a formal court session is indisputably that of an adjudicatory judge, not a compromise-working mediator engaged in "didactic conciliation."

As for the concrete meaning of adjudicating by law, Fang Dashi provided a clear and plain illustration in his recommendations on the handling of debt cases:

In debt cases, . . . if they are clearly supported by documents and contracts [*juan yue*], then the magistrate should of course act according to the code and enforce repayment. If he does not, then the rich dare not lend money, and in times of hunger, or the gap between the old harvest and the new one, the small people will be at a loss. As for enforcing payment, the code stipulates that private loans may not exceed a monthly interest of 3 percent and the total interest, no matter how long the time period, should not exceed the amount of the original principal. (Fang Dashi 1878, 3: 31a)

For Fang, there was no doubt about the magistrate's role as a judge adjudicating by the letter of the law.

Thus, although in the moral culture of the magistrate, lawsuits over trivial matters were not to exist at all, the practical culture of the office acknowledged the reality of such lawsuits and called for their unequivocal adjudication by law. The coupling of the two outlooks was predicated on the coexistence of formal and informal justice. It was a coupling that was consistent with the paradoxical combination within the code itself of moralistic statutes (*lü*) with highly practical substatutes (*li*).

Formal Adjudication

The handbooks contained specific instructions about how to adjudicate. Adjudicating by law, first of all, did not mean to adjudge harshly or to resort simply to punishment. According to Wang Huizu, courts should take care to temper their sentences with the kind of humane compassion (qing) that made for good relations among people (renqing). To make the point, he singled out the ruling of a certain Jiangsu magistrate surnamed Zhang who was known to be particularly strict. The offender was a youth (*tongzi*) who was caught trying to cheat on an examination by bringing in sample essays. The magistrate ordered, in accordance with the law, that he be cangued and placed on public exhibit. The young man's relatives beseeched the magistrate for leniency, pleading for a month's postponement because the youth was newly wed (just a day before the examination). But Magistrate Zhang refused. On learning of the decision, the bride committed suicide. Even though Zhang immediately released the youth, the damage was already done: the young man followed his bride in suicide by jumping into the river. Wang Huizu commented: "If the magistrate had allowed the postponement of the punishment, he would have been compassionate without going against the law. There was no reason not to do it" (Wang Huizu 1794: 6).

With disputes over minor matters, Wang Huizu stressed, the magistrate must rely not on force but on making the parties understand and agree with the court's judgment. By Wang's reasoning, if both parties understood what was right (*yili*),

there would be no reason for a lawsuit. The start of a lawsuit stems from one party's being blind to what is right and insisting on his view. That is why they must come for resolution to the official. If the official analyzes the dispute clearly and distinguishes between right and wrong, the litigants' emotions will calm. (Wang Huizu 1793: 12)

Wang then spelled out the thinking behind the standard requirement that litigants file pledges of willingness to accept the court's
judgment and close a case (*ganjie*). Even when punishment was
called for, he said, the magistrate could be more effective if he did not
use it but instead explained to the offender "why he should be flogged
[*ta*] but was not being flogged, so that he would understand and re-
gret his actions, and be fearful and grateful." Such an approach, he
believed, exemplified "the lodging of genuine love in the application of the law." Here Wang reconciled the representation of "minor"
offenses as punishable with the actual practice of not using punishment. For Wang, the exception to his general principle was an offender "who is truly evil and cruel, who uses his poverty to make
trouble for the rich . . . or uses his superior position to abuse the
inferior . . . so that they cause endless trouble for their [agnatic and
affinal] relatives [*zuyin*]. . . . When faced with such a person, [the
magistrate] must apply the law to its limit and punish him severely."
But even then, he must take care to "explain over and over again to
make the person understand why he is being flogged" (Wang Huizu
1793: 12–13).

We might observe here that, in attitude and approach, what Wang
advocated was entirely consistent with the moral ideal of the magistrate as the father-mother official toward his subjects. He would be
kindly and benevolent like the mother toward the good children-
subjects, the better to promote harmony and good relations among
them, but also strict and severe like the father faced with truly un-
ruly behavior, to make sure that no wayward child spoil the good
relations among the others.

Once again, such instructions for tempering law with compassion
should not be read as calling for magisterial mediation rather than
adjudication. The point was not to forgo clear-cut adjudication in favor of compromise-working, but rather to take human feeling and
relations into account when considering the use of punishment, and
to persuade litigants of the correctness of the court's opinion, *after*
having come to a clear-cut judgment (*duan* or *pan*) based in law.

In the legal discourse of the handbooks, the term qing had to do
not just with compassion but also with "facts" (as in shiqing or qingshi), as opposed to falsehood. Getting at the truth was the second
important principle in adjudicating. Yuan Shouding put it this
way: "When hearing a case, [the magistrate] must clear his mind, so
that it is a blank and without any preconceptions. . . . If he interro-

gates carefully and pays close attention to details, he will naturally come to see the [true] facts [*qing*]. But if he . . . harbors preconceptions about who is right and wrong, and allows first impressions to dominate his thinking, makes judgments hastily and is impressed with his own intelligence, then he is likely to err" (*Muling shu*, 17: 20a).

Wang Zhi, a jinshi of 1721 and himself a magistrate, likened such attention to empirical details to the techniques of writing, no doubt in order to communicate better with his colleagues of a scholarly bent: "Hearing a case is like writing. One must research and delve deeply into the subject. In going back and forth [between research and writing], one can come to new understanding. Only thus can one comprehend the facts of a subject, and only thus can one come to the heart of a matter. In hearing cases, I have been able to be patient and not fear painstaking work" (*Muling shu*, 18: 7a). Yuan and Wang, clearly, were not asking for a fuzzy-headed compromise-working approach aimed only at smoothing over differences. There can be no mistaking that the purpose of sorting out the real facts of a case was to determine the truth and decree what was right and wrong in the eyes of the law.

The compound "qingli," as we have seen, could likewise convey not just the moralistic meanings of tianli and renqing (the use to which the Qianlong emperor put it, for example, in his preface to the code of 1740), but the more mundane meaning of a common-sense consideration of the facts (the li now being used as in daoli). This is the sense in which Fang Dashi, for instance, used the term when he said that "matters generally contain their *qingli*." To illustrate what he meant, Fang cited the case of Gu Zhengli from his own service in Xiangyang. Gu charged that his father-in-law, Wei Daoheng, had borrowed 340,000 wen from a shop in Gu's name. After Wei died, the widow, to relieve Gu of the burden of the debt, pledged 60 mu of the family land to Gu as security. But the son, Wei Binggong, refused to acknowledge and repay the debt, and Gu had therefore brought suit. Fang analyzed the plaint from the standpoint of qingli: Binggong's father was a well-to-do man; the loan had allegedly been made 24 years earlier, when the plaintiff, Gu, was just fourteen years old. This was most unlikely, Fang reasoned: why would a well-to-do man borrow money in the name of his young son-in-law? Moreover, the document allegedly executed by the widow was not witnessed or guaranteed by any of the Wei relatives, only an outsider. That too was most unlikely, Fang figured: Wei's patrilineal kin certainly would have been involved in a transaction of such a scale. By Fang's account, the plaintiff, Gu, faced with Fang's compelling analysis, had no choice but to admit to bringing a false accusation (Fang Dashi 1878, 3: 22a).

From the point of view of these handbooks, it was crucial for the magistrate to demonstrate that he was in command of the law and the facts. As Huang Liuhong explained: "When two litigating parties are confronted with the magistrate, if the one at fault always loses [*wangzhe changfu*] and the one in the right is always upheld [*zhizhe changshen*], then unreasonable and untrue plaints [*wuqing zhi ci*] will not gallop about" (Huang Liuhong 1694, 11: 14a). Since "litigation instigators," "litigation mongers," and false accusers were responsible for the malfunctioning of the legal system, the way to check their abusive behavior was to ensure knowledgeable, clear-cut, and efficient adjudication.

Comments on Plaints

The handbooks would have the magistrates take essentially the same approach in commenting on plaints (*pici*). The magistrate must from the start be perfectly clear about the law, while considering matters from both the standpoint of moral principles–human compassion and the standpoint of common sense–facts. Then his comments would be on the mark. "If the comments are not on the mark," Wang Huizu observed, "then either the plaintiff will feel still more aggrieved or the defendant will feel still more emboldened," with the result that "the lawsuit might be aggravated rather than avoided" (Wang Huizu 1786b: 1). The purpose of these preliminary comments on plaints, as he makes clear, was not to dodge a court decision but to keep the matter from coming to court at all by encouraging outside mediation. "If the comments are on the mark, and take into account both *li* and *qing* [*zhuoli zhunqing*]," so that "the emotions of the weak will be calmed, and the temper of the strong checked, then the relatives and neighbors would be able to mediate." Such a resolution would "settle matters at the start of the plaint and maintain good relations among relatives." It would also be much better for the litigants if they could settle things early rather than "after the plaint has been accepted and after they have spent money in payments to the clerks' offices" (ibid.).

Wang Huizu, we may note, was talking in effect about what has been termed in this book that intermediate sphere of Qing justice where judicial officials and community mediators collaborated. As has been seen, magistrates' comments had considerable influence in the operation of that "third realm" system. Wang was reiterating the preference of Qing legal ideology for settling disputes through extrajudicial mediation if at all possible; court adjudication was to be only a final resort. In the eyes of Qing magistrates, encouraging compromise through community/kin-group mediation was not at all inconsistent with making an unequivocal adjudication in court.

Wang Youhuai, an eighteenth-century legal specialist "of the mid-Qianlong period," spelled out at some length the techniques for writing good comments in his handbook for legal secretaries, *Ban'an yaolue* (Important strategies for handling cases):

In commenting on plaints, [the legal secretary] needs to be able to surmise the feelings and facts of people [*renqing*] and the reason of things [*wuli*], to discern false pretenses, understand big principles [*ming dayi*], and be familiar with the code. The words should be simple but the meaning encompassing, and the text clear and fluid. Only then can the comments hit the mark and be appropriate for the particular case. (Wang Youhuai n.d.: 27b)

It was important to compose the plaints skillfully, Wang said, so that "the cunning rogues would have respect and the litigation instigators would not dare try their tricks." If the legal secretary was "undiscriminating in accepting and rejecting cases, and reversed himself right and left, then the aggrieved will not be able to obtain justice and the innocent will be falsely implicated." The consequence would be "the accumulation of more and more plaints day by day" (ibid.).

Wan Weihan explained things in the practical terms of the concern for a favorable review of one's performance:

Litigation instigators and crafty people are always testing the magistrate. If [the magistrate's comments and judgments] do not penetrate to the heart of the matter, then they will not submit willingly. That will mean appeals, and then small matters will become big matters, and the minor [*zili*, i.e., "self-managed"] cases will become major cases. Even if things do not reach the point of appeals, since [the plaints, comments, and judgments] are included in the case registers, they might well be questioned or rejected, leading to investigations. That is why the comments [*pici*] must be written by people qualified to handle . . . cases. (Wan Weihan 1770: 5b)

The magistrate, in other words, must act like a judicial expert even while encouraging extrajudicial mediation. That was consistent with the paradoxical combination of formal with informal justice in the justice system. It was also the surest way to minimize his caseload and ensure good evaluations for his job performance.

The Acceptance of Plaints

Upon the receipt of plaints about minor matters, the handbooks agreed, the magistrate "should not accept them lightly" (*bu qing zhun*). We have seen how Wang Huizu estimated that the majority of the 200-odd plaints and petitions he received on a minor-matter day were counterplaints and prompting petitions, and that the court generally accepted no more than 10 cases. Both Chen Qingmen and Liu Heng, as one might expect, given their view that a magistrate should see every suit through to unequivocal judgment, emphasized the need to be discriminating in accepting plaints. Rejecting a plaint, we might say, was the magistrate's first line of defense against the problem of an excessive caseload and unfavorable upper-level reviews.

Wang Huizu advocated that the magistrate comment on plaints in the "big hall" (*datang*) of the yamen in public sessions, rather than in the "inner yamen" (*neiya*) in closed sessions. Most magistrates, he knew, preferred to work in the more informal environment of the inner room where they could dress casually and get up and move about as they pleased. That choice over the alternative of dressing in formal garb and sitting stiffly throughout the proceedings was understandable. But the problem with working out of the inner yamen, it seemed to him, was that the magistrate's words were heard only by the litigants. In the big hall, on the other hand, he would have an audience of hundreds, and the effect of his judgment would resonate across all similar cases and would-be cases. That way, the skillful magistrate could use every comment and judgment as educational and warning devices against potential troublemakers (*Muling shu*, 1848, 17: 27a).

Liu Heng, too, favored the public forum. He also favored magistrates acting swiftly. A magistrate who waited three or five days before taking up a plaint, Liu counseled, would find himself inundated. New plaints would pile up on old plaints not yet acted on; and evildoers would find ways to abuse the system, even to try to purchase desired comments. Liu would instead have the magistrate receive personally a plaint in the big hall and interrogate the plaintiff immediately as needed. He would also have the magistrate post his comments immediately [*jixing bangshi*] for all to see.

But Fang Dashi, who quoted Liu Heng on this point (1878, 2: 30a), was troubled by this approach. The problem was that a less than expert and self-assured magistrate could find himself embarrassed in public. Like all other writers, he was convinced that abusers of the system were always on the lookout for weaknesses in the magistrate. A magistrate not thoroughly familiar with the code or discerning about truth and falsehood would accordingly find himself inundated with fabricated charges and false accusations. The problem was especially serious for a neophyte, not yet familiar with the law or seasoned in the ways of human nature. For this reason, Fang Dashi observed, only old hands could follow the kind of procedure advocated by Wang Huizu and Liu Heng. A man new to the bench, with no good grasp of the code or of the human condition, and unfamiliar with the local situation, would not be able to comment on the spur of the moment in the big hall. What he should do instead was to wait until the court was closed and then go over that day's plaints one by one with the legal secretary before trying to comment on them. Over time, he would become more expert and would then be able to act on his own (ibid.).

In fact, even as Fang Dashi wrote this, in the late nineteenth century, he was pointing to the typical practice (*tongli*) in local yamens (or at least the more heavily burdened ones): a plaint would go first to the legal secretary, who would draft a preliminary comment on the duplicate copy and pass it on to the magistrate for approval; the comment would then be copied onto the original form by the "brush clerk" (*mobi*); he in turn passed that form on to be transcribed onto a "plaint placard" (*zhuangbang*) for public view. Fang advocated modifying the procedure somewhat: he thought the posting process should be speeded up by directly transcribing the plaint and comment from the approved draft instead of waiting for the clerk to copy it onto the original form (Fang Dashi 1878, 2: 31b).

The posting of the magistrate's comments on a plaint, of course, initiated the second stage of a lawsuit, in which the voice of the court came to figure in the ongoing processes of informal mediation. That is what this book has characterized as the middle stage of a lawsuit, during which the formal and informal systems worked together.

That stage continued until just before the formal court session, the final stage of a case.

Abusers of the System

Most of the handbook writers addressed the problem of litigation abuse, and the more fully as mounting caseloads came to snarl up many local courts. Some saw a conspicuous difference in this respect between "the North" and "the South," similar to the differences I outlined in Chapter Six between Baodi and Danshui-Xinzhu. Wan Weihan put it this way: "The people of the northern provinces are simple and coarse. Even the devious among them can be easily seen through. The southern provinces have the largest number of crafty people. [There are lots of] untrue plaints that do not make sense [*wuqing zhi ci*], often entirely beyond belief. Only two or three of 10 narrate the facts in a straightforward manner" (Wan Weihan 1770: 3a). Wan's contemporary Yuan Shouding made a similar observation and attributed the difference to litigation instigators:

The South is litigious. Even the peripheral and mountainous counties always have litigation instigators. They concoct stories out of thin air, and there are so many plaintiffs. . . . The North is different. The plaints tend to be simple. The plaintiffs tend to tell the facts straight, in just a few lines. Even when they hide or dress something up, they quickly tell the truth. This is a difference between the cultures of the peoples of the North and South." (*Muling shu*, 1848, 17: 26b-27a)

Such a view is of course entirely consistent with the Qing code's ascribing all such evils to immoral litigation instigators/mongers; good people simply did not litigate.

The practical advice about how to handle litigation abuse is given within this discursive structure. Most have to do with methods for checking the problem and minimizing the number of lawsuits. As has been seen, the first line of defense was to not "accept plaints lightly." The magistrate would try to discern falsehoods and reject the untrue plaints. He would make judicious comments on the plaints, to deter potential abusers and in the hope that his comments would help facilitate successful informal mediation. If the disputes were not settled informally, then the magistrate must investigate the facts carefully and separate out truth from falsehood. He would then adjudicate clearly and unambiguously, by law, to show potential abusers the futility of attempting to deceive the court.

The handbooks would also have the magistrates check the original claims in a plaint by interrogating the plaintiff immediately on receipt of the form, the better to forestall the fabrications of abusers. Though the magistrate was to resort to punishment as little as possible in dealing with minor matters, he should deal harshly with these people once identified, in order to deter others. He should do this in the big hall in public to make examples of the offenders.

Although these writers placed the blame for the courts' difficulties for the most part on immoral people in the society at large, some traced the problem also to immoral yamen clerks and runners. Wang Huizu put it this way: "The litigation instigators and the clerks of the different offices of the yamen [*chaifang*] all want to see more lawsuits." Why? Because "the clerks like the troubles of the people, because that is how they profit" (Wang Huizu 1786a: 4–5). So far as he was concerned, "there [were] no upright people" (*duanren*) at all among the yamen runners; they were "like wolves and tigers when they [went] down to the countryside" (Wang Huizu 1793: 18). The clerks were hardly better. As the saying went, "Honest officials cannot escape the clasp of unscrupulous clerks." By contrast, the legal secretary on the magistrate's personal staff was interested in "harmony among the people, because that is how he can feel at ease, not burdened by cases." It was up to him and the magistrate to control abuse by the clerks and runners (Wang Huizu 1786a: 4–5).

Though Yuqian spoke of the clerks and runners more sympathetically than Wang, he still arrived at the same picture of them. He began by noting the sad fact that their pay was not even enough to provide subsistence for just one person, for these men had parents, wives, and children like everyone else. They too needed food and clothing. How could they be expected to serve with empty stomachs? For Yuqian, this line of sympathetic reasoning led to the conclusion: "How can it be demanded of them that they maintain their integrity under conditions of starvation?" (Quoted in Fuma 1993: 480, n. 6.) By Yuqian's reasoning, these functionaries could hardly help being corrupt.

Wu Guangyao, who served as Xiushan county magistrate in the late nineteenth and early twentieth centuries, similarly, offered sympathetic explanations only to arrive at the same conclusion. In the old days, he said, officials earned enough to cover their subsistence. But these days (his preface is dated 1903), the quotas for the numbers of clerks and runners did not begin to meet the real needs of the yamen, and they were paid only a nominal sum. Since in these circumstances, no man of good family was willing to serve in such a capacity, ne'er-do-wells among the poor had to be gathered to do the job. And since these men were not able to support themselves on their statutory pay, they had to resort to corrupt practices inside and outside the yamen to make a living (Wu Guangyao 1903: 1b–2a). Like Wang Huizu and Yuqian, Wu saw clerks and runners as bound to be corrupt.

This image had its roots, first of all, in the institutionalized opposition in interests between the magistrate and the yamen staff. As noted in the preceding chapter, as the gap between the statutory funding for and the actual needs of the yamen staff widened, fees charged on legal cases became the principal source of revenue for the yamen's operating expenses. That practical reality dictated an adversarial relationship between the magistrate and the clerks and runners. The magistrate's interest was in minimizing the number of lawsuits, because his performance rating depended on how well he kept his caseload down and how efficiently he disposed of his docket. But from the point of view of the clerks and runners, the more lawsuits, the higher their income. Given such a clash of interests, it is small wonder that the magistrates and legal secretaries should have been disposed toward a vilified image of clerks and runners.

In addition, official discourse characteristically employed a binary construct of the ideal of moral governance by superior men and its counter of immoral "yamen worms," similar to the pairing of nonlitigious moral gentlemen with "litigation instigators/mongers." There was little or no intermediate conceptual space between the two. In the discursive structure of the handbooks, there could be no decent extrastatutory clerks and runners, just as there could be no decent litigants.

However, practical instructions in the handbooks, though given within this discursive structure, reveal a different operational reality. They show that the yamen generally worked according to routinized rules and procedures. Scribes, for example, had to pass an examination to qualify for their jobs. Liu Heng made a point of urging new magistrates to observe the practice rigorously when they took up their posts. To keep out the unqualified and uncertified, Liu advocated issuing a seal to each properly qualified scribe, drawing up a list of those so certified, and posting the list outside the yamen for all to see. He would require a scribe to put his name and seal to each and every plaint. If, on interrogation, the magistrate should find discrepancies between the plaintiff's oral account and the written text of the plaint, he would be able to identify and punish the scribe responsible (*Muling shu*, 1848, 17: 34b–35a).

Fang Dashi, as we saw, described the standardized procedures in the late nineteenth century for recopying and transcribing the comments on a plaint. He wanted to speed up the process by going directly from the draft to the posting placard. According to him, the purpose of the modification was not simply to move things along; it was to prevent yamen clerks from leaking or selling information about the magistrate's reaction before the documents were posted (Fang Dashi 1878, 2: 31b).

Huang Liuhong, to give another example, told about the standard practice of rotating assignments of runners among different groups. He urged that the practice be carefully observed (Huang Liuhong 1694, 11: 11a). Although Huang did not spell out his reasons, if we consider things from the perspective of Bradly Reed's analysis (1993) of the complex contestations among different groups of runners for access to the income that legal cases provided, it becomes clear that the practice was intended to minimize conflict inside the yamen by equalizing the distribution of income.

Huang also urged that, in a minor case, if a plaintiff ran off when summoned (presumably because of the suspicion of possible fraud), the magistrate should promptly cancel the summons as he issued an order for the person's arrest. This seemed prudent to Huang because the clerk who held a still valid summons might use it to extort money from the defendants named in the complaint (Huang Liuhong 1694, 11: 13a).

Practical instructions like these tell us a good deal about the operational realities of local government. They are predicated on the expectation of routine procedures; they contain specific suggestions on how to improve upon those procedures in order to minimize abuse or corruption. They tell about the "paper-shuffling" side of yamen clerks as bureaucratic functionaries. They belie the caricatured image of those men as somehow bent on unbridled evil.

This is not the place, however, to try to provide a detailed account of the workings of the yamen. My purpose is only to show that the handbooks blamed evil yamen clerks and runners for the failures of local government in ways and for reasons similar to their blaming of evil litigation instigators/mongers for mounting caseloads. In that respect, they are similar to the moralistic representations we find in the Qing code. But they also contain practical advice that reveal much about the operational realities of local government. And in that also they are similar to the Qing code, with its practical substatutes.

"Minor" Versus "Civil" Matters

We saw earlier how the handbooks, while confirming the lack of any clear distinction between civil and criminal matters in theory, also indicate a distinct separation between the two in practice. Indeed, the evidence in them suggests that there was something of an institutionalized separation between the two. In Xinzhu county in the late Qing, for example, "all debt, land, marriage and such cases were sent to the tax secretary [*qiangu muyou*], while robbery and theft, assault and battery, and gambling were sent to be read by the legal secretary" [*xingming muyou; Xinzhu xianzhi,* 1957, 4: 307]. The corresponding bureaucratic division was generally between the Tax and Punishment offices of the yamen.*

The two-tracked practice dated back at least to the eighteenth century, as shown by the following passage from Wang Youhuai, the "mid-Qianlong-period legal expert":

Cases that fall into the overlapping area between punishment and tax [*xing qian jiaoshe shijian*] are often difficult to separate out, leading to disputes and competition [among the different yamen offices]. The way to separate them is to look at the intentions of the plaintiff. If the dispute concerns land and house, the repayment of debts, exchange, taxes, deeds, and so on, even if there are a couple of references to assault and battery but without injury, or to gambling but without proof, or to other illegal matters, and involve burial grounds, disputes over inheritance or succession, they should go to the Tax Office. If the plaints are about assault and battery, fraud, burial grounds, inheritance, marriage and all other major matters related to crucial moral obligations [*gangchang*] and [Confucian] teachings [*mingjiao*], even if they contain references to debts and land and house, they should go to the Punishment Office. (Wang Youhuai n.d.: 29a)

What Wang Youhuai was trying to do here was to suggest conceptual criteria for practices already in place.

To begin with, one had to determine whether the case involved a

---

* In Baxian in the late Qing, as Reed 1993 shows, there was a three-way division: marriage and family cases went to the Rites Office (Li fang), debt and property cases to the Tax Office (Hu fang), and criminal cases to the Punishment Office (Xing fang).

minor matter. In Wang's view, even if there were passing references to some major violation like assault or gambling, if there was no injury or no proof, and the nub of the plaint had to do with property or debt, then the case should go to the Tax Office. Here he was coming close to the suggestion that minor offenses would not be punishable.

The problem is that so far as the Qing code was concerned, there was no such qualitative distinction between minor and major offenses. Both were punishable; the difference between them was only a matter of degree of punishment. Thus, unpaid debts and the improper occupation of another's land and house were punishable by graduated degrees of caning depending on the amounts involved. Wang therefore could not come to an explicit formulation that would distinguish minor from major offenses in terms of whether they were punishable or not. Such an idea would have run directly counter to the conceptual foundations of the Qing code.

The other criterion Wang suggested was determining whether the case involved crucial moral principles. If not, it should go to the tax secretary and the Tax Office. If so, it should go to the legal secretary and the Punishment Office. Here the difficulty is what to do with marriage and inheritance cases. By the Qing code, minor matters included "household, marriage, and land [and debt]" (*hu, hun, tiantu xishi*) cases. If that was to be the distinction, then marriage and inheritance cases should go to the Tax Office. By the criterion Wang suggested, however, they involved moral principles and should go to the Punishment Office. The confusion was not resolved by Wang; he placed inheritance cases under both offices, without attempting to specify which types should go to which.

It remained for the Republican code, using imported concepts and language, to do away with the minor/major distinction and introduce instead the civil/criminal distinction. The former encompassed "people's matters" that were not of direct concern to the state and hence generally not punishable in theory or in fact; the latter encompassed "punishable matters" of direct concern to the state. That distinction was what finally took civil relations out of the conceptual frame of offenses against the social and moral order distinguished from major offenses only by degree of punishment.

Wang Youhuai's efforts are much of a piece with Wang Youfu's attempt in the early nineteenth century (discussed in Chap. 6) to distinguish between benign "litigation masters" and the evil "litigation sticks" of official Qing legal discourse, a distinction that hovered on the edges of the modern conception of private lawyers. But constrained by the structure of Qing legal discourse, Wang Youfu could not think in terms of legitimate private specialists serving the legitimate interests of private clients, for that would have gone against the fundamental precept in the official representation of Qing law that litigation constituted a breakdown in the familial social and moral order. In the end, Wang Youfu's benign litigation master remained the exceptional "songshi" of the Qing code: someone who helped to right a grievous wrong within the existing system. Wang could not go on to question the conceptual foundations of the entire legal system by suggesting the autonomy of law and the legitimacy of private legal service.

The passage from Wang Youhuai cited above, then, is chiefly important for demonstrating the institutional separations in practice between minor and major cases. That laid the practical, if not the conceptual, basis for the later Republican separation between civil and criminal cases. When we look across the Qing and Republican periods, the paradox was the coupling of striking changes in representational construction with basic continuities in legal practice. That, however, is the story of my sequel volume on justice in the Republican period. The story of this volume is the paradoxical disjunction in the Qing legal system between a representation that allowed for no concept of civil law but a legal practice that routinely handled civil disputes, and between a representation that allowed for no concept of property or contractual rights independent of the patriarchal authority of the state but a practice that routinely protected such "rights." The Qing legal system, we might say, embodied the practical reality of civil law and property rights without their representational realities.

In sum, magistrate handbooks when read with an eye to distinguishing between representation and practice put the finishing touches on the central arguments of this book. Though the moral ideal espoused was that minor cases did not exist, the practical instructions suggested how they should be handled; though magistrates ideally did not adjudicate, the practical instructions detailed how they should study the code and adjudicate accordingly; though the system was ostensibly strictly penal in its approach, the practical instructions took for granted that punishment would seldom be used in civil cases; though justice was ostensibly governed by morality more than by law, the practical instructions drew clear distinctions between informal justice based on compromise and formal justice based on law; though adjudication was in theory governed at once by moral principles, human compassion, and law, the practical instructions were unequivocal about the primacy of law; though the "qing" of renqing was represented in its moralistic guise, the practical instructions called for an operative interpretation closer to "facts" (qingshi); though the law was conceived as making no distinction between the civil and criminal, the practical instructions separated the two quite clearly; and, finally, though there was no conception of property rights in theory, the practical instructions called for consistent adjudication to protect and uphold them.

The handbooks, moreover, took for granted the interaction between informal and formal justice, in what I have termed the intermediate sphere or third realm of Qing justice. The authors advocated the deliberate use of preliminary comments on plaints and petitions to encourage the workings of informal justice and gave priority to informal justice over formal. However, if matters had to go to a formal court session, then the magistrate's task was to adjudicate unequivocally on the basis of the law and of true facts.

These handbooks, finally, evidence the same kind of discursive structure observed in the preceding chapter about the Qing code. Moralistic ideals were accompanied by equally moralistic counter-ideals. Local governments were portrayed as either exemplary of the benevolent government of moral men or as the corrupted operations of immoral clerks and runners, just as society was seen as comprising either morally superior gentlemen who would not stoop to litigation or immoral litigation instigators/mongers who did. In that binary structure, there could be no acknowledgment of decent functionaries who were neither morally superior nor rapacious, just as there could be no acknowledgment of decent people who were neither so moral as to be above litigation nor so immoral as to be abusive litigators.

Nevertheless, the handbooks tell of a different operational reality. Though they depict clerks and runners as immoral evildoers, checked only by the moral rectitude of magistrates and their legal secretaries, the practical instructions talk about them as paper-shuffling functionaries who could be made to conform with routine procedures.

The handbooks show, then, that magistrates operated by both a moral culture and a practical culture, in a paradoxical combination that I have called practical moralism. And they demonstrate that the justice system was a paradoxical and multilayered one, comprising a formal system based on law, an informal one based on compromise, and the intermediate third space between them. The handbooks, in short, confirm the major arguments made in the preceding chapters.

CHAPTER NINE

Max Weber and the Qing Legal and Political Systems

H OW THEN ARE WE TO understand the nature of the Qing legal system? And how are we to characterize it in terms of contemporary Western scholarly discourse? This chapter uses the still influential ideas of Max Weber as the springboard for some theoretical suggestions about the Qing and some comparative observations about late imperial China and the West.

The Legal System

Weber developed a typology of legal systems to serve as a clarifying and comparative device. In particular, he dichotomized formalism and rationality on the one hand and instrumentalism and irrationality on the other. In the first, law comes to be highly formalistic, in the sense of being derived by logical reasoning from abstract legal propositions (to be distinguished from my usage of the term formal to mean simply official), hence the equating of formalism with rationalism. In such a system, law comes to take on an autonomy of its own, standing above the will of the ruler and the caprices of chance and circumstance. It gives rise also to formalist proceduralism, in which "truth" itself comes to be defined as that which can be established within the procedural parameters set by the court. That operative legal truth comes to be the only truth recognized by the court. Herein for Max Weber lies the essential character of modern Western law. And herein of course lie also the roots of modern liberal law, of the assertion of the rights of individuals against arbitrary interference by the state.

The polar opposite of such formalism-rationalism-liberalism in law is what Weber termed variously substantive or instrumental law—law that derives not from logical reasoning based on consistent abstract legal propositions, but from the whims of the ruler. Such law is at best Solomonic, at worst arbitrary. Weber, in fact, tended to equate it with "irrationality." He called it, among other things, kadi justice (e.g., Weber 1968, 3: 976–78; 2: 644–46, 812–14, 844–48).

It should be clear from the preceding chapters that neither of Weber's ideal-types fits the Qing legal system. It was surely not formalist and rational in Weber's sense of those words. But it was just as surely not kadi justice. As I hope I have shown, it was not arbitrary, or inconsistent, or irrational.

Weber himself actually moved beyond these simple dichotomies with a tentative formulation that he termed "substantive rationality" (Weber 1968, 2: 656–58; see also 868–70). Though he did not elaborate on the concept at any length, he left some hints about its possible content. Since he had equated formalism with rationalism, and substantive justice with irrationality, the term substantive rationality suggests immediately a paradoxical coupling of his two varieties of justice. Anglo-American common law, he pointed out, with its reliance on a jury system of laymen, as opposed to continental (European) law's reliance on professional judges alone, contains strongly substantive characteristics. By implication, Weber would have viewed Anglo-American common law as combining formalist and substantive characteristics. He stopped well short, however, of explicitly stating that his "substantive rationality" might be understood as a paradoxical formulation.

At the same time, Weber hinted at a breaking up of his own ideal-typical concept of "rationality." His equation of modern Western law with rationalism unavoidably suggests a teleological and Western-centric scheme, in which the modern West's becomes the only possible "rational" law. As if to qualify that kind of unilinear teleology, Weber suggested that modern socialist states might have developed "substantive natural law," with an emphasis on workers' rights to the fruits of their labor, in contrast to the "formal natural law" of bourgeois states, with its emphasis on the bourgeoisie's right to individual property (Weber 1968, 2: 868–71). In this, he came close to suggesting a major reconceptualization of his own binary typology, holding out the possibility of multiple varieties of rationalities and multiple directions for the development of law in the modern age.

I believe "substantive rationality" can be a useful category for conceptualizing the Chinese legal system, if we think of it as a paradoxical formulation and if we allow for multiple varieties of rationality. "Substantive" has the virtue of conveying, first of all, the role that the will of the ruler played in the legal system. It is manifested in the official Chinese system in the representational insistence that the emperor was the sole legitimate source of authority for all laws. Thus, the Yongzheng emperor claimed in the preface to the code of 1725 to have "personally read and reflected on every word and sentence," and the Qianlong emperor similarly wrote in the preface to the code of 1740 of having personally relied on "estimations of heavenly principles and considerations of human compassion" (cited in Zheng Qin 1993: 41, 56).

But it does not follow that Chinese justice was in consequence simply unpredictable and arbitrary. Qing law never claimed that the ruler should be completely free to act on his own whim, in the manner of Weber's kadi justice. Instead, the ruler's will, as expressed in stipulations in the code, was meant to embody universal and unchanging moral principles that would serve as consistent guides to legal practice. Accumulated over time, those alone served as powerful checks on the scope for arbitrary actions by any individual emperor. The only change of statutes in the entire Qing period came in 1725, when the original code's 459 statutes were reduced to 436; they remained untouched thereafter (Zheng Qin 1993: 41). Indeed, individual emperors were specifically enjoined from making "special edicts" aimed at particular crimes or "ad hoc administrative rulings" into statutes; statutes had to be of general applicability and valid for all times (ibid., p. 62). The theoretical absolutism of imperial power did not mean unchecked arbitrary power in practice.

This brings us to the second important characteristic that the term substantive can convey: the notion that law should be guided by moral principles. The emperor's will was supposed to embody such principles, which was why the Qianlong emperor wrote of having based himself "solely on the most just [of principles]" and having "aimed to attain the most [morally] correct" (cited in Zheng Qin 1993: 56). State laws, we have seen, were meant to work in conjunction with qingli, or moral and humane considerations.

In addition, "substantive" conveys the emphasis in the Qing judicial process on the real truth, as opposed to settling for its approximation in the courtroom under formalistic procedures. Conceptually, Qing law did not concede the existence of any higher truth that could not be discerned by the ruler/judge, and hence never conceptualized the idea of settling for its approximation or substitution in a courtroom truth. By extension, it never developed the elaborate rules of evidence that characterize the formalist proceduralism of modern Western law. Hearsay and facial expressions, for example, were considered perfectly acceptable evidence on which a magistrate might base his judgment.

Such a system should not be seen as simply irrational in all the meanings Weber associated with that word. To be sure, Weber intended a very specific meaning for his term formal rationality: it was meant to convey a legal system guided by the requirement that "every concrete legal decision be the 'application' of an abstract legal proposition to a concrete 'fact situation'" (Weber 1968, 2: 867). Nevertheless, he also associated more general characteristics like consistency and predictability with "formal rationality," as opposed to arbitrary and unpredictable kadi justice. As Zheng Qin clearly demonstrates, Qing law in fact searched for rationality in the sense of consistency and universality. The statutes of the code were meant to be immutable, "not to be changed in ten thousand generations" (*wanshi buyi*). The state adapted to social change mainly by adding substatutes, which grew from 449 in the Shunzhi reign (1644–61) at the start of the Qing to 1,892 by the Tongzhi reign (1862–74; Zheng Qin 1993: 71).

Qing law was intended to be rational also in the sense of practical or instrumental rationality. As we have seen, imperial law did not consist merely of high-flown moralizing and ideologizing (as embodied on the whole in the code's unchanging statutes), but was also intended to provide practical and consistent guides for the resolution of real problems and disputes. The preceding chapters have examined a large number of those practical civil stipulations in the code.

Weber's "formal rationality," then, needs to be taken apart to separate out its associated meanings from its core meaning. Qing law was clearly rational in the sense of being consistent and predictable, though not in the sense of being formalist. It was also rational in the sense of being practical. And contemporary Chinese law, we might further point out along the lines Weber hinted at, can be seen as rational in its substantive emphasis on workers' rights to the fruits of their labor, as opposed to the formalist and bourgeois emphasis on the absolute rights of individual property.

To the extent that "rationality" is understood only in the narrow meaning of law based on formalist logic, however, the term substantive rationality does convey a particular tension that Weber intended to posit between "substantive" and "formalist" justice. The theory of the absolute power of the ruler (or of the contemporary Chinese Communist Party) left little room for a theory of the supremacy of abstract propositions and of logical reasoning following from them. By extension, it left little room for the development of a theory of law as autonomous and independent of the will of the ruler. It also left little room for the kind of formalist proceduralism that has come to govern modern Western law, in which the truth established in the courtroom rather than the substantive truth discerned by the ruler/judge is seen as the only acceptable basis for adjudication.

"Substantive rationality," then, can be used to capture the substantive and rational dimensions of Chinese justice, while also conveying the tensions between "substantive justice" and "formal rationality" that Weber intended to spotlight. Like Weber, we do not need to be forced into the oversimplified dichotomy between ideal-typical kadi justice and rational justice when thinking about a real-life legal system. We can retain the insight of his theoretical typology without doing violence to the reality of imperial Chinese law.

The insistence on maintaining the twin paradoxical dimensions of substantivism and rationality, of course, produced the consequence of a law of much lesser "infrastructural reach" than modern law.* Weber himself did not explicitly link substantive law to his political ideal-type of "patrimonialism"—in which the ruler enjoys absolute power predicated on inherited and personal ownership of the domain—but to the extent that we equate substantive law with the concerns of patrimonial rule, we might call on some of the characteristics that Weber attributed to that ideal-type. The greatest challenges to patrimonial rule, Weber suggested, would be two: the parcelization of patrimonial authority, as in decentralized local satrapies or feudalism; and bureaucratic routinization, as in modern government. To cope with the one, patrimonial rule typically sharply restricts the elaboration of the state apparatus, the better to control through personal dependency. To cope with the other, it typically re-

*I am indebted here to Michael Mann's (1984, 1986) distinction between the "despotic power" and the "infrastructural power" of the state, although I am intentionally using the term infrastructural reach in a more limited sense than Mann intends by his term infrastructural power. I mean here simply the degree of the state's reach into society.

stricts the full elaboration of bureaucratic routinization, the better to protect against a direct challenge to the power of the ruler (Weber 1968, 3: 1047–1051).

Applied to law, we might think of "substantive rationality" as carrying similar dictates. To retain the discretionary latitude of administrative authority, legal stipulations are intentionally kept general and relatively sparse, lest their specificity constrain the ruler's authority. Hence the reliance on judgments by analogy and the resistance to the kind of fuller elaboration that has occurred with modern civil codes. At the same time, to maintain the patrimonial ruler's personalized control over the state apparatus, the infrastructural reach of the bureaucratic system is intentionally kept thin and sparse, lest its elaboration outrun the ruler's ability to control through the personal dependency of his officials. Hence the reliance on nonofficial justice and the decision to leave "minor matters" to society as much as possible. While formalist justice, à la Weber, carries powerful imperatives for elaboration and infrastructural expansion, and consequent specialization and professionalization, justice of the substantive rationality variety, we might say, comes with the logic for limited infrastructural reach. It results in the paradoxical coupling of official justice with informal justice, as under the Qing.

We must not imagine a simple relationship of domination/subordination between formal and informal justice. By its own ideology, the official system of the Qing was to defer to the nonofficial on "minor matters." Government was to be kept sparse and thin, not intrusive and all-pervasive. Wherever possible, minor civil disputes were to be resolved by the informal justice of society itself rather than by the formal legal system. That was especially true of family and descent-group disputes. Such an ideological construct resulted in a relationship between the formal and informal justice systems that was more equal than the presumption of a state-dominated society would suggest. It contained, as I indicated in Chapter Four, a negotiatory dimension as well.

Yet informal justice should not be seen as somehow autonomous and independent of the formal system. Informal justice in the Qing afforded litigants a relatively wide scope of choice not because civil society had wrested concessions from the state but because the state wished to keep from overburdening its legal system with trivial matters. There was never any question that the formal system, or the administrative will of the officials, could and would prevail over the informal if and when it chose to. That informal justice was largely left to its own should not be mistaken for a system of political rights under liberal-democratic rule.*

The Qing's paradoxical combinations of substantivism with rationality, and official with nonofficial justice, then, can be thought of as elaborations of Weber's provocative but undeveloped concept of "substantive rationality." I believe such a formulation provides a much better characterization of Chinese justice than either of Weber's simple ideal-types. It frees us from the Eurocentric and teleological implications of the simple dichotomy between the rational justice of the modern West and the kadi justice of much of the non-Western world. It breaks out of the discursive trap of arguing for one or the other side of a binary formulation, of looking to the early-modern and modern West as *the* master narrative against which all modernization or development must be measured. But it still allows for useful comparisons between China and the West.

The Political System

The nature of the Qing legal system, of course, tells us a good deal about the nature of the political system as a whole. Like tax payments, lawsuits brought the populace into direct contact with the state apparatus; unlike taxes, however, lawsuits entailed contacts not only on the level of practice but also on the level of representation. And they involved of necessity both the structure of the system and the agency/choices of individual litigants and magistrates. The workings of the legal system seen through case records are in fact arguably the most telling prism through which to view the political system.

Here again Max Weber's ideal-types, closely connected to his typology of legal systems, is a useful starting point for discussion. On one pole of his dichotomous typology were patrimonialism and feudalism; on the other pole was rational modern bureaucracy.[†]

In the patrimonial state, government is patterned on the relationship between a patriarch and his household servants. The officials are personally dependent on and loyal to the emperor. Their offices are given to them by the emperor much like personal property; there is

---

* For a fuller discussion of these issues, and those raised by the application of Jürgen Habermas's notion of "public sphere" to the Qing, see P. Huang 1993a.
† The following discussion is based on Weber 1968, 3: 1006–1097.

no separation between office and person. Such rule does not lead to formalization, specialization, and professionalization of the sort that characterizes modern, "rational" bureaucracy.

The biggest threat to the patrimonial state is decentralization or feudalization. Relationships of personal dependency centering around the ruler can easily break up and lead to parcelization. Hence, as noted above, the patrimonial state does what it can to keep the state apparatus to a minimum, to avoid too many layers of personal dependency. The government apparatus tends to remain sparse and shallow, again in contrast to the modern bureaucratic state. Feudalism, by contrast, is a kind of parcelized patrimonialism. The reach of the state under feudalism is deeper than under centralized patrimonialism, precisely because it is more decentralized. The feudal lord's reach vis-à-vis the peasant is greater than the patrimonial emperor's because of his proximity; he is not separated from the peasant by multiple layers of personal dependency relationships.

Juxtaposed against both patrimonialism and feudalism is modern bureaucracy. It is formalized rather than personalized, specialized and professionalized rather than generalized. It is based on a separation of the officeholder from the office, rather than on an entwining of the two. Bureaucrats are salaried, rather than depending on a benefice (fee for service) or a prebend (ownership of an income-yielding office), as under patrimonial rule. Everything is regularized and predictable and consistent, rather than arbitrary and subject to the whim of the patrimonial ruler. That was what Weber meant by rationalization.

As with his speculations on Chinese law, Weber did not remain bound to his simplified ideal-types when it came to the empirical reality of the Chinese state. Instead of reducing the Chinese state to a single type, he worked with a preliminary paradoxical formulation in the concept of "patrimonial bureaucracy" (Weber 1968, 3: 1047–1051). Patrimonialism, he recognized, had only limited survivability, ever subject to the threat of parcelization. What would ensure its survival was bureaucracy, the development of standardized rule with legitimacy, independent of personal loyalty to the ruler. Though he did not develop the idea at any length, it seems to me that here, as with the notion of "substantive rationality," Max Weber suggested a direction of thinking that goes beyond his own typology.

As with the legal system, I would argue here for a conception of the Chinese state that would identify the paradoxical combination of patrimonialism with bureaucracy as *the* defining characteristic of the state system. No emperor could see to the long-term survival of simple patrimonial rule without routinized bureaucracy, yet all feared the threat to their powers that routinized bureaucracy could pose. What China's dynastic rulers opted for was a combination. Patrimonial power would be built into the system—the emperor would remain in theory the ultimate source of all laws and appointments.* That way bureaucratization could be checked before it threatened to evolve into the kind of formalized and semiautonomous power that characterizes modern bureaucracies. At the same time, however, imperial Chinese rule obviously went a long way in developing a bureaucracy with Weberian characteristics. It was no accident that the Qing code gave much of its attention to laws and regulations on administration. It was also no accident that China was the first state to develop a civil service examination system, long before the rise of modern bureaucracy in the West.

It was neither simply patrimonialism nor bureaucracy but the paradoxical coupling of the two that defined the essential characteristics of the late imperial state.† Indeed, the Confucian political ideal of the benevolent rule of moral men may be seen as the ideology of patrimonialism. It came complete with an explicit analogy between the polity and the family and between the ruler and the patriarch. Legitimacy was established by the claim to moral superiority. Legalism and the "rule of law," on the other hand, may be seen as the ideology of bureaucracy, with its emphasis on routinized administration and regulations. The imperial state, of course, was neither simply Confucian nor simply Legalist, based neither simply on the rule of men nor on the rule of law. The very suppleness and longevity of the Chinese imperial state were the consequence of the coupling of the two.

Some of the distinctive and perplexing characteristics of Qing lo-

---

*Even the constraint against an individual emperor's use of "special edicts" of limited applicability as the basis for legal statutes was qualified by preserving at the same time his authority to issue special edicts that might go outside of or contravene existing laws (Zheng Qin 1993: 62).

†Although Philip Kuhn (1990: 188–89) explicitly distances himself from Weber (and aligns himself more closely with Hans Rosenberg's distinction between the "dynastic absolutism" of the pre-Napoleonic Prussian state and the "bureaucratic absolutism" of the post-Napoleonic Prussian state), his concept of "bureaucratic monarchy" bears substantial resemblance to Weber's "patrimonial bureaucracy." Kuhn, however, stops well short of the explicitly paradoxical formulation that I have proposed here. His emphasis is instead on the opposition between monarchy and bureaucracy: how the Qianlong emperor might have exploited the sorcery scare of 1763 as a way to whip his bureaucracy into shape (see especially his chap. 9). My emphasis here is on their systemic interdependence.

cal government may be seen as products of patrimonial bureaucracy. Patrimonial ideology led directly to the conception of the local magistrate as the "father-mother official," whose power was intended to be total, like the emperor's at the center. Legitimacy for such patrimonial rule was predicated on the magistrate's moral superiority, the cornerstone of the Confucian ideology of moral governance by the rule of men. In addition, the imperatives of patrimonialism for low infrastructural reach were manifested in the representation that the local yamen contained few if any staff; if yamen clerks and runners must exist, they would be kept to an absolute minimum and on nominal pay.

On the other hand, the fact of bureaucratic government meant that the magistrate was the low man on the totem pole of an apparatus that emphasized regulations and routine procedures. He was a functionary in an elaborate bureaucratic system, who was kept in close check by a meticulous review system, and who had little choice but to operate according to standard rules. The burdens of his office, moreover, dictated that his yamen develop a highly elaborate administrative apparatus to cope with the complex day-to-day tasks of local government. He was the head of a local government that required a bureaucracy to do its work.

One wonders whether magistrates themselves ever fastened on the curious nature of their office. Of an office in which the theoretical absolutism of magisterial power was checked in practice by bureaucratic regulations and procedures. Of an office in which the moralistic rule of the magistrate was accompanied by the bureaucratic rule of law. Of an office in which government by the example of the magistrate's person was implemented, perhaps even checked and balanced, by the bureaucratic apparatus of the yamen clerks and runners. Even the disjunctions between representation and practice were part of the very structure of the office; moralistic representations were meant to be accompanied by practical adaptations. The system was built on the mutual dependencies of paradoxical dimensions.

It was a system that also built *in* certain inevitable tensions, in particular between the transient magistrates and their personal staffs and the entrenched clerks and runners of their yamens. Magistrates were evaluated for their ability to minimize lawsuits; clerks-runners, on the other hand, depended on those lawsuits for their income.

The relationship was hardly improved by an official discourse that paired the moral magistrate with the evil yamen clerk-runners, just as the moral gentleman who was above lawsuits was paired with the evil litigation instigator/monger who abused the legal system. The result was the otherwise perplexing phenomenon in which magistrates habitually vilified the yamen clerk-runners as rapacious "worms" even while relying on them for the routine operations of bureaucratic government. No matter the actual bureaucratic nature of local government, magistrates portrayed themselves as moral gentlemen who had to battle constantly the moral depravity of the staff on which they relied for day-to-day operations. That was their way of espousing the patrimonial ideology of moral governance even while behaving like a bureaucrat.

The nature of local justice followed closely that of local government. The patrimonial ideology of moral governance, with the familial simile for magistrate rule, led to the denial of the legitimacy of civil lawsuits; it made no sense to speak of children under parental authority going to court. The actual imperatives of bureaucratic administration, however, led to the constant and heavy involvement of the magistrates in these so-called minor matters. While portraying themselves as disdainful of trivial lawsuits, the magistrates habitually spent much of their time with them. This paradoxical phenomenon can also be readily explained by the interdependencies and tensions between patrimonial and bureaucratic rule.

The same is true of what magistrates said and did about their handling of civil cases. By the patrimonial ideology of moral governance, it made no sense to speak of parents relying on a law code to deal with the squabbles of their children. The magistrate's power, like the emperor's and the family head's, was supposedly absolute, checked only by his personal moral predilections. He ostensibly adjudged civil disputes without reference to laws. On the other hand, as the basic-level official in a complex and routinized bureaucracy, the magistrate of necessity operated according to prescribed rules and regulations. As might be expected of any bureaucratic functionary, he adjudged cases according to written laws and regulations.

The same is true, finally, of the paradoxical coexistence of informal and formal justice. Patrimonial rule dictated that bureaucracy be kept to a minimum, lest it outrun controls based on personal dependency; hence the reliance on informal justice. Bureaucracy, on the other hand, demanded codification and regularization; hence the development of the formal legal system. The collaboration and ten-

sions between informal and formal justice were direct manifesta-
tions of the collaboration and tensions between patrimonial rule and
bureaucratic rule.

The Qing legal system of substantive rationality, in other words,
was intimately related to its political system of patrimonial bureaucracy. The workings of the legal system not only document and illustrate well the nature of the political system; they may be seen also as
the consequences of the political system. Substantive rationality in
the legal system, we might even say, is explained by patrimonial bureaucracy in the political system.

"Domination" and "Rights"

As students of Weber will have noted, my discussion of "substantive rationality" and "patrimonial bureaucracy," even as it builds on
Weber's insights, departs from his central concern—the relations
and modes of domination. Patrimonialism and feudalism were for
Weber ideal-types of the principal varieties of traditional domination,
and rational bureaucratic rule the distinguishing characteristic of
modern domination. He was interested only secondarily, and even
then just implicitly, in the empowerment of modern citizens through
legal rights. Indeed, he viewed even rational formalist law mainly
from the point of view of "legal domination" under modern bureaucratic rule. To be consistent with his concerns, the imperial Chinese
legal system must be seen first and foremost as an instrument of
domination.

That is precisely the analytical perspective, as well as the principal contribution, of most of the past scholarship in our field. Ch'ü
T'ung-tsu (1962) and Bodde-Morris (1967), in particular, made crystal
clear how imperial Chinese law extended the hierarchical relations
of the patriarchal family to the polity and society as a whole by
analogizing the power relations of ruler/subject and superior/inferior
to those of parents/children and husband/wife. They showed how
law reinforced the relations of domination in society at the same
time that it applied their principles to the political domination of
society by the state. That story is a familiar and well-known one in
our field, and it formed the starting point for this book.

The Qing code, I have suggested along those same lines, should
be seen as a multilayered text whose most prominent and exterior
layers were made up of Legalist and Confucian ideologies of political

and social domination. Beyond that, I have showed how the informal justice system, though it worked well to resolve civil disputes among relative equals, could do little to redress gross imbalances in power. A daughter-in-law, for example, could not turn to either the informal or the formal system to redress maltreatment at the hands of her husband's family without the backing of her natal parents to equalize the imbalance in status/power between her and her in-laws. Tensions between the meek/poor people and the powerful/rich were largely contained by relations of domination-subordination, preventing them from erupting into open disputes, much less becoming lawsuits. Cases pitting an inferior against a superior rarely appeared in the formal courts. These points should be seen as elaborations of the Weberian theme of domination.

The case records examined in this book, however, drew my main attention to the neglected story of "rights" or "empowerment" by law even more than to domination—to the power of the common people to assert legitimate claims even more than to the power that the ruler and the elites exercised over them. The more I delved into them, the more I came to appreciate that local courts dealt regularly and consistently with civil disputes, and that magistrates in fact routinely adjudged cases according to the law. Despite the official ideology of absolute power for the ruler and his administrators, which has led us to the impression of arbitrariness, in practice the Qing legal system routinely protected the legitimate claims of common litigants to property, contracts, inheritance, and old-age support. The most skeptical of my colleagues, I hope, will now concede that large numbers of even simple peasants used the courts to assert and enforce their legitimate claims; for them, those powers amounted to rights in practice, even if not in theory.

Those civil rights, to be sure, did not include political rights. A conception of civil law that assumed the "minor matters" of the populace were of no concern to the state would find little need to dwell on power relations between state and society. In that respect, things are not much different today. "Civil law" in the modern Chinese conception deals only with the horizontal relations between equal citizens, not the vertical relations between them and the state.

Those civil rights also did not include the social rights of the weak and poor versus the elites. Unlike the modern Western civil tradition, which is predicated on the equality of all citizens before the law, the Qing code upheld and reinforced social hierarchy. Neither formal law nor informal justice, therefore, offered much in the way of recourse against one's superiors and the powerful. Social justice did not become an explicit concern until the legal reforms of the twentieth century.

"Substantive rationality" as a shorthand characterization for Qing civil justice, then, must be understood as paradoxical in these senses as well as those outlined earlier in the chapter. It tells about the presence in Qing China of proprietary, contractual, and inheritance civil rights without political and social civil rights. Those civil rights were allowed by patrimonial authority, not wrested from absolutist rule by civil society. Nevertheless, they served to empower the common people in major areas of their daily lives.

In the end, my use of Weber perhaps departs from his original ideas as much as it draws on them. His preoccupation with vertical relations of domination does not work well with a subject like civil law, which is centrally concerned with horizontal relations among the people. And his binary construction of rational law versus kadi justice violates Qing realities no matter which side one chooses to emphasize. Yet we cannot therefore turn to Qing constructions alone, or to a simple objectivist equation of Qing civil law with its application. We need instead to focus on the disjunctions between representation and practice. It is finally Weber's tentatively paradoxical formulations that prove to be useful. The Qing legal and political systems can be seen as a combination of patrimonial-substantive representations with bureaucratic-rational practices. Moralism and practical orientations were entwined in the code, the magistrates, and local government. Rights were denied in theory but protected in practice. Twentieth-century legal reformers would have to work with both the limitations and the promises of that legacy.

Reference Material

Village and County Data

The Dan-Xin data are based on all the cases catalogued as "civil" by Dai Yanhui; the Baodi data, on all the cases categorized under "land," "debt," "marriage," and "inheritance" that were in a reproducible condition in the spring of 1988; and the Baxian data, on the cases provided to me by the Sichuan Provincial Archive staff in the summer of 1990. (For Shunyi, I drew on all the extant civil cases in the county archive.)

TABLE A.1

Cases Studied, by County and Decade

Decade	Baxian	Baodi	Dan-Xin	Total
1760–1769	20			20
1770–1779	82			82
1780–1789	40			40
1790–1799	38			38
1800–1809	0			0
1810–1819	3	2		5
1820–1829	60	7		67
1830–1839	6	18	1	25
1840–1849	3	10	1	14
1850–1859	56	11	10	77
1860–1869		25	8	33
1870–1879		12	62	74
1880–1889		14	102	116
1890–1899		8	18	26
1900–1909		11		11
TOTAL	308	118	202	628

TABLE A.2

Baxian, Baodi, and Dan-Xin Cases, by Decade and Category

Year	Land	Debt	Marriage	Inheritance	Total
Baxian, 1760's–1850's					
1760–1769	7	13	0	0	20
1770–1779	38	37	7	0	82
1780–1789	0	0	40	0	40
1790–1799	19	0	18	1	38
1800–1809	0	0	0	0	0
1810–1819	0	0	0	3	3
1820–1829	19	26	15	0	60
1830–1839	0	0	2	4	6
1840–1849	0	0	0	3	3
1850–1859	17	20	17	2	56
TOTAL	100	96	99	13	308
Baodi, 1810's–1900's					
1810–1819	0	1	1	0	2
1820–1829	0	3	4	0	7
1830–1839	6	7	4	1	18
1840–1849	1	5	3	1	10
1850–1859	1	4	3	3	11
1860–1869	6	8	7	4	25
1870–1879	3	6	2	1	12
1880–1889	5	5	4	0	14
1890–1899	0	5	2	1	8
1900–1909	1	7	2	1	11
TOTAL	23	51	32	12	118
Dan-Xin, 1830's–1890's					
1830–1839	1	0	0	0	1
1840–1849	0	0	0	1	1
1850–1859	9	1	0	0	10
1860–1869	6	1	0	1	8
1870–1879	38	14	2	8	62
1880–1889	61	30	6	5	102
1890–1899	10	5	1	2	18
SUBTOTAL	125	51	9	17	202
Missing	6	1	0	0	7
Other[a]	3	2	0	0	5
TOTAL	134	54	9	17	214

NOTE: Mainland Chinese archivists have not used modern legal categories to classify (the Baxian and Baodi) Qing cases but have simply grouped them by content. Though Dai Yanhui used modern categories to classify the Dan-Xin archives, his civil category is roughly the same as mine, with 214 of its 222 cases falling readily under the four main groups. The main departure has to do with adultery and the sale of wives and daughters, which the mainland archivists (and I) include in the marriage category, but which he puts in the criminal category. I have made some minor adjustments in Dai's civil category to bring certain cases more in line with the Baxian and Baodi classifications, as follows: 10 cases involving the conditional sale of land from his category "debt," subcategory "dian and pawn" (*diandang*), to "land"; 13 cases from "land and houses—property disputes" (*zhengcai*) to "succession"; 1 case from "land and houses—collective property" (*gongye*) to "succession"; 2 cases from "land and houses—forcible removal" (*chaoya*) to "debt"; and 1 case each from "debt—buying and selling" (*maimai*) and "debt—retrieval" (*taowu*) to "land."

   [a] Fragments only.

TABLE A.3

Outcomes of Baxian, Baodi, and Dan-Xin Cases, by Category

Outcome	Land	Debt	Marriage	Inheritance	Total
	Baxian, 1760's–1850's				
Informally settled	22	13	17	1	53
By mediation	22	13	17	1	53
By litigants	0	0	0	0	0
Rejected	0	0	0	1	1
Adjudicated[a]	32	28	33	5	98
Incomplete	46	55	45	6	152
Other[b]	0	0	4	0	4
TOTAL	100	96	99	13	308
	Baodi, 1810's–1900's				
Informally settled	10	19	13	3	45
By mediation	10	15	8	3	36
By litigants	0	4	5	0	9
Rejected	0	2	0	0	2
Adjudicated[a]	8	17	15	5	45
Incomplete	5	13	4	4	26
TOTAL	23	51	32	12	118
	Dan-Xin, 1830's–1890's				
Informally settled	14	12	1	1	28
By mediation	13	10	1	1	25
By litigants	1	2	0	0	3
Rejected	4	2	1	0	7
Adjudicated[a]	55	12	0	11	78
Incomplete	50	24	7	5	86
Other[b]	2	1	0	0	3
TOTAL	125	51	9	17	202
GRAND TOTAL	248	198	140	42	628

[a]Includes court-arbitrated cases.

[b]For instance, the court treated the case as a criminal case (e.g., assault and battery, rape) or dismissed it.

TABLE A.4
Breakdown of Incomplete Baxian, Baodi, and Dan-Xin Case Files,
by Category

Reason	Land	Debt	Marriage	Inheritance	Total
		Baxian			
Records damaged or lost[a]	9	0	10	1	20
Magistrate would not handle[b]	0	0	0	0	0
Plaintiff or defendant not found	7	10	5	0	22
File ends with summons	30	45	30	4	109
Other[c]	0	0	0	1	1
TOTAL	46	55	45	6	152
		Baodi			
Records damaged or lost[a]	0	1	0	0	1
Magistrate would not handle[b]	1	2	0	3	6
Plaintiff or defendant not found	2	6	4	0	12
File ends with summons	2	3	0	1	6
Other[c]	0	1	0	0	1
TOTAL	5	13	4	4	26
		Dan-Xin			
Records damaged or lost[a]	5	3	0	0	8
Magistrate would not handle[b]	22	4	3	2	31
Plaintiff or defendant not found	0	3	1	0	4
File ends with summons	21	12	3	3	39
Other[c]	2	2	0	0	4
TOTAL	50	24	7	5	86
GRAND TOTAL	101	92	56	15	264

[a]Evidenced by absence of earlier stage documents when later stage ones present, by damaged sheets, and the like.

[b]That is, passed the case on to a *xiangbao* or a runner to act as his surrogate. Such cases rarely went any farther.

[c]For instance, the case ended because the deadline set by the court expired.

TABLE A.5

Baxian Court Cases, by Category and Basis of Ruling

Ruling	Land	Debt	Marriage	Inheritance	Total
For plaintiff	13	19	14	1	47
By law	13	18	14	1	46
On extralegal grounds	0	1	0	0	1
With compromise[a]	(3)	(2)	(0)	(0)	(5)
For defendant	10	4	6	2	22
By law	9	4	6	2	21
False accusation	5	4	6	0	15
Other	4	0	0	2	6
On extralegal grounds	1	0	0	0	1
With compromise[a]	(1)	(0)	(1)	(0)	(2)
No winner	5	2	6	1	14
By law	1	0	3	0	4
By arbitration	4	2	3	1	10
No ruling pending further investigation[b]	4	0	1	0	5
Other	0	3	6	1	10
TOTAL	32	28	33	5	98

NOTE: Where there were multiple court sessions and more than one court judgment, the case is counted by the first judgment.

[a]Compromises are given in parentheses because they are already counted among the cases for each category; that is, they do not constitute additional cases. Rulings for one or the other party did not preclude minor face-saving compromises, even if only symbolic.

[b]Includes only those not followed by another court session.

[c]For instance, the court treated the case as a criminal case (rape, kidnapping) or made no clear ruling.

TABLE A.6

Baodi Court Cases, by Category and Basis of Ruling

Ruling	Land	Debt	Marriage	Inheritance	Total
For plaintiff	4	5	8	4	21
By law	4	4	8	4	20
On extralegal grounds	0	1	0	0	1
With compromise[a]	(0)	(0)	(1)	(0)	(1)
For defendant	3	10	3	1	17
By law	3	10	3	1	17
False accusation	1	6	1	0	8
Other	2	4	2	1	9
On extralegal grounds	0	0	0	0	0
With compromise[a]	(0)	(0)	(0)	(0)	(0)
No winner	0	2	4	0	6
By law	0	2	3	0	5
By arbitration	0	0	1	0	1
No ruling pending further investigation[b]	1	0	0	0	1
TOTAL	8	17	15	5	45

NOTES: See Table A.5.

TABLE A.7

Dan-Xin Court Cases, by Category and Basis of Ruling

Ruling	Land	Debt	Marriage	Inheritance	Total
For plaintiff	32	9	0	3	44
By law	30	9		3	42
On extralegal grounds	0	0		0	0
With compromise[a]	(2)	(0)		(0)	(2)
For defendant	12	2	0	5	19
By law	12	2		5	19
False accusation	6	2		5	13
Other	6	0		0	6
On extralegal grounds	0	0		0	0
With compromise[a]	(1)	(0)		(0)	(1)
No winner	10	1	0	3	14
By law	9	1		3	13
By arbitration	1	0		0	1
No ruling pending further investigation[b]	0	0	0	0	0
Other[c]	1	0	0	0	1
TOTAL	55	12	0	11	78

NOTE: Where there were multiple court sessions and more than one court judgment, the case is counted by the first judgment

[a]Compromises are given in parentheses because they are already counted among the cases for each category; that is, they do not constitute additional cases. Rulings for one or the other party did not preclude minor face-saving compromises, even if only symbolic.

[b]Includes only those not followed by another court session.

[c]The court ordered the kin group to settle the dispute.

Weights and Measures

1 mu = 0.164 acre
1 jia = 11.3 mu

10 dou = 1 shi
1 shi = ca. 160 catties = ca. 176 pounds
1 dan = 133.3 pounds

1,000 (copper) wen (*cash*) = 1 (copper) diao = 1 (copper) chuan
1 (silver) yuan = 800 to 2,000 (copper) wen

References

The Mantetsu surveys (*Chūgoku nōson kankō chōsa*) are cited by the abbreviation KC.

All references to the Qing code are to the 1970 version of Xue Yunsheng's 1905 compilation, annotated and edited by Huang Tsing-chia. The first number refers to the statute as numbered by Huang, the second, if any, refers to a substatute. All references to the Republican civil code, by article number, are to *The Civil Code of the Republic of China* (1930).

The Baxian files are cited by category number, subcategory number, juan (bundle) number, and year, lunar month, and day, if available (e.g., Baxian 6:1:1062, 1789.2.23); the Baodi files by just juan number and lunar date (e.g., Baodi, 194, 1839.2.23); the Dan-Xin files by cataloguer's number and lunar date (e.g., Dan-Xin 22615, 1893.7.4); and the Shunyi files by category number, juan number, year, solar month, and day (e.g., Shunyi 3:483, 1931.5.21). For all of the above, the date is of the original plaint or, if that is unavailable, of the first dated document. The final bracketed letter and number when given are my own file references, by category ("l" for land, "d" for debt, "m" for marriage, and "i" for inheritance) and case number.

Alford, William P. 1984. "Of Arsenic and Old Laws: Looking Anew at Criminal Justice in Late Imperial China," *California Law Review*, 72.6: 1180–1256.

———. 1986. "The Inscrutable Occidental? Implications of Roberto Unger's Uses and Abuses of the Chinese Past," *Texas Law Review*, 64: 915–72.

Allee, Mark Anton. 1994. "Code, Culture, and Custom: Foundations of Civil Case Verdicts in a Nineteenth-Century County Court." In Bernhardt and Huang 1994b: 122–41.

———. 1987. "Law and Society in Late Imperial China: Tan-shui Subprefecture and Hsin-chu County, Taiwan, 1840–1895." Ph.D. dissertation, University of Pennsylvania.

Annual Report of the Director of the Administrative Office of the United States Courts, 1981. Washington, D.C.: U.S. Government Printing Office.

Baodi xian 寶坻縣. *Cisong anjian bu* 詞訟案件簿 (Register of litigation cases). 1833–35, 1861–81. In Baodi xian dang'an, juan 329.

Baodi xian dang'an 寶坻縣檔案 (Baodi county archives). In Diyi lishi dang'an guan 第一歷史檔案館, Beijing. [Classified under Shuntianfu; cited by juan no. and lunar date.]

Baxian dang'an 巴縣檔案 (Baxian county archives). In Sichuan sheng dang'an guan 四川省檔案館, Chengdu, Sichuan. [Cited by category no., juan no., and lunar date.]

Baxian zhi xuanzhu 巴縣志選注 (Gazetteer of Baxian County, with Selective Annotations). 1989. Chongqing.

Bernhardt, Kathryn. 1994. "Women and the Law: Divorce in the Republican Period." In Bernhardt and Huang 1994b: 187–214.

———. 1992. *Rents, Taxes, and Peasant Resistance: The Lower Yangzi Region, 1840–1950.* Stanford, Calif.: Stanford University Press.

Bernhardt, Kathryn, and Philip C. C. Huang. 1994a. "Civil Law in Qing and Republican China: The Issues." In Bernhardt and Huang 1994b: 1–12.

———, eds. 1994b. *Civil Law in Qing and Republican China.* Stanford, Calif.: Stanford University Press.

Bodde, Derk, and Clarence Morris. 1967. *Law in Imperial China, Exemplified by 190 Ch'ing Dynasty Cases.* Cambridge, Mass.: Harvard University Press.

Bourdieu, Pierre. 1977. *Outline of a Theory of Practice.* Cambridge, Eng.: Cambridge University Press.

Brockman, Rosser H. 1980. "Commercial Contract Law in Late Nineteenth-Century Taiwan." In Jerome A. Cohen, Randle Edwards, and Fu-mei Chang Chen, eds., *Essays in China's Legal Tradition,* pp. 76–136. Princeton, N.J.: Princeton University Press.

Buxbaum, David. 1971. "Some Aspects of Civil Procedure and Practice at the Trial Level in Tanshui and Hsinchu from 1789 to 1895," *Journal of Asian Studies,* 30.2 (Feb.): 255–79.

Chūgoku nōson kankō chōsa 中國農村慣行調查 (Investigations of customary practices in rural China). 1952–58. Comp. Chūgoku nōson kankō chōsa kankōkai. Ed. Niida Noboru 仁井田陞. 6 vols. Tokyo: Iwanami.

Ch'ü T'ung-tsu. 1962. *Local Government in China Under the Ch'ing.* Cambridge, Mass.: Harvard University Press.

———. 1961. *Law and Society in Traditional China.* Paris: Mouton.

Cihai 辭海. 1979. 3 vols. Shanghai: Shanghai cishu chubanshe.

Cohen, Jerome A. 1967. "Chinese Mediation on the Eve of Modernization," *Journal of Asian and African Studies,* 2.1 (April): 54–76.

Conner, Alison Wayne. 1994. "Lawyers and the Legal Profession During the Republican Period." In Bernhardt and Huang 1994b: 215–48.

———. 1979. "The Law of Evidence During the Qing." Ph.D. dissertation, Cornell University.

Crook, David, and Isabel Crook. 1959. *Revolution in a Chinese Village: Ten Mile Inn.* London: Routledge & Kegan Paul.

Dai Yanhui [Tai Yen-hui] 戴炎輝. 1979. *Qingdai Taiwan zhi xiangzhi* 清代

台灣之鄉治 (Township government in Taiwan during the Qing). Taibei: Lianjing.

Dan-Xin dang'an 淡新檔案 (Danshui subprefecture and Xinzhu county archive). Microfilm copy, UCLA East Asian Library. Catalogued by Dai Yanhui.

Daxue 大學 (The great learning). N.d. In *Sishu jizhu*. Taibei: Shijie shuju, 1964.

Ebrey, Patricia Buckley, and James L. Watson, eds. 1986. *Kinship Organization in Late Imperial China, 1000–1940*. Berkeley: University of California Press.

Fairbank, John King. 1983. *The United States and China*, 4th ed. Cambridge, Mass.: Harvard University Press.

Fan Zengxiang 樊增祥. 1910. *Fanshan zhengshu* 樊山政書 (Records of Mr. Fanshan's administration). N.d. 3 vols. Taiwan: Wenhai chubanshe.

Fang Dashi 方大湜. 1878 (date of Preface). *Pingping yan* 平平言 (Plain words).

Fei Hsiao-tung. 1939. *Peasant Life in China: A Field Study of Country Life in the Yangtze Valley*. New York: Dutton.

Fuma Susumu 夫馬進. 1993. "Min-Shin jidai no shōshi to soshō seido" 明清時代の訟師と訴訟制度 (Litigation instigators and the litigation system in the Ming-Qing period). In Umehara Kaoru, ed., *Chūgoku kinsei no hōsei to shakai*. Kyoto: Kyōtō daigaku jinbun kagaku kenkyūjo.

Gamble, Sidney. 1963. *North China Villages: Social, Political, and Economic Activities Before 1933*. Berkeley: University of California Press.

Gangyi 剛毅. 1889. *Muling xuzhi* 牧令須知 (What a magistrate should know). Taibei xian: Wenhai chubanshe reprint, n.d.

"Geji shenpanting shiban zhangcheng" 各級審判廳試辦章程 (Provisional regulations for the different level courts). 1907. In *Xin Faling jiyao*. Shanghai: Shangwu yinshuguan.

The German Civil Code. 1907. Translated and annotated, with a Historical Introduction and Appendixes, by Chung Hui Wang. London: Stevens & Sons.

Habermas, Jürgen. 1989. *The Structural Transformation of the Public Sphere: An Inquiry into a Category of Bourgeois Society*. Tr. Thomas Burger. Cambridge, Mass.: M.I.T. Press.

Henderson, Dan Fenno. 1965. *Conciliation and Japanese Law: Tokugawa and Modern*. Seattle: University of Washington Press.

Henderson, Dan Fenno, and Preston M. Torbert. 1992. "Tranditional Contract Law in China and Japan." In *International Encyclopedia of Comparative Law*, 7: *Contracts in General*, 6-2–6-40. Dordrecht: Mohr, Tübingen, and Jijhoff.

Hong Huanchun 洪煥椿, ed. 1988. *Ming Qing Suzhou nongcun jingji ziliao* 明清蘇州農村經濟資料 (Source materials on the rural economy of Suzhou during the Ming and Qing). Jiangsu: Jiangsu guji chubanshe.

Hsiao Kung-ch'üan. 1979. "Compromise in Imperial China." Seattle: School of International Studies, University of Washington.

Huang Liuhong 黃六鴻. 1694 (date of Preface). *Fuhui quanshu* 福惠全書

(A complete book concerning happiness and benevolence). Translated in part as *A Complete Book Concerning Happiness and Benevolence: "Fu-hui ch'üan-shu:" A Manual for Local Magistrates in Seventeenth Century China* by Djang Chu. Tucson: University of Arizona Press, 1984.

Huang, Philip C. C. 1994. "Codified Law and Magisterial Adjudication in Qing China." In Bernhardt and Huang 1994b: 142–86.

———. 1993a. "'Public Sphere'/'Civil Society' in China? The Third Realm Between State and Society," pp. 216–40 of Huang, ed. "'Public Sphere'/ 'Civil Society' in China? Paradigmatic Issues in Chinese Studies, III," *Modern China*, 19.2 (April): 107–240.

———. 1993b. "Between Informal Mediation and Formal Adjudication: The Third Realm of Qing Justice," *Modern China*, 19.3 (July): 251–98.

———. 1991a. "The Paradigmatic Crisis in Chinese Studies: Paradoxes in Social and Economic History," *Modern China*, 17.3 (July): 299–341.

———. 1991b. "Civil Justice in Rural China During the Qing and the Republic." Paper presented at the conference on Civil Law in Chinese History, UCLA, Aug. 12–14, 1991.

———. 1990. *The Peasant Family and Rural Development in the Yangzi Delta, 1350–1988.* Stanford, Calif.: Stanford University Press.

———. 1985. *The Peasant Economy and Social Change in North China.* Stanford, Calif.: Stanford University Press.

———. 1982. "County Archives and the Study of Local Social History: Report on a Year's Research in China," *Modern China*, 8.1 (Jan.): 133–43.

Jing Junjian. 1994. "Legislation Related to the Civil Economy in the Qing Dynasty." In Bernhardt and Huang 1994b: 42–84.

——— 經君健. 1981. "Lun Qingdai shehui de dengji jiegou" 論清代社會的 等級結構 (On the structure of [legal] status in Qing society). In *Jingji yanjiusuo jikan* 經濟研究所集刊, 3. Beijing: Zhongguo shehui kexue chubanshe.

Jones, William C. 1987. "Some Questions Regarding the Significance of the General Provisions of Civil Law of the People's Republic of China," *Harvard International Law Journal*, 28.2 (Spring): 309–31.

———, tr. (with the assistance of Tianquan Cheng and Yongling Jiang). 1994. *The Great Qing Code.* New York: Oxford University Press.

Karasawa Yasuhiko. 1994. "Between Speech and Writing: Textuality of the Written Record of Oral Testimony in Qing Legal Cases." Seminar paper, UCLA.

———. 1993. "Composing the Narrative: A Preliminary Study of Plaints in Qing Legal Cases." Paper presented at the conference on Code and Practice in Chinese Law, UCLA, Aug. 8–10, 1993.

Kuhn, Philip A. 1990. *Soulstealers: The Chinese Sorcery Scare of 1768.* Cambridge, Mass.: Harvard University Press.

Lan Dingyuan 藍鼎元. 1765. *Luzhou gong'an* 鹿州公案 (Mr. Luzhou's cases). Taibei xian: Wenhai chubanshe reprint, 1971.

Li Wenzhi, Wei Jinyu, and Jing Junjian 李文治, 魏金玉, 經君健. 1983. *Ming Qing shidai de nongye zibenzhuyi mengya wenti* 明清時代的農業資本

主義萌芽問題 (The problem of the sprouts of capitalism in agriculture during the Ming-Qing period). Beijing: Zhongguo shehui kexue chubanshe.

Liang Zhangju 梁章鉅. 1837. *Tui'an suibi* 退菴隨筆 (Mr. Tui'an's notes). Taibei xian: Wenhai chubanshe reprint, n.d.

Linhai xianzhi 臨海縣志 (Gazetteer of Linhai county). 1989. Hangzhou: Zhejiang renmin chubanshe.

Macauley, Melissa A. 1994. "Civil and Uncivil Disputes in Southeast Coastal China, 1723–1820." In Bernhardt and Huang 1994b: 85–121.

———. 1993. "Trickster Tales: A Preliminary Discussion of Non-Official Sources Concerning Litigation Brokers." Chap. 6 of Macauley, "The Civil Reprobate: Pettifoggers, Property, and Litigation in Late Imperial China, 1723–1850." Ph.D. dissertation, University of California, Berkeley.

Mann, Michael. 1986. *The Sources of Social Power, 1: A History of Power from the Beginning to A.D. 1760.* Cambridge, Eng.: Cambridge University Press.

———. 1984. "The Autonomous Power of the State: Its Origins, Mechanisms and Results," *Archives européennes de sociologie,* 25: 185–213.

Minshi anjian yuebao biao 民事案件月報表 (Monthly tabulated reports of [Shunyi county branch court's] civil cases). 1927. In Shunyi xian dang'an, 2: juan 458.

Minshi susong anjian nianbao biao 民事訴訟案件年報表 (Annual tabulated report of [Shunyi county branch court's] civil litigation cases). 1930. In Shunyi xian dang'an, 3: juan 281.

Mu Han 穆翰. 1845. *Mingxing guanjian lu* 明刑管見錄 (My limited opinions to clarify the law).

Muling shu 牧令書. 1848. (Compendium on magisterial service).

Ningdu xianzhi 寧都縣志 (Gazetteer of Ningdu county). 1986.

Qian Xiangbao 錢祥保. 1920. *Bangshu* 謗書 (Works of a maligned [magistrate]). Taibei xian: Wenhai chubanshe reprint, 1976.

Reed, Bradly. 1994. "Scoundrels and Civil Servants: Clerks, Runners and Local Administration in Late Imperial China." Ph.D. dissertation, University of California, Los Angeles.

———. 1993. "Clerks, Runners, and Local Judicial Administration: A Study of Baxian County, Sichuan, in the Late Qing." Paper presented at the conference on Code and Practice in Chinese Law, UCLA, Aug. 8–10, 1993.

Ruan Benyan 阮本焱. 1887. *Qiumu chuyan* 求牧芻言 (Humble words of one seeking official service). Taibei xian: Wenhai chubanshe reprint, 1968.

Scogin, Hugh T., Jr. 1990. "Between Heaven and Man: Contract and the State in Han Dynasty China," *Southern California Law Review,* 63.5: 1325–1404.

Shanghai shi sifaju 上海市司法局. 1991. *Shanghai shi renmin tiaojie gongzuo shouce* 上海市人民調解工作手冊 (Handbook for Shanghai municipality's people's mediation work). Shanghai: Shanghai shi xinwen chubanju.

Shiga Shūzō 滋賀秀三. 1984. *Shindai Chūgoku no hō to saipan* 清代中國の 法と裁判 (Law and justice in Qing China). Tokyo: Sōbunsha.

————. 1981. "Shindai soshō seido ni okeru minjiteki hōgen no gaikatsuteki kentō" 清代訴訟制度における民事的法源の概括的檢討 (A general analysis of the origins of civil law in the litigation system of the Qing), *Tōyōshi kenkyū*, 40.1: 74–102.

————. 1974–75. "Criminal Procedure in the Ch'ing Dynasty—With Emphasis on Its Administrative Character and Some Allusion to Its Historical Antecedents," *Memoirs of the Research Department of the Tōyō Bunko*, (2 parts), 32: 1–45; 33: 115–38.

Shunyi xian dang'an 順義縣檔案 (Shunyi county archives). In Shunyi xian dang'an guan 順義縣檔案館. [Cited by category no., juan no., and Western date.]

Sifa tongji, 1936 司法統計 (Judicial statistics, 1936), 2: *Minshi* (Civil); 3: *Xingshi* (Criminal). In Di'er lishi dang'an guan 第二歷史檔案館, (category) 7: juan 7078.

Skinner, G. William. 1977. "Cities and the Hierarchy of Local Systems." In G. William Skinner, ed., *The City in Late Imperial China*. Stanford, Calif.: Stanford University Press, pp. 275–351.

Sommer, Matthew Harvey. 1994. "Sex, Law, and Society in Late Imperial China." Ph.D. dissertation, University of California, Los Angeles.

Songjiang xianzhi 松江縣志 (Gazetteer of Songjiang county). 1991. Shanghai: Shanghai renmin chubanshe.

State Court Caseload Statistics: Annual Report, 1980. Court Statistics and Information Management Project, 1984 (National Center Publication No. R-092).

Suizhou zhi 隨州志 (Gazetteer of Suizhou county). 1988. Beijing: Zhongguo chengshi jingji shehui chubanshe.

Unger, Roberto M. 1976. *Law in Modern Society*. New York: Free Press.

Usui Sachiko. 1981. 臼井佐知子 "Shindai fuzei kankei sūchi no ichi kentō" 清代賦稅關係數值の一檢討 (An examination of statistical data pertaining to land taxes during the Qing), *Chūgoku kindaishi kenkyū*, no. 1 (July): 43–114.

Wakefield, David. 1992. "Household Division in Qing and Republican China: Inheritance, Family Property, and Economic Development." Ph.D. dissertation, University of California, Los Angeles.

Wan Weihan 萬維翰. 1770 (date of Preface). *Muxue juyao* 幕學舉要 (Important aspects of the skills of serving as a private secretary).

Wang Huizu 汪輝祖. 1800 (date of Preface). *Xuezhi shuozhui* 學治說贅 (Tiresome views on learning governance). In *Congshu jicheng*. Shanghai: Shangwu yinshuguan, 1939.

————. 1796. *Bingta menghen lu* 病塌夢痕錄 (Traces of dreams from a sickbed). N.p.: Guangwen shuju reprint, n.d.

————. 1794 (date of Preface). Xuezhi xushuo 學治續說 (Further views on

learning governance). In *Congshu jicheng*. Shanghai: Shangwu yinshuguan, 1939.

———. 1793 (date of Preface). *Xuezhi yishuo* 學治臆說 (Subjective views
on learning governance). In *Congshu jicheng*. Shanghai: Shangwu yinshuguan, 1939.

———. 1786a (date of Preface). *Zuozhi yaoyan* 佐治藥言 (Admonitions on
assisting [a magistrate] with governance). In *Congshu jicheng*. Shanghai: Shangwu yinshuguan, 1937.

———. 1786b (date of Preface). *Xu zuozhi yaoyan* 續佐治藥言 (Sequel to
"Admonitions on assisting with governance"). In *Congshu jicheng*.
Shanghai: Shangwu yinshuguan, 1937.

———. N.d. Miscellaneous excerpts in *Muling shu* (q.v.).

Wang Yeh-chien. 1973. *Land Taxation in Imperial China, 1750–1911*. Cambridge, Mass.: Harvard University Press.

Wang Youfu 王有孚. N.d. Miscellaneous excerpts in *Muling shu* (q.v.).

Wang Youhuai 王又槐. N.d. *Ban'an yaolue* 辦案要略 (Important strategies
in handling cases). In *Rumu xuzhi wuzhong* 入幕須知五種 (Five volumes of essential knowledge for those entering private secretary work).
Ed. Zhang Tingxiang 張廷驤. 1892. N.p.: Zhejiang shuju.

Watson, Alan. 1981. *The Making of the Civil Law*. Cambridge, Mass.: Harvard
University Press.

Weber, Max. 1968. *Economy and Society: An Outline of Interpretive Soci-
ology*. 3 vols. New York: Bedminster Press.

———. 1954. *Max Weber on Law in Economy and Society*. Ed. Max Rheinstein.
Cambridge: Harvard University Press.

Wu Guangyao 吳光耀. 1903 (date of Preface). *Xiushan gongdu* 秀山公牘
(Official documents from [my service as magistrate of] Xiushan county).

Xin faling jiyao 新法令輯要 (Important new laws and regulations). 1911
(1910). Shanghai: Shangwu yinshuguan.

Xinzhu xianzhi 新竹縣志 (Gazetteer of Xinzhu county). 4 vols. 1957. Taibei:
Chengwen.

Xue Yun-sheng 薛允升. 1905. *Duli cunyi* 讀例存疑 (Doubts remaining after
perusing the substatutes). Taiwan reissue, ed. Huang Tsing-chia. 5 vols.
Taipei: Chinese Materials and Research Aids Service Center, 1970.

Yang, C. K. 1959. *Chinese Communist Society: The Family and the Village*.
Cambridge, Mass.: M.I.T. Press.

Yang, Martin. 1945. *A Chinese Village: Taitou, Shantung Province*. New
York: Columbia University Press.

Zelin, Madeleine. 1986. "The Rights of Tenants in Mid-Qing Sichuan: A
Study of Land-Related Lawsuits in the Baxian Archives," *Journal of
Asian Studies*, 45.3 (May): 499–526.

Zhang Jinfan 張晉藩 ed. 1994. *Qingchao fazhi shi* 清朝法制史 (A history of
the legal system of the Qing dynasty). Beijing: Falü chubanshe.

Zheng Qin 鄭秦. 1993. "Qingchao falü: lü he li de xingcheng ji yunxing" 清
代法律: 律和例的形成及運行 (Qing law: the formation of statutes and
substatutes and their application). Paper presented at the conference on

Code and Practice in Chinese Law, UCLA, Aug. 8–10, 1993. Published in slightly abridged form in *Modern China*, 21.3 (July 1995): 310–45.

———. 1988. *Qingdai sifa shenpan zhidu yanjiu* 清代司法審判制度研究 (A study of the trial system of the Qing). Changsha, Hunan: Hunan jiaoyu chubanshe.

Zhongguo falü nianjian 1990 中國法律年鑑 (Law yearbook of China, 1990). N.p.: Zhongguo falü nianjian she.

Zhongguo tongji nianjian 1990 中國統計年鑑 (Statistical yearbook of China, 1990). Beijing: Zhongguo tongji chubanshe.

Zhou Guangyuan. 1993. "Narrative and Action: A Study of Qing Case Reports and Reviews." Paper presented at the conference on Code and Practice in Chinese Law, UCLA, Aug. 8–10, 1993.

Character List

Not included in this list are names and titles appearing in the "References," well-known place-names, and the names of individual litigants and disputants.

ai nan zhun li 礙難准理
baiqi 白契
bangshu 幫書
bao 保
Baodi xian 寶坻縣
Baoji xian 寶雞縣
baojia 保甲
baoren 保人
baosong 包訟
baozhang 保長
baozheng ren 保證人
Baxian 巴縣
Beifaxin (*cun*) 北法信 (村)
bici jianmian fu / pei li 彼此見
面服/陪禮
bing 兵
bing wu jiuge 并無糾葛
bing wu yishuo 并無異說
binggong lichu 秉公理處
bobo 餑餑
boze 薄責
bu deyi 不得已
bu qing zhun 不輕准
bushou wobei 不守臥碑
butou 埠頭

buzhun 不准
caili 財禮
chaduan 查斷
chafu 查覆
chaifang 差房
Changan xian 長安縣
Changli xian 昌黎縣
Changwu xian 長武縣
Chaoyi xian 朝邑縣
chaqing 查情
chaqing lichu 查情理處
chaoya 抄押
Chaoyang xian 潮陽縣
Chen Hongmou 陳宏謀
Chen Qingmen 陳慶門
Chengcheng xian 澄城縣
Chenggu xian 城固縣
chi 飭
chi chai chuanxun 飭差傳訊
chuan 串
chuan'an 傳案
chuan'an xun jiu 傳案訊究
chuanjiu 傳究
chuanpiao 傳票
chuanxun 傳訊

chuanxun jiu 傳訊究
cisong anjian bu 詞訟案件簿
cizhuang 詞狀
congzhong suonong 從中唆弄
cuichai chafu 催差查覆
cuichai chali 催差查理
cuichai chuanxun 催差傳訊
cuicheng 催呈
cuici 催詞
daishu 代書
Dali xian 大荔縣
Daming fu 大名府
dan 擔
danbao 擔保
dang 當
Danshui fenfu 淡水分府
Danshui ting 淡水廳
daoli 道理
daomai tianzhai 盜賣田宅
dashi hua xiao, xiaoshi hua liao
 大事化小, 小事化了
datang 大堂
datie 大帖
dazu 大租
de minxin 得民心
dengji 登記
dian 典
diandang 典當
dianmai tianzhai 典賣田宅
dianxin 點心
diao 刁
diao 吊
diaosong 刁訟
dibao 地保
difang fayuan 地方法院
digun 地棍
dilin 地鄰
dingqin 定親
Dingyuan xian 定遠縣
diyue 地約
dongshi 董事
dou 斗
dou'ou 鬥毆
duan 斷
duanjie 斷結
duanren 端人
duo 奪

duyi 蠹役
Enxian 恩縣
er 爾
fa 法
fanjian 犯姦
fanren 凡人
fanyu zhi tu 販鬻之徒
fazhi 法治
feili 非理
fen 分
fenjia 分家
fenjiadan 分家單
fumu 父母
fumu guan 父母官
Funing xian 阜寧縣
Fuping xian 富平縣
fuqin 父親
fuxun 復訊
gaichai, rengchi 改差, 仍飭
gailiang tubu 改良土布
gangchang 綱常
ganjie 甘結
gaodeng fayuan 高等法院
gong 工
gongshi 工食
gongye 公業
gu congkuan 姑從寬
guahao 掛號
guanli shoucai 官吏受財
guanxi 關係
gugongren 雇工人
Guiji xian 會稽縣
guofa 國法
guren wugao zhe 雇人誣告者
hanhu 含糊
Hatada Takashi 旗田巍
Hayakawa Tamotsu 早川保
heduo 核奪
Heyang xian 郃陽縣
Hongli 弘曆
hongqi 紅契
hou tangxun 候堂訊
Houjiaying (cun) 侯家營 (村)
Houxiazhai (cun) 後夏寨 (村)
houxun, wu du 候訊, 勿瀆
hu 戶
Hu fang 戶房

hu, hun, tiantu 戶, 婚, 田土
hu, hun, tiantu xishi 戶, 婚, 田土細事
huanxun 喚訊
Huayin xian 華陰縣
huishou 會首
hulü 戶律
hunyin 婚姻
jia 甲
jia dangjia 加當價
jiagun 夾棍
jian 間
jian 姦
jianmian fuli 見面服禮
jianmin 賤民
jianqing 姦情
jiansheng 監生
jiansong 健訟
jiansong buxiu 健訟不休
jiaosuo cisong 教唆詞訟
Jiaqing 嘉慶
jiazhang 家長
jiazhang 甲長
jiazhuang 嫁妝
jicheng 繼承
jie 結
jie'an 結案
jieshaoren 介紹人
jiguan 積慣
jing qinyou/lin shuohe 經親友/鄰說合
jingzhong shuohe 經中說合
jiu 究
jiuduan 究斷
jiujiu 舅舅
jixing bangshi 即行榜示
jixun 集訊
ju 拘
ju ganjie 具甘結
ju'an 拘案
juan yue 卷約
juemai 絕賣
junzi 君子
juren 舉人
juyuan xisong 俱愿息訟
kaidan songshen 開單送審
kanzhang 勘丈

ken en mianxun 懇恩免訊
kongqing 控情
kui zhu tianli, zhun zhu renqing 揆諸天理, 准諸人情
lairen 來人
lan zhun 濫准
laogu zhengshi 牢固正實
Lengshuigou (*cun*) 冷水溝 (村)
li 吏
li 禮
li 例
li 理
li dizi weifa 立嫡子違法
Li fang 禮房
liangren 良人
Liangxiang xian 良鄉縣
Licheng xian 歷城縣
lichu 理處
Lintong xian 臨潼縣
Liu Heng 劉衡
liupin 六品
liyi 離異
lizhi zhe 理直者
long 壟
Luancheng xian 欒城縣
lüe 略
lüeren lüemai ren 略人略賣人
lüli 律例
Luonan xian 雒南縣
maimai 買賣
maixiu maixiu 買休賣休
maixiu weilü 買休違律
mianxun/jiu 免訊/究
mianzi 面子
minfa 民法
ming dayi 明大義
mingbai pouxi 明白剖析
mingjiao 名教
minjian cisong 民間詞訟
minshi 民事
mobi 墨筆
mu 畝
muqin 母親
neiya 內衙
neizheng 內政
niangao youde 年高有德
Nijing (*zhen*) 泥井 (鎮)

tianli 天理
tiaochu 調處
ting duan 聽斷
tingsong 聽訟
tongli 通例
tongsheng 童生
tongzi 童子
Tongzhi 同治
tudi 土地
tugun 土棍
Wang Zhi 王植
wangjie 妄訐
Wangquan (cun) 望泉 (村)
wangzhe changfu 枉者常負
wanshi buyi 萬世不移
weijin quli 違禁取利
weili zhifu ren 威力制縛人
weiyan songting 危言聳聽
wen 文
wu du 勿瀆
wu yong song du 勿庸聳瀆
Wudian (cun) 吳店 (村)
wugao 誣告
wugao zhe 誣告者
wukong 誣控
wuli 物理
wuqing zhi ci 無情之詞
xian you yinni bieqing 顯有隱
　匿別情
xiangbao 鄉保
xianglin 鄉鄰
xiangshi 鄉試
Xiangxiang xian 湘鄉縣
xiangyue 鄉約
Xianning xian 咸寧縣
Xianyang xian 咸陽縣
xiaopiao 銷票
xiaoren 小人
xiaotie 小帖
xiaozu 小租
xin xianzhi 新縣志
xing 刑
Xing bu 刑部
Xing fang 刑房
xing qian jiaoshe shijian 刑錢交
　涉事件

xingming muyou 刑名幕友
xingshi 刑事
xingzheng 行政
xinshou 新收
Xinzhu xian 新竹縣
xishi 細事
xixiao 息銷
xun 訊
xunduan 訊斷
xunjian 巡檢
ya 押
yadu 衙蠹
yahang 牙行
yan 嚴
yancheng 嚴懲
yanchuan 嚴傳
yanglaodi 養老地
yangshan 養贍
yanju 嚴拘
yayaoqian 押腰錢
yayi 衙役
yi pishi chuanxun 已批示傳訊
Yichuan xian 宜川縣
Yijun xian 宜君縣
yili 義理
yiqu zhe 義曲者
yixiang shanshi 一鄉善士
Yongzheng 雍正
you 誘
you xinyong 有信用
youguai 誘拐
yuan 元
yuan 冤
Yuan Shouding 袁守定
yuandi 園地
yue 約
yuelin 約鄰
Yuqian 裕謙
zai qianwang shefa chuli 再前
　往設法處理
zaitao 在逃
zhaishi 摘釋
zhaiwu 債務
zhangze 掌責
zhaojia 找價
zhaotie 找貼

zhengcai　爭財

zhenqing　眞情

zhenqing zhuoli　斟情酌理

zhenzhang　鎮長

zhidi jieqian　指地借錢

Zhili　直隸

zhixun　質訊

zhiyuan　治原

zhizhe changshen　直者常伸

zhong'an　重案

zhongbaoren　中保人

zhongjianren　中間人

zhongqing　重情

zhongren　中人

zhongshi　重事

zhongshuoren　中說人

zhouxian zili　州縣自理

zhuangbang　狀榜

zhun　准

zhun xiao'an　准銷案

zhuoli zhunqing　酌理准情

zhuoyong　酌用

zigao　自稿

zigao shanbian　自稿繕便

zilaigao　自來稿

zili　自理

zili cisong yuebao　自理詞訟月報

zimin　子民

zongbao　總保

zongli　總理

zongshu　總書

zulin　族鄰

zuqin　族親

zuoge renqing　做個人情

zupi　租批

zuyin　族姻

Index

In this index an "f" after a number indicates a separate reference on the next page, and an "ff" indicates separate references on the next two pages. A continuous discussion over two or more pages is indicated by a span of page numbers, e.g., "57–59." *Passim* is used for a cluster of references in close but not consecutive sequence.

Library of Congress Cataloging-in-Publication Data

Huang, Philip C., 1940–
Civil justice in China : representation and practice in the Qing /
Philip C. C. Huang.
    p.   cm.—(Law, society, and culture in China)
    Includes bibliographical references and index.
    ISBN 0-8047-2740-6 (cl.) : ISBN 0-8047-3469-0 (pbk.)
    1. Justice, Administration of—China—History.   2. Civil law—
China—History.   3. Dispute resolution (Law)—China—History.
    4. Practice of law—China—History.   I. Title.   II. Series.
KNN 1572.H83 1996
347.51—dc20
[345.107]   96-14807   CIP

∞This book is printed on acid-free, recycled paper.

Original printing 1996

Last figure below indicates year of this printing:

05   04   03   02   01   00   99   98